W9-BVM-535

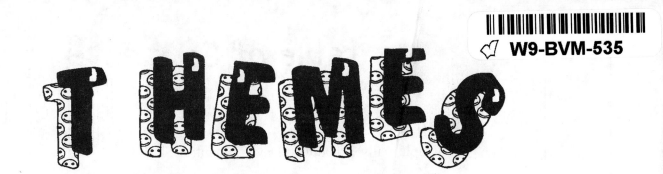

THEMES
Through the Year

September	October	November	December
January	February	March	April
May	June	July	August

Written by **Debbie Thompson and Darlene Hardwick**

Edited by Ina Massler Levin

Illustrated by Blance Apodaca, Cheryl Buhler, Sue Fullam, Keith Vasconcelles and Teresa Wright

Teacher Created Resources

Teacher Created Resources, Inc.
6421 Industry Way
Westminster, CA 92683
www.teachercreated.com

ISBN: 978-1-55734-146-4

©1993 Teacher Created Resources, Inc.
Reprinted, 2008

Made in U.S.A.

Table of Contents

Introduction

Teachers of young children will love organizing their curriculum using a thematic approach. Children and their parents will love it, too. Thematic teaching enhances learning by allowing children to make connections between the various experiences during a school day. This book provides the busy teacher with ideas, follow up materials, sample schedules, and weekly calendars.

The beginning pages of *Early Childhood Themes Through the Year* will prove invaluable to the busy teacher. In them you will find detailed instructions for making teaching materials that you will use throughout the school year. These include detailed directions for file folder activities, art recipes, glove puppets, fishing poles, and feelie boxes.

Each section of the book is arranged around a theme appropriate to the early childhood classroom. This theme is carried throughout the entire week. The section is introduced with a weekly activities calendar. The calendar is designed to serve many purposes. It will help you to organize your week. Use the calendar not only to plan, but also to check off what you have completed. The calendar is designed to be reproducible. Parents will love receiving a copy outlining their child's school week so that they can discuss and reinforce school experiences.

Each weekly section contains suggestions for:

Materials needed for the week:	these are items not considered standard classroom supplies but necessary for the weekly theme
Sharing Time:	questions, ideas, stories, and objects about the theme that can be discussed by and with the children
Art:	fun and simple projects to extend the theme
Story Time:	book titles appropriate to the theme and early childhood classroom; activities to go along with stories
Circle Time:	games, songs, stories, and more that children can experience together
Food Experiences:	opportunities to both prepare and sample theme appropriate foods
Theme Activities:	an assortment of activities that allow for further enjoyment and extension of the theme

Classroom additions include complete listings of materials that will enrich your classroom environment, a teachers' aid section, bulletin board ideas and patterns, tips to send home to parents, and a related thematic bibliography.

A sample of the activity portion of an early childhood classroom is shown below. It does not encompass an entire day. The amounts of time shown are only approximate since each school's master schedule varies. Remember that flexibility will serve to enhance an existing program, or add to a new one.

Sample Daily Schedule

Arrival—Opening Activities 15 minutes

Sharing Time—15 minutes

Free Activity—15-30 minutes

(Child may choose from activities including centers in the classroom. This might be done twice during the day.)

Clean Up—10 minutes

Art—15 minutes

Snack—15 minutes

Story Time—15 minutes

Large/Small Muscle Activities—30-45 minutes (Outside Play)

Circle Time—15 minutes

Food Experience—15 minutes

Lunch—30 minutes

Quiet Time—15 minutes

Theme Activity—15-30 minutes

Development of Skills

The activities listed in this book will help encourage and promote various developmental skills for children in early childhood classrooms. Since all of the skills are inter-related, it would be too lengthy to name each activity and the skills associated. Therefore, you will find a sample listing of some of the various skills used throughout the book.

Gross/Fine Motor

Children will develop both gross and fine motor skills through activities such as: Dancing, Hopping, Games, Pretending, Outside Play, Taking Walks, Cutting, Pasting, Painting, Writing, Coloring, Finger Plays, File Folder Activities, and Puzzles.

Cognitive

Children will learn sequencing, pre-writing, classification, visual/object discrimination, language, math, and science skills through the use of: Books, Flannel Stories, Poems, Finger Plays, Discussions, File Folder Activities, Songs, Science Activities, Puppets, Food Experiences, and Field Trips.

Health Safety/Social

Children will learn health, safety, and social skills through the use of: Food Experiences, Field Trips, Classroom Visitors, Books, Puppets, Art, Dramatic Play, and Multi-Cultural Themes.

Instructions For Making Teaching Materials

How To Make File Folder Games

These file folder activities can be used during circle time as a group activity, by parents and teachers as a one-to-one activity, and/or as a free activity choice for a child. Before beginning, you will need to explain to the child the proper way to use the activity and how to care for the pieces. These file folder activities can also be sent home for parents to use with their child.

The following directions for making file folder activities can be followed whenever it is necessary to make a file folder game.

Materials Needed: file folders (these are available in colors), markers, tag board, wallpaper sample books, scissors, crayons, construction paper, rubber cement, carbon paper, colored stick-on dots. For durability, cover the completed file folder and loose matching pieces with laminating or clear contact film.

(Discarded wallpaper sample books can often be obtained from interior decorating and wallpaper stores. These are valuable resources for making file folder activities, bulletin board letters, and displays.)

Types of File Folder Activities

Color Matching

Choose a pattern appropriate for the weekly theme and trace it onto the eight basic colors of construction paper. You will need to have two cutouts for each of the colors. Cut pieces out and glue one set onto the inside of a file folder. The other set will be used for matching. Add details to your pieces with markers. For durability, cover the completed file folder and loose matching pieces with laminating or clear contact film. Staple a resealable baggie or envelope onto the back side of the Me folder to store the matching pieces.

Dot Number Matching

Choose a pattern appropriate for the weekly theme and trace it onto the construction paper. You may use different colors of construction paper, if desired. On two pieces you will place the same number of stick-on dots. Place dots on as many sets of pieces until you reach the desired number. Glue one set of patterns with the dots onto the file folder. The other set is used for matching. The numeral that matches the number of dots may be written on the back of each piece. Staple a resealable baggie or envelope onto the back side of the file folder to store the matching pieces.

Introductions For Making Teaching Materials (cont.)

Shape Matching

Instead of adding dots, you will now draw shapes on the pieces. Two will have squares, two will have circles, and so on. Glue one set onto the file folder. Use the other set for matching.

Pattern Matching

Use wallpaper samples to cut two pieces of any pattern pieces you wish. One group of patterns will be glued onto the file folder. The other group will be used for matching the wallpaper patterns.

General Teaching Aids

Fingerpaint Recipe

- Soap Flakes
- Water
- Food Coloring
- Mixer

Add small amounts of water to the soap flakes until the desired consistency is obtained. Add food coloring. Use on fingerpaint paper or a table top.

Play Dough

- 1 cup (263 mL) salt
- 2 cups (472 mL) flour
- 1 cup (236 mL) water
- 2 tablespoons (30 mL) alum
- 2 tablespoons (30 mL) salad oil
- food coloring

Mix together until smooth. Add food coloring of your choice. Seal in a resealable plastic baggie.

Smelly Play Dough

Follow the recipe above but add liquid flavorings for smell.

Puzzles

Reproduce any pattern in the book. Glue it onto index or tagboard. Laminate it. Cut into several large pieces. Store pieces in an envelope.

Lacing Cards

Reproduce any pattern in the book. Glue it onto index or tagboard. Laminate it. Use a hole punch and punch holes around. Provide shoe laces or yarn with ends flattened with tape for lacing.

Instructions For Making
Teaching Materials (cont.)

Funny Putty

- 2 parts white glue
- 1 part liquid starch
- tempera paint

Mix together. If it is too sticky, add more starch until the right consistency is obtained. Add paint for color.

Sparkle Garden

- Charcoal briquettes
- 6 tablespoons (90 mL) salt
- 6 tablespoons (90 mL) blueing
- 6 tablespoons (90 mL) water
- 1 tablespoon (15 mL) ammonia

Place charcoal into a foil pan. Mix ingredients and pour over charcoal. Add bits of cotton, wood, or string. Drop food coloring onto mixture. Place near heat and observe.

Gooey Mixture

- ½ cup (118 mL) water
- 1½ cups (354 mL) cornstarch

Pour cornstarch into a bowl. Slowly add the water and stir. Let children handle the mixture. If they knead it, what happens? If they just hold it in their hands, what happens?

Glove Puppets

Attach velcro® to the underside of each fingertip of a gardening glove. Cut out felt figures. The felt will stick to the velcro®. This technique can be used wherever a glove puppet is listed.

Fishing Poles

Make fishing poles from ½ inch (1.3 cm) wooden dowel rods which can be purchased at a hardware or craft store. Cut a groove around one end of the dowel rod about one inch (2.5 cm) from the end. Tie a short length of yarn into the groove. Tie a small magnet onto the other end. (Magnetic strips are available at craft stores.)

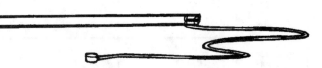

Feelie Box

To make a feelie box, cover a shoe box with contact paper and cut a hole in one end. The hole should be no larger than a child's hand. Place assorted items inside the box, then have the children take turns placing their hands through the hole and guessing what they are feeling. Ask questions such as: Is it hard? Is it soft? Is it round? Does it bend?

Weekly Theme: _____	Week of: _____			
	Monday	**Tuesday**	**Wednesday**	**Thursday**	**Friday**

	Monday	Tuesday	Wednesday	Thursday	Friday
Date					
Sharing Time					
Art					
Story Time					
Circle Time					
Food Experiences					
Theme Activities					

Weekly Theme: *Getting Acquainted*   Week of: _____

	Monday	Tuesday	Wednesday	Thursday	Friday
Date					
Sharing Time	Introduce the children to each other. Discuss school.	Classroom Rules	Review Safety Rules	Song: Good Morning To You	Book: *School Bus*
Art	Finger Painting	Play Dough	Easel Painting	Drawing and Coloring	Cutting and Pasting
Story Time	Book: *Blue Bug Goes To School*	Book: *Berenstain Bears Go To School*	Book: *Will I Have A Friend?*	Book: *My Teacher Sleeps In School*	Book: *Starting School*
Circle Time	Family Photos	Song: Friends	Song/Activity: Hokey Pokey	Activity: The Freeze	Activity: Name Game
Food Experiences	Salty Foods	Sour Foods	Crunchy Foods	Soft Foods	Sweet Foods
Theme Activities	Song/Activity: If You're Happy	Flannel Activity: The People Who Live At My House	Book: *The Flying School Bus*	Book: *I Like Me*	Song: The Wheels On The Bus

Monday

Materials Needed for the Week:

- old magazines, camera and film, different textured sandpapers, rocks of various textures, sizes, and colors, shape note pads (available at school supply stores)

Sharing Time: Introductions

- Introduce the children to one another and also to the staff. Discuss what we do at school and show children the learning centers. Show children where the bathroom is located and answer any questions they may have.

Art: Finger Painting

- Use the recipe on page 6. Let children paint a picture for the bulletin board.

Story Time: Book

- Read the *Blue Bug Goes To School* by Virginia Poulet.

Food Experience: Salty Food

- Let children become acquainted with different types of foods this week. Have them try some salty foods today such as soda crackers with salted tops or pretzels.

Circle Time: Photographs

- Take photographs of children with their mothers and fathers as they arrive or leave school. Have double prints made. Hang one set on the bulletin board in the classroom and place the second set in a photo album in the book corner.

Theme Activity: Sing a song.

- Have children perform the movements in the song as they sing.

"If You're Happy" (Traditional)

If you're happy and you know it, clap your hands.
If you're happy and you know it, clap your hands.
If you're happy and you know it,
Then your face will surely show it.
If you're happy and you know it, clap your hands.

If you're happy and you know it, stamp your feet, etc.
If you're happy and you know it shout, "Hurray!," etc.
If you're happy and you know it, do all three, etc.

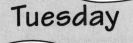

Tuesday

Our Class Rules

1. Share with others
2.

Sharing Time: Classroom Rules

Let children help you make up the rules for the classroom. Keep them very simple and only have two or three. Make sure you discuss safety rules. Print them for all to see.

Art: Play Dough

Let children play with play dough. Use the recipe on page 6. Let them create something for the classroom and display it for all to see the first week.

Story Time: Book

Read the *Berenstain Bears Go To School* by Stan and Jan Berenstain

Circle Time: Song

Sing "Friends" from the record *On The Move With Greg and Steve.* Afterwards, talk about making new friends at school.

Food Experiences: Sour Food

Taste some sour foods, such as lemons.

Theme Activities: Flannel Board

"The People Who Live At My House"

Make flannel figures of different family members. Include an adult male, adult female, boy, girl, and baby. See patterns on page 17. Discuss who lives at each child's house. Have children take turns choosing the characters that live at their house and then move the characters around. Encourage them to tell a story about their family. Have available several figures that can represent family members.

Wednesday

Sharing Time: Review safety rules.

Ask the children what type of emergencies would require them to leave the classroom. Talk about why it would be very important for them to listen and follow all directions. Then discuss and practice exiting the classroom in case of an emergency.

Art: Easel Painting

Have children become acquainted with easels and painting. Provide four colors: red, yellow, blue, and green, and let them paint pictures with these colors.

Story Time: Book

Read the story *Will I Have A Friend?* by Miriam Cohen.

Circle Time: Song and Dance

Have children sing "The Hokey Pokey" while following the movements.
"The Hokey Pokey" (Traditional)
You put your right hand in, you put your right hand out,
You put your right hand in, and you shake it all about.
You do the Hokey Pokey and you turn yourself around,
That's what it's all about.
You put your left hand in, etc.
You put your right foot in, etc.
You put your left foot in, etc.
You put your head in, etc.
You put your whole self in, etc.
You do the Hokey Pokey, you do the Hokey Pokey,
You do the Hokey Pokey.
That's what it's all about!

Repeat for each verse, substituting with the correct body part.

Food Experiences: Crunchy Food

Try some crunchy foods. These can include carrots, celery, or apples.

Theme Activities: Book

Share the story *The Flying School Bus* by Seymour Reit.

Thursday

Sharing Time: Song

"Good Morning to You" (Traditional)
Good morning to you,
And how do you do?
We're all in our places,
With sun shiny faces.
And this is the way,
We start a new day.

Art: Drawing and Coloring

Have children become acquainted with your procedures for
passing out and using materials as you pass out paper and
large crayons. Discuss the different colors with the children
and suggest they draw something they learned this week.

Story Time: Book

Read *My Teacher Sleeps In School* by Leatie Weiss.

Circle Time: Movement Activity

Do "The Freeze" from the record *We All Live Together, Vol. 2.* As the children listen to the second,
have them follow the directions.

Food Experiences: Soft Food

Taste some soft foods. Yogurt, pudding, and cottage cheese are some good ones to try.

Theme Activities: Book.

Read the book *I Like Me* by Nancy Carlson. Let children decide on ways they like themselves.
Encourage them to share this with the class.

Friday

Sharing Time: Book

Review safety rules. Talk about how to handle scissors safely. Read *School Bus* by Donald Crews.

Art: Cutting and Pasting

Emphasize the safe use of scissors. Let the children cut pictures out of magazines and paste them onto construction paper. Use the opportunity to observe the children's cutting skills.

Story Time: Book

Read and discuss the story *Starting School* by Janet and Allan Ahlberg. Let the children talk about their first week of school.

Circle Time: Name Game

Play this name game. The first child says his or her name, then the next child says his or her name and repeats the first child's name. Play continues until the last child or the teacher has repeated everyone's name.

Food Experiences: Sweet Food

Let children taste some naturally sweet foods. Ripe fruit and unsweetened applesauce are good choices.

Theme Activities: Song

Ask children if they ride the bus to school or have ever taken a bus ride before singing this song. As they sing, make up movements to go with the actions mentioned in the song.

"The Wheels On The Bus" (Traditional)

The wheels on the bus go round and round,
Round and round, round and round.
The wheels on the bus go round and round,
All through the town.
The horn on the bus goes beep, beep, beep, etc.
The money on the bus goes clink, clink, clink, etc.
The people on the bus go bump, bump, bump, etc.

14

Classroom Additions

Center Ideas

As the students are getting acquainted with each other and with the classroom, try some of the following suggestions to make their introductions to learning centers easier.

• Have only a few toys and educational items out in each learning center so children won't be overwhelmed. Gradually add more and rotate items as the year progresses.

• Have the classroom arranged attractively.

• Have all displays at the children's eye level, if possible.

• The room should be arranged so you can see all areas of the classroom where the children will be interacting.

• Clearly mark each learning center with the number of children who may enter at one time. Use figures of children. (See patterns on page 17.)

• All materials and activities should be placed on a low shelf where they can be easily reached by the children.

• Have fire exits clearly marked with diagrams that children will understand. Put up a list of classroom and safety rules. Safety posters will help here.

Science

Let children get acquainted with different types of science equipment. Place some of these items in your science area:

• Magnifying glass

• rocks of various sizes, colors, textures

• sandpaper of different textures

• smooth piece of tile

• fish aquarium or terrarium

Teachers' Aids

Prepare these extras in advance of introducing your unit so they are ready to work with during the week. For directions see page 5.

File Folder Activities:

Choose the skills you wish to emphasize this week. See directions on pages 5-6.

• School Bus and School House

• Back-to-School Child to School House

• Back-to-School Child to School Bus

Classroom Additions (cont.)

• Back to School Name Tags

Cut shapes from construction paper, purchase shape note pads, or use patterns throughout this book. On the name tags write children's names, their parent's names, and children's birthdates. Laminate all tags so they can be reused. Write information with a wipe-off marker or crayon. These tags can be placed on the bulletin board or on a section of a wall. They may also be left up all year. Add the children's and parents' pictures and it becomes an appropriate first week of school bulletin board.

Bulletin Board Ideas:

• Continue the theme in your classroom by using some of the bulletin board ideas and patterns.

• Welcome to School Materials   • Children and Parents Photographs

• School House   • School Bus

• Information Tags

For Parents

Send these tips home to help parents enrich their child's education.

• Talk to your child about going to school.

• Talk about what he/she will learn at school.

• Talk about why we go to school.

• Read to your child daily.

• Play learning games with your child.

• Reinforce classroom, safety, and bus rules at home with your child.

• Offer to volunteer and share ideas with the teachers.

• Ask teacher to share nutritional snack recipes with you.

Bibliography

Children's Books
Ahlberg, Janet and Allen. ***Starting School.*** Viking Press, 1988
Berenstain, Stan and Jan. ***The Berenstain Bears Go To School.*** Random House, 1978
Carlson, Nancy. ***I Like Me.*** Trumpet Club, 1988
Cohen, Miriam. ***Will I Have A Friend?*** Macmillan, 1967
Crews, Donald. ***School Bus.*** Greenwillow, 1984
Poulet, Virginia. ***Blue Bug Goes To School.*** Children's Press, 1985
Reit, Seymour. ***The Flying School Bus.*** Western Publishing, 1990
Weiss, Leatie. ***My Teacher Sleeps In School.*** Frederick Warne, 1984

Records
Steve Millang and Greg Scelsa. ***We All Live Together, Vol.2.*** Youngheart Records, 1978
Steve Millang and Greg Scelsa. ***On The Move With Steve and Greg.*** Youngheart Records, 1983
Steve Millang and Greg Scelsa. ***We All Live Together, Vol.3.*** Youngheart Records, 1979

Patterns

Patterns

18

© *Teacher Created Resources, Inc.*

Weekly Theme: *Pets*   Week of: _____

	Monday	Tuesday	Wednesday	Thursday	Friday
Date					
Sharing Time	Fingerplay: This Kitty	Fingerplay: Two Little Puppy Dogs	Fingerplay: Goldfish	Fingerplay: I Saw A Little Bird	Book: *Herbie Hamster, Where Are You?*
Art	Cat Ears	Paper Plate Dog	Fish and Fish Bowl	Seed Collage	Draw Your Favorite Pet
Story Time	Song: Three Little Kittens	Flannel Story: The Dog and the Bumblebee	Fingerplay: I Caught A Fish Alive	Fingerplay: Five Little Robins	Book: *Pet Show*
Circle Time	Fingerplay: Five Kittens	Song: B-I-N-G-O	Activity: Fishing	Fingerplay: Blackbirds	Book: *The Sesame Street Pet Show*
Food Experiences	Milk	Doggie Bones	Fish Crackers	Sunflower Seeds	Animal Crackers
Theme Activities	Book: *Millions of Cats*	Fingerplay: This Little Doggie	Book: *A Fish Out of Water*	Flannel Story: The Bird, The Mouse, and The Bat	Field Trip

Monday

Materials Needed For The Week:

large white paper plates, various types of seeds, unshelled sunflower seeds, edible sunflower seeds, milk, animal crackers, paper cups, construction paper

Sharing Time:

Finger Play: "This Kitty"

Discuss children's pets, especially cats. Let children tell their pets' names. Then do the finger play with the children.

"This Kitty"
This kitty said, "I smell a mouse,"
This kitty said, "Let's hunt through the house."
This kitty said, "Let's go creepy creep."
This kitty said, "is the mouse asleep?"
This kitty said, "Meow, meow, I saw him go through
This hole just now."

(Start by holding up all five fingers. At each line take one away. On the last line have the final finger run through a hole made by the left hand.)

Art: Cat Ears

Let children cut out cat ears from construction paper. Glue onto a two inch (5 cm) wide band that fits the child's head. Let them wear their headbands as they sing the "Three Little Kittens."

Story Time: Song

Sing the traditional English song "Three Little Kittens" with the children.

1 Three little kittens
They lost their mittens
And they began to cry,
Oh, Mother dear,
We sadly fear
Our mittens we have lost.

2 What! Lost your mittens,
You naughty kittens!
Then you shall have no pie.
Mee-ow, mee-ow, mee-ow
No, you shall have no pie.

3 The three little kittens
They found their mittens,
And they began to cry,
Oh, Mother dear,
See here, see here,
Our mittens we have found.

4 Put on your mittens,
You silly kittens,
And you shall have some pie.
Purr-r, purr-r, purr-r,
Oh, let us have some pie.

Monday (cont.)

5 The three little kittens
Put on their mittens
And soon ate up the pie;
Oh, Mother dear,
We greatly fear
Our mittens we have soiled.

6 What! Soiled your mittens,
You naughty kittens!
Then they began to sigh,
Mee-ow, mee-ow, mee-ow,
Then they began to sigh.

7 The three little kittens
They washed their mittens,
And hung them out to dry;
Oh, Mother dear,
Do you not hear;
Our mittens we have washed.

8 What! Washed your mittens,
Then you're good kittens,
But I smell a rat close by.
Mee-ow, mee-ow, mee-ow,
We smell a rat close by.

Circle Time: Finger Play

"Five Kittens" (Traditional)

Five little kittens standing in a row, (Hold up five fingers.)
They nod their heads to the children so. (Bend fingers.)
They run to the left; they run to the right. (Run fingers to the left and then to the right)
They stand up and stretch in the bright sunlight. (Stretch fingers out tall.)
Along comes a dog who's in for some fun. (Hold up one finger from opposite hand.)
ME-OW! See those little kittens run! (Let fingers run.)

Food Experiences: Milk

Discuss why milk is good for you. Which pets love milk? Find out if milk is good for all pets. Serve each child a glass of milk.

Theme Activities: Book

Read *Millions Of Cats* by Wanda Gag. Ask questions about the book. Discuss all of the cats. Make sure all questions asked have more than one correct answer.

Tuesday

Sharing Time: Finger Play

"Two Little Puppy Dogs"

Two little puppy dogs *(Hold up two fingers.)*
Lying in a heap, *(Let two fingers fall down.)*
Soft and wooly *(Pet two fingers with opposite hand.)*
And fast asleep. *(Lay hands against the
side of your face and close eyes.)*
Along came a pussycat *(Hold up one
finger from opposite hand and move
toward the two fingers.)*
Creeping near, "Meow,"
She cried right in their ear.
Two little puppy dogs *(Hold up two fingers.)*
After one cat, *(Two fingers chase the one finger.)*
Did you ever play tag like that? *(Point to children.)*

This finger play may also be done as a flannel activity. Discuss how children should care for their pets.

Art: Paper Plate Dog

Let the children make a paper plate dog. Have ready for each child two dog ears cut from construction paper. Children draw a dog's face on a paper plate then glue one ear on each side of the paper plate.

Story Time: Flannel Story See patterns on page 29-30.

"The Dog and The Bumblebee" (Traditional)

A little dog set out one day, adventuring was he—
When what did he meet upon the way but a great big bumblebee!
"Bzz, bzz, bzz," said the bumblebee,
"Little dog—stay away from me."
The little dog laughed, "Silly fly—you can't give me a scare.
Afraid of no little bug am I—and I will bite you there!"
"Bzz, bzz, bzz," said the bumblebee.
"I'm warning you-stay away from me."
But the little dog opened his mouth up wide—and just as you'd suppose—
"Very well," the bee replied-and stung the little dog's nose!
The little dog yelped, "Oh-oh-oh," and the bee replied, "I told you so."
So the little dog turned-and ran did he-as fast as he could go—
fast as he could go
Now—he nevermore will bite a bee! Absolutely NO!

Tuesday (cont.)

Circle Time: Song

Sing the traditional song "Bingo" about the farmer and his dog. Children will love when you add additional verses and just have them clap the letters you leave out.

"Bingo"

There was a farmer had a dog
And BINGO was his name-o
B-I-N-G-O, B-I-N-G-O,
B-I-N-G-O, and Bing-o was his name-o.

Food Experiences: Doggie Bones

Make a soft pretzel dough and let each child shape it into a bone. Bake and eat when cool. Canned biscuits can be molded into a dog bone shape. Allow one biscuit per child.

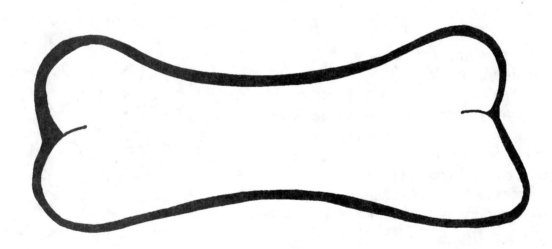

Theme Activities: Finger Play

"This Little Doggie"

(Start by holding up five fingers.)

This little doggie ran away to play. *(Take one finger away.)*
This little doggie said, "I'll go too some day." *(Take next finger away.)*
This little doggie began to dig and dig. *(Pretend to dig with next finger, then take it away.)*
This little doggie danced a funny jig. *(Pretend to dance with next finger, then take it away.)*
This little doggie cried, "Ki! Yi! Ki! Yi!
I wish I were big." *(Take last finger away.)*

Wednesday

Sharing Time: Finger Play

Discuss what children should feed their pets, especially fish. Then share the finger play with them.

"Goldfish"

My darling little goldfish *(Wiggle one finger.)*
Hasn't any toes. *(Point to your toes.)*
He swims around without a sound *(Pretend one finger is swimming.)*
And bumps his hungry nose. *(Point to nose.)*
He can't get out to play with me *(Point to yourself)*
Nor I get in to him. *(Point to children.)*
Although I say, "Come out and play," *(Motion finger to come out.)*
He says, "Come in and swim." *(Pretend you are swimming.)*

Art: Fish and Fish Bowl

Cut off about two inches (5 cm) from a paper plate. This is the fish bowl. Children can either draw or cut out colored fish from construction paper. Fish can be glued to paper plate. Attach string and hang from ceiling.

Story Time: Finger Play

"I Caught A Fish Alive" (Traditional)
One, two, three, four, five, *(Hold up five fingers, one at a time.)*
I caught a fish alive. *(Imitate holding up fish.)*
Six, seven, eight, nine, ten, *(Raise up fingers of other hand.)*
I let it go again. *(Imitate throwing fish back.)*
Why did I let it go? *(Hold up hands, looking puzzled.)*
Because it bit my finger so! *(Shake right hand.)*
Which finger did it bite? *(Hold up right hand.)*
The little finger on the right. *(Hold up little finger.)*

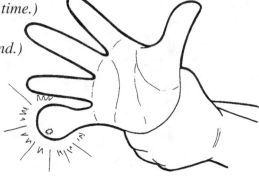

Circle Time: Fishing

Use fish patterns on page 30 to make several different colored fish to use with this activity. See page 7 for directions on making fishing poles.

Food Experiences: Goldfish Crackers

Give children several different flavored fish shaped crackers to try.

Theme Activities: Book

Ask the children what they think it would mean to be a fish out of water. Then read the story A *Fish Out Of Water* by Helen Palmer. Ask open-ended questions about the book.

Thursday

Sharing Time: Rhyming Finger Play

Discuss the importance of being careful around strange pets. Talk about how children would react to a stray bird, then do the Mother Goose rhyming finger play.

"I Saw a Little Bird"

Once I saw a little bird, come hop,
Hop, hop. *(Make one finger go up and down.)*
So I cried "Little bird, will you stop,
Stop, stop." *(Hold up flat hand.)*
I was going to the window to say "Howdy-do,
Howdy-do." *(Wave hello.)*
But he shook his little tail, and away he flew,
Flew, flew, away he flew. *(Make hand go up and down as if flying.)*

Art: Seed Collage

Explain that birds like to eat seeds. Then provide different types of seeds for the children to glue onto construction paper and create a collage.

Story Time: Finger Play

"Five Little Robins"
Five little robins in a sycamore tree, *(Hold up five fingers.)*
A father, *(Hold up thumb.)*
A mother, *(Hold up pointer finger.)*
And babies three; *(Hold up remaining fingers.)*
Father brought a worm, *(Point to thumb.)*
Mother brought a bug, *(Point to pointer finger.)*
The three baby robins started to tug;
This one ate the bug, *(Point to middle finger.)*
This one ate the worm, *(Point to ring finger.)*
This one sat and waited for his turn. *(Point to little finger.)*

Circle Time: Finger Play

"Blackbirds" (Mother Goose)
Two little blackbirds sitting on a hill, *(Hold up index fingers.)*
One named Jack and one named Jill. *(Bend one finger at a time.)*
Fly away Jack. *(Hand behind back.)*
Fly away Jill. *(Hand behind back.)*
Come back Jack. *(Bring hand back to front.)*
Come back Jill. *(Bring hand back to front.)*

Food Experiences: Sunflower Seeds

Show sunflower seeds in their shells. Crack a few open for children to see. Then give them some shelled seeds to taste. How do they taste? What pets eat sunflower seeds?

Theme Activities: Flannel Story

Use patterns on page 29 to help tell the following story.

"The Bird, The Mouse, And The Bat" (Anonymous)

BIRD: What a strange mouse that is. It can fly.

MOUSE: What a strange bird it is. It has fur.

BIRD: Oh, no! That is not a bird. We never show our ears.

MOUSE: I am sure that it is not a mouse. Mice cannot fly.

BIRD: But look at its fur!

MOUSE: But look at its wings!

BIRD: But look at its ears!

MOUSE: I think it is more like a mouse than a bird; but whoever heard of a mouse that could fly?

BAT: Are you talking about me?

BIRD: Yes; please tell us who you are.

BAT: My name is Bat. I heard you talking about me, but you called me a bird.

BIRD: Oh, no! I called you a mouse.

BAT: What can a mouse do best?

MOUSE: I can run.

BAT: But I cannot run at all.

MOUSE: Then you are a poor kind of mouse.

BAT: I will tell you what I can do. I can fly as well as a bird.

BIRD: But do you lay eggs in a nest?

BAT: No! I have no nest and no eggs.

BIRD: Then you are a poor kind of bird.

MOUSE: Where do you sleep?

BAT: Oh, I hang by my toes in a barn.

BIRD: What a way to sleep!

MOUSE: Who takes care of your little ones?

BAT: I carry them about with me until they are old enough to care for themselves.

MOUSE: What a way to keep house!

BIRD: Your wings are not like mine.

BAT: No, my wings are my hands too. I feel my way with them.

BIRD: You fly as if you do not see very well.

BAT: That's true, but I can fly by listening to the echoes of my sounds. This means that even though I can't see, I can fly at night and in the darkest caves. That's something Mrs. Bird or Mrs. Mouse can't do!

BIRD: True. But what are you eating?

BAT: I am catching flies for supper.

MOUSE: Your eyes are small, and your ears are large. Can you hear better than you can see?

BAT: Yes, but I can touch better than I can see or hear. I would not give my wings for pretty ones like Mrs. Bird's, nor would I give them for feet like those of Mrs. Mouse.

BIRD: I would not give up my nest to hang by my toes.

MOUSE: Are your teeth as sharp as mine?

BAT: I have sharp teeth.

MOUSE: I am afraid that you will bite.

BAT: I bite when anyone tries to hurt me.

MOUSE: Good-by, Mrs. Bat. See how fast I can run!

BIRD: Good-by, Mrs. Bat. I am going home to my nest and my little ones.

BAT: Good-by. Please don't think that I would bite you. Why is everyone afraid of me? I do not wish to hurt anyone.

Friday

Sharing Time: Book

Discuss what the children have learned about different pets this week. Read *Herbie Hamster, Where Are You?* by Terrence Blacker.

Art: Draw Your Favorite Pet

Provide children with various drawing media. Encourage them to draw their favorite pets. Write on their paper the name and type of each child's pet. Hang them up for all to see.

Story Time: Book

Read the book *Pet Show* by Ezra Jack Keats.

Circle Time: Book

Discuss all the types of pets students have talked about this week. Let them take turns telling about their favorite pets. Share the book *The Sesame Street Pet Show* and discuss the different types of pets in the book.

Food Experiences: Animal Crackers

Give each child a handful of animal crackers. Let children decide which ones would make good pets before they eat them.

Theme Activities: Field Trip

Take a field trip to the local pet store. Discuss the different pets the children see. If taking a field trip is not possible, then show the children a filmstrip about pets or re-read their favorite books from this week on pets.

Classroom Additions

Center Ideas

These materials can be placed in the learning centers in addition to your regular materials.

- Housekeeping: small brushes and combs for grooming pets, stuffed animals for grooming
- Circle: pictures of different pets, felt board, and pieces for the different stories
- Books: books about pets, stuffed animals to read to
- Music: records about pets or animals, stuffed animals
- Table Activities: file folder activities listed, animal lotto games, animal puzzles
- Blocks: fishing poles, fish cutouts, plastic animals
- Art: paper plates, crayons, markers, paints, paper, paste, various types of seeds
- Puppets: various animal puppets
- Science: pets to observe, aquarium or plastic fish bowl with plastic fish if a real one is not possible
- Science Activities: During the week, bring in live pets. Note: Observe closely while children are touching any animal. Have available pictures of each animal that the children are able to observe. Let them discuss what the animals eat and where they might live.

Teachers' Aids

Prepare these extras in advance of introducing your unit so they are ready to work with them during the week.

- Pet File Folder Activities
- Kittens and Matching Mittens
- Matching Dog to Bones/Matching Dogs to Spots
- Matching Fish Sizes/Matching Fish to Worms
- Match the Hamsters/Match the Birds Bulletin Board Ideas
- Pictures or photos of different animals
- Display children's art work done during the week

For Parents

- Take your child to the local animal shelter to look at or to pick out a pet. Encourage your child to be responsible for his/her pet including feeding, grooming, and giving it attention.
- Go to the library. Let your child pick out books about animals.
- Visit a pet store to look at different types of pets.
- Discuss the names of each pet and also what type foods they eat.

Bibliography

Children's Books

Blacker, Terrence. *Herbie Hamster, Where Are You?* Random House, 1990

Crawford, Thomas. *A Bath For A Beagle.* Troll, 1970

dePaola, Tomie. *Tomie dePaola's Mother Goose.* G.P. Putnam's Sons, 1985

Gag, Wanda. *Millions of Cats.* Putnam, 1928

Keats, Ezra Jack. *Pet Show.* Macmillan, 1972

Kingsley, Emily Perl. *The Sesame Street Pet Show. Western. 1980*

Palmer, Helen. *A Fish Out Of Water.* Random House, 1961

Patterns

Patterns

Patterns

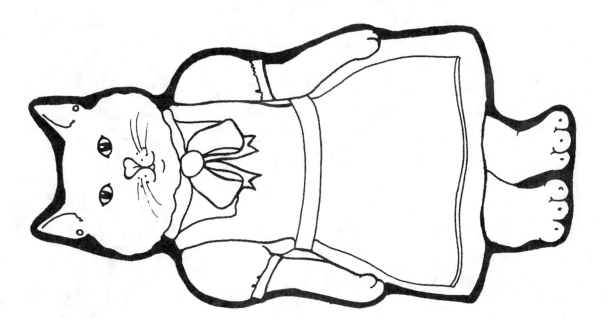

Patterns

Weekly Theme: *Apples and Worms*   Week of: _____

	Monday	**Tuesday**	**Wednesday**	**Thursday**	**Friday**
Date					
Sharing Time	Discussion About Apples	Fingerplay: The Apple Tree	Fingerplay: Five Red Apples	Book: *Wilbur Worm*	Fingerplay: Dancing Apples
Art	Classroom Apple Tree	Apple Picture	Fingerpaint with Red	Easel Paint with Yellow	Green Play Dough
Story Time	Book: *Apples*	Book: *Rain Makes Applesauce*	Book: *I Can Read About Johnny Appleseed*	Flannel Story: The Boy and the Worm	Book: *The Season's of Arnold's Apple Tree*
Circle Time	Leaf Walk	Fishing for Apples	Musical Apples	Song: Walter the Waltzing Worm	Pretend to be Worms
Food Experiences	Tasting Different Kinds of Apples	Apples with Other Foods	Apple Sauce	Apple Smiles	Apple Juice
Theme Activities	Planting Apple Seeds	Book: *Apples and Pumpkins*	Counting Apples on Flannel Apple Tree	Finding Objects in Apple Tree	Fishing for Apples and Worms

Materials Needed For The Week:

apples: two red, two yellow, and two green; two inch (1.3 cm) wooden dowels; two small magnets; small metal paper clips; wicker baskets of various sizes; plastic apples; potting soil; small drinking cups

Sharing Time: Discussion about Apples

Where do apples come from? What different colors are apples? Do you like red, yellow, or green apples the best? Which apples are sweet? Which apples are tart?

Art: Classroom Apple Tree

Use a large piece of bulletin board paper. Draw a tree with branches. Children can use an apple shaped sponge or use paint and a brush to put apples on the tree. When paint is dry, write the children's names on their apples. Hang apple tree art in the classroom or on a bulletin board.

Story Time: Book

Read *Apples* by N. Hogrogian.

Circle Time: Leaf Walk

Take a leaf walk outside and collect apple leaves. If this is not possible, cut leaves from construction or tissue paper and place them around your room or building before taking the walk. Have children find the leaves.

Food Experiences: Tasting Different Kinds of Apples

Provide three types of apples-red, yellow, and green. Wash the apples and cut them into pieces, and place on three separate paper plates. Tell children the name of each apple. Have them compare the color, texture, and taste of each type of apple.

Theme Activities: Planting Apple Seeds

Provide small paper drinking cups, apple seeds, potting soil or dirt, and water. Save seeds from the apples used for the food experience. Give each child a cup and have the children fill their cups with soil. Place finger in soil to make a small hole and drop in the seed. Dampen the soil with a small amount of water. Place cups in a well lighted place and water occasionally; then read the children the book *The Tiny Seed* by Eric Carle.

Tuesday

Sharing Time: Finger Play

> ***"The Apple Tree"*** (Traditional)
> Away up high in an apple tree, *(Raise arms high.)*
> Two red apples smiled at me. *(Smile and hold up two fingers.)*
> I shook that tree as hard as I could; *(Shake hands.)*
> Down came those apples, *(Bring hands down.)*
> And mmmmm, were they good. *(Rub tummy.)*

Art: Apple Pictures

Have children cut out apples from red, yellow, or green construction paper. Glue onto another sheet of paper. Glue on tissue paper leaves or real leaves collected on Monday's leaf walk. While children are doing this activity, reinforce the colors of different apples.

Story Time: Book Read

Rain Makes Applesauce by J. Schew.

Circle Time: Fishing For Apples

Make fishing poles according to the directions on page 7. Cut apple shapes from red, yellow, and green construction paper. Attach a metal paper clip to each apple shape. Place apples on a large piece of blue butcher paper which has been cut into the shape of a pond. Lay the items on the floor and ask children to fish for different colored apples or to pick up a certain number of apples.

Suggestions: Apple shapes can be laminated or covered with clear contact paper first so they will

last longer. Shapes or dots can be written on the apples and used for shape recognition or counting activities.

Food Experiences: Apples with Other Foods

Slice apples. Spread with peanut butter or cheese spread and let children taste them.

Theme Activities: Book

Wednesday

Sharing Time: Finger Play or Flannel Activity

"Five Red Apples"
Five red apples hanging in a tree, *(Hold up five fingers.)*
The juiciest apples you ever did see.
The wind came by and gave an angry frown, *(Fingers flutter downward.)*
And one little apple came tumbling down. *(One finger falls.)*
Four red apples, hanging in a tree, etc.
(Hold up four fingers and continue until no apples are left.)

This poem can be adapted for children to count from ten red apples down. Red apples can be cut from flannel or construction paper and used as a flannel activity. See page 41 for an apple pattern. Then cut a large green cloud shape for the top of the tree and a brown rectangular shape for the tree trunk.

Art: Fingerpaint with Red Paint

Use the fingerpaint recipe on page 6. Add red food coloring. Use on fingerpaint paper or a table top.

Story Time: Book

Read I *Can Read About Johnny Appleseed* by J.I. Anderson.

Circle Time: Musical Apples

Make an apple necklace for each child playing. Cut a small apple shape from red, yellow, and green construction paper. Punch a small hole in the top of the apple and attach a piece of yarn large enough to loosely go over the child's head.

Let the children wear their necklaces while playing Musical Apples. This is played like musical chairs. Place a picture of an apple on each chair. Put out one less chair than children who will be playing. Play some marching music, and have children sit on the chairs as the music stops. Each time you play the music eliminate a chair. The child who doesn't get a seat needs to wait until the game starts over. The winner is left when there is only one child on one chair.

Food Experiences: Making Applesauce

Wash and peel five apples. Cut into quarters and remove the cores. Put the pieces into a saucepan, and add ¾ cup (177 mL) of water. Cover and simmer until tender. Let the apples cool. Let children take turns mashing the apples with a potato masher or mixer. Add sugar and cinnamon to taste.

Theme Activities: Counting Apples on a Flannel Apple Tree

Make a large flannel apple tree. Follow directions given at Sharing Time and make several different colored apples. Let children count the number of apples on the tree or let them name the colors.

Thursday

Sharing Time: Book

Read *Wilbur Worm* by Richard and Nicky Hale, and Andre Amstutz.

Art: Easel Paint with Yellow Paint

Different shades of yellow can be obtained by adding small amounts of white paint for lighter shades or orange paint for darker shades. Let the children help make these different shades and discuss which is lighter and which is darker.

Story Time: Flannel Story

Make flannel pieces of grass, a boy, and a worm. (See page 42 for patterns.)

"The Boy and the Worm" (Anonymous)

One time a little boy was playing in his backyard. In the grass he saw a worm. He watched the worm for a long time. Then he said, "What an ugly thing you are! You have no hair, no legs, and I don't think you have any eyes."

That doesn't matter," said the worm. "All worms are like that. We get a along fine."

"But do you know how to do anything?" said the boy. "The animals run about, and the birds fly and sing. You cannot do any of those things."

"True," said the worm. "I cannot do those things."

"I know how to do everything," said the boy. "I even know how to read and write."

"I do not need to know how to read and write," said the worm. "But, tell me, do you know how to live in the world all by yourself? Can you feed yourself and take care of yourself without the help of your parents?"

"No, but I am still very young," said the boy.

"But I am much younger than you, and yet I can feed myself and take care of myself without any help. And besides, did you every see a worm that could talk?"

Circle Time: Song

Play "Walter the Waltzing Worm" form the record *Walter the Waltzing Worm.* Let the children sing along.

Food Experiences: Apple Smiles

Core and slice an apple. Spread peanut butter on one side of each apple slice. Place four tiny marshmallows on top of the peanut butter of one slice. Top with another apple slice, peanut butter side down. Gently squeeze together.

Theme Activities: Finding Object in an Apple Tree

Draw a large apple tree on construction paper. (Or use the flannel apple tree made on Wednesday.) Add leaves, apples, apple halves, apple cores, apple seeds, and worms. Children can find the objects at your request. Children can also be asked to place the apple on the tree, the worm under the tree, the leaves above the tree, etc.

Friday

Sharing Time: Finger Play

Use the following with the children.

"Dancing Apples" (Traditional)

Four little apples dancing in a tree, *(Let four fingers dance.)*
They danced so long that they set themselves free. *(Fingers fall.)*
They continued to dance as they fell to the ground.
And there by some children these apples were found.
"Oh! Look at the rosy one! *(Hold up one finger.)*
It almost bounced!"
"I'll take the red one!" *(Hold up second finger.)*
Another announced.
The third child laughed as he chose the yellow one. *(Hold up third finger.)*
"I'll take it to Mother, 'cause she lets me have fun."
The fourth child put the last one on a tray *(Put fourth finger in palm of left hand.)*
And carefully carried the green apple away.

Art: Green Play Dough

See page 6 for the recipe. Add green food coloring. Let children make green apples.

Story Time: Book Read *The Seasons of Arnold's Apple Tree* by Gail Gibbons.

Circle Time: Pretend To Be Worms

Children can wiggle on the floor and be worms. Make a large apple cutout from poster board or cardboard. Cut the hole large enough for children to crawl through.

Food Experiences: Apple Juice Tasting

Compare sweetened to unsweetened apple juice, and if possible, compare fresh apple juice to canned or frozen. Discuss with the children how apple juice may be bought in different forms.

Theme Activities: Fishing for Apples and Worms

See Circle Time on Tuesday. Use construction paper cutouts of worms and apples of different sizes.

Classroom Additions

Center Ideas

These materials can be placed in the learning centers in addition to your regular materials.

• Housekeeping: wicker baskets of various sizes, plastic apples

• Circle: classroom apple tree made in art on Monday, felt board with apple tree and apple cutouts

• Books: books about apples and worms

• Music: records about apples and worms

• Table Activities: file folder activities, apple and worm puzzles, apple lacing boards

• Blocks: fishing activity

• Art: provide different colors of red, yellow, and green paint and play dough

• Puppets: apple and worm, stick puppets, apple face masks made from paper plates

• Science: Display different types of apples. These include Granny Smith, Yellow Delicious, Red Delicious, McIntosh.

• Science Activities: Try some of the following:

  • Plant apple seeds.

  • Find earthworms and put them in a jar. Study how they move. Return them to the ground.

  • Collect leaves from different types of apple trees.

  • Conduct a science experiment. Cut an apple in half crosswise to show design of the seeds. How are they formed? What do they look like? Ask children questions about the apple such as: What design does the apple make? Were you surprised? Do you think any other fruit has a special shape inside it?

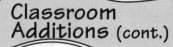

Classroom Additions (cont.)

Teachers Aids

Prepare these extras in advance of introducing your unit so they are ready to work with during the week.

File Folder Activities: Choose which skills you wish to emphasize this week. See directions on pages 5-6.

• Apple Tree and Apples Matching

• Apples and Worms
• Worms to Worms
• Apple Puzzle
• Apple cutouts of construction paper or felt

• Apples to Apples
• Worm Puzzle

Bulletin Board Ideas:

• Continue the theme in your classroom by using some of the bulletin board ideas and patterns.

• Apple Tree
• Apple Basket
• Large apple from poster board or cardboard

• Worms
• Apples of different colors

For Parents

• Make apple pies with your child.

• Serve applesauce and apple juice at home this week.

• Plant an apple seed with your child. Water it together and discuss its growth.

• Provide apples for snacks at home.

Bibliography

Children's Books

Anderson, J.I. *I Can Read About Johnny Appleseed.* Troll, 1977
Carle, Eric. *The Tiny Seed.* Picture Book Studio, 1987
Gibbons, Gail. *The Seasons of Arnold's Apple Tree.* Harcourt Brace Jovanovich, 1984
Hale, Richard & Nicky and Andre Amstutz. *Wilbur Worm.* Willowisp Press, 1986
Hogrogian, N. *Apples.* Macmillan, 1972
Rockwell, Anne. *Apple & Pumpkins.* Macmillan, 1989
Schew, J. *Rain Makes Applesauce.* Holiday House, 1964

Records

Hap Palmer. *Walter the Waltzing Worm.* Educational Activities, Inc., 1982.

Patterns

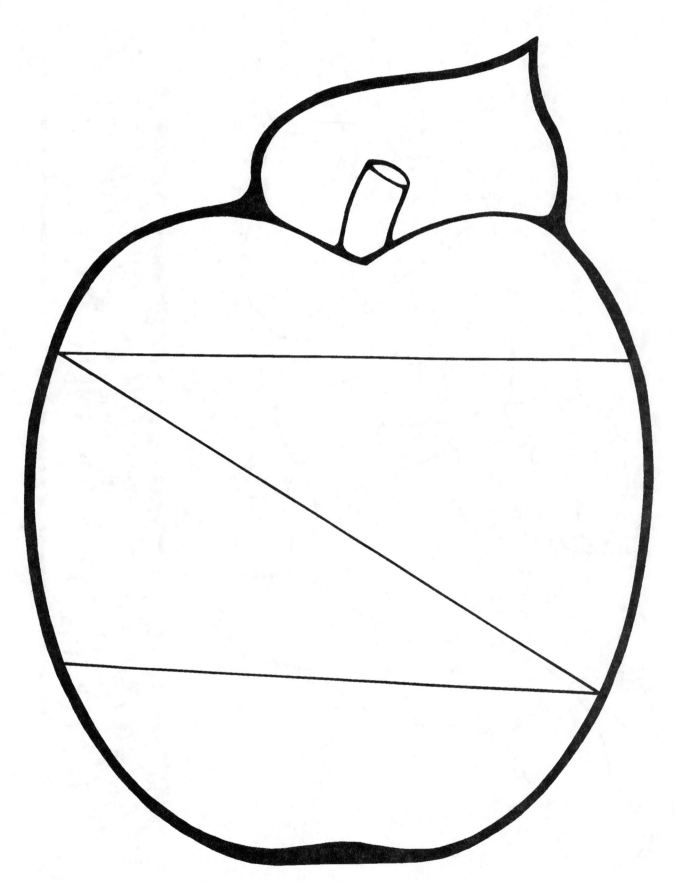

Patterns

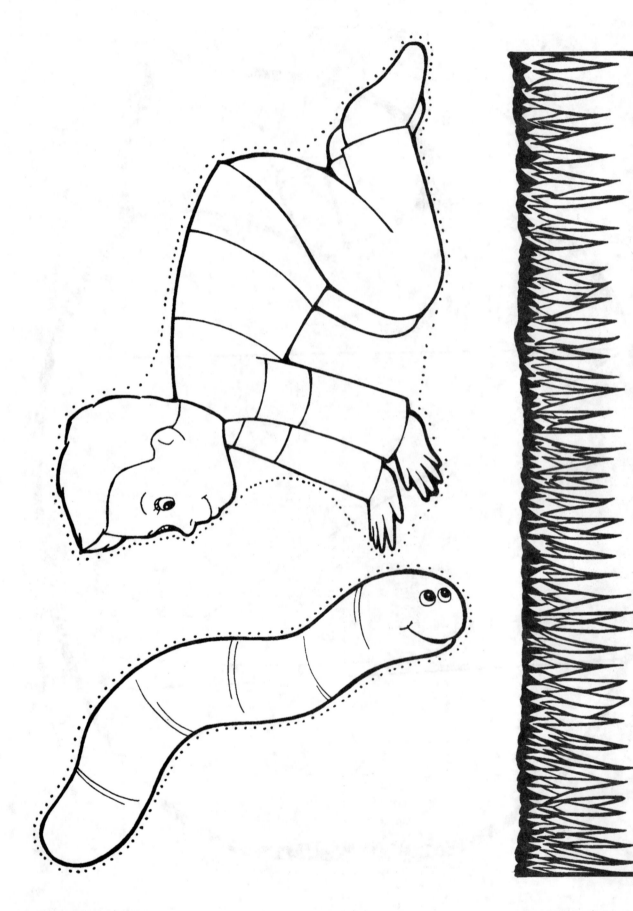

Patterns

Apples and Worms

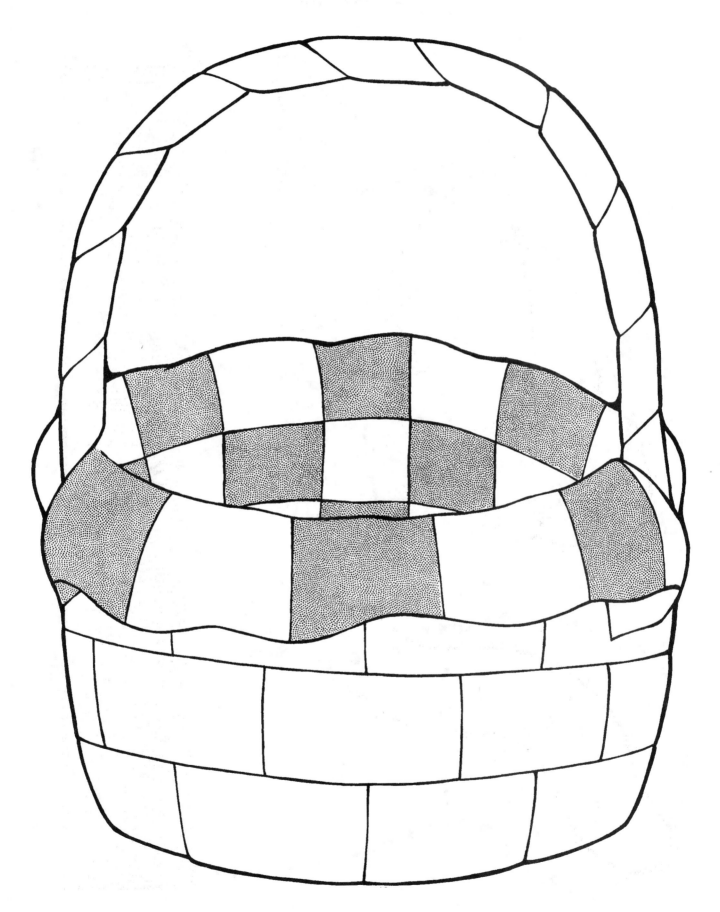

Patterns

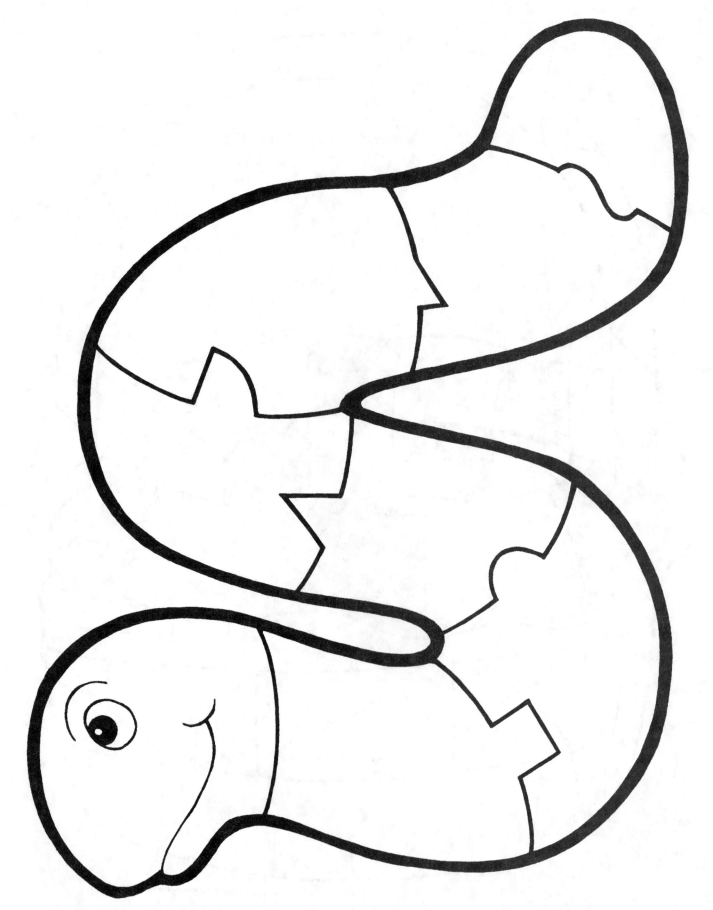

Patterns

Weekly Theme: _Fall_   Week of: _____

	Monday	Tuesday	Wednesday	Thursday	Friday
Date					
Sharing Time	Fingerplay: Leaves	Fingerplay or Flannel Activity: Five Little Squirrels	Fingerplay: I'm a Nut	Discussion: Colors of the Season	Discussion: Fall Weather
Art	Leaf People	Squirrel Puppet	Nut Stick Puppet	Leaf Rubbings	A Fall Tree
Story Time	Fingerplay: Squirrels in a Tree	Book: _Frederick_	Song: I Had a Little Nut Tree	Poem: "Harvest Home"	Book: _The Cinnamon Hen's Autumn Day_
Circle Time	Activity: Bowling in the Tree	Activity: Forest Animals	Activity: Musical Nuts	Falling Leaves	Activity: What I Like Best About Fall
Food Experiences	Turnip Greens	Cracking Nuts	Coconut Tasting	Honey	Squash
Theme Activities	Book: _Leaves_	Book: _Squirrels_	Fingerplay: Whisky, Frisky	Adopt a Tree	Activity: Crunching Leaves

Monday

Materials Needed For The Week:

various nuts and leaves, craft sticks, large cardboard box, large cut-out leaves from construction paper, can of turnip greens, honey, crackers, a whole coconut, a nut cracker, squash

Sharing Time: Finger Play

"Leaves" (Traditional)
The leaves are whirling round and round. *(Wave fingers.)*
The leaves are falling to the ground, *(Wave fingers downward.)*
Round and round, round and round, *(Roll one hand over the other.)*
Falling softly to the ground. *(Slowly wave hands downward.)*

Art: Leaf People

Cut out large leaves or use pattern on page 53. Have the children decorate the leaves with facial features, arms, and legs to create leaf people.

Story Time: Finger Play

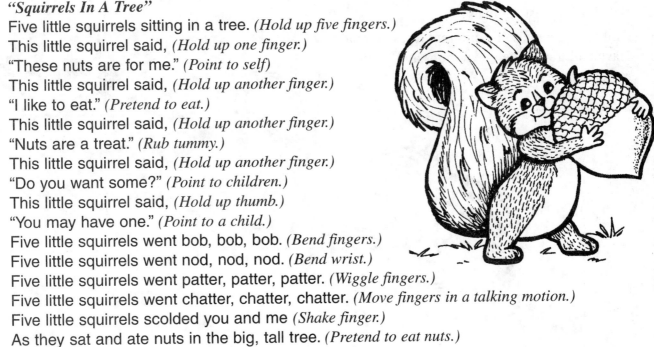

"Squirrels In A Tree"
Five little squirrels sitting in a tree. *(Hold up five fingers.)*
This little squirrel said, *(Hold up one finger.)*
"These nuts are for me." *(Point to self)*
This little squirrel said, *(Hold up another finger.)*
"I like to eat." *(Pretend to eat.)*
This little squirrel said, *(Hold up another finger.)*
"Nuts are a treat." *(Rub tummy.)*
This little squirrel said, *(Hold up another finger.)*
"Do you want some?" *(Point to children.)*
This little squirrel said, *(Hold up thumb.)*
"You may have one." *(Point to a child.)*
Five little squirrels went bob, bob, bob. *(Bend fingers.)*
Five little squirrels went nod, nod, nod. *(Bend wrist.)*
Five little squirrels went patter, patter, patter. *(Wiggle fingers.)*
Five little squirrels went chatter, chatter, chatter. *(Move fingers in a talking motion.)*
Five little squirrels scolded you and me *(Shake finger.)*
As they sat and ate nuts in the big, tall tree. *(Pretend to eat nuts.)*

Circle Time: Leaves Blowing in the Wind

Children pretend to be leaves blowing in the wind. Play a soft tempo piece of music while children dance, sway, and fall gently to the floor as if they were leaves.

Food Experiences: Turnip Greens

Try turnip greens or other leafy vegetables for a tasting experience.

Theme Activities: Book

Read *Leaves* by Fulvio Testa.

Tuesday

Sharing Time: Finger Play or Flannel Activity

"Five Little Squirrels" (Traditional)

Five little squirrels sat up in a tree; *(Hold up all five fingers.)*
This little squirrel said, "What do you see?" *(Wiggle thumb.)*
This little squirrel said, "I smell a gun!" *(Wiggle pointer finger.)*
This little squirrel said, "Oh, let's run!" *(Wiggle middle finger.)*
This little squirrel said, "Let's hide in the shade." *(Wiggle ring finger.)*
This little squirrel said, "I'm not afraid." *(Wiggle little finger.)*
Then BANG went the gun! *(Clap hands together.)*
And away the little squirrels ran, every one. *(Run all five fingers behind back.)*

Art: Squirrel Puppet

Cut several squirrels out of light brown construction paper. (Use the pattern on page 53.) Let children decorate and attach a craft stick to the back of the squirrel and make a stick puppet.

Story Time: Story Time

Read *Frederick* by Leo Lionni.

Circle Time: Forest Animals

Children pretend to be different forest animals. Have children make the motions and sounds of forest animals.

Food Experiences: Cracking Nuts

Provide children with walnuts and nut crackers. Show them how to crack the walnuts and very carefully remove the seed. Let them try eating a few pieces. (You may need to crack the nuts for the children.)

Theme Activities: Book

Read the book *Squirrels* by Brian Wildsmith.

Wednesday
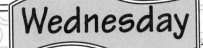

Sharing Time: Rhyme Time

"I'm a Nut" (Traditional)
I'm an acorn, small and round,
Lying on the cold, cold ground.
People pass and step on me,
That's why I'm all cracked, you see.
I'm a nut, *(Clap, clap.)*
I'm a nut, *(Clap, clap.)*
I'm a nut, *(Clap, clap.)*
I'm a nut. *(Clap, clap.)*

Art: Nut Stick Puppet

Use nut pattern on page 53. Cut several out of construction paper and attach a craft stick to the back of the nut. Use puppets while reading rhymes.

Story Time: Song

"Little Nut Tree" (Traditional)
I had a little nut tree
And nothing would it bear
But a silver nutmeg, and a golden pear.
The queen of Spain's daughter
Came to visit me
And all because of my little nut tree.

Circle Time: Musical Nuts

Play this like musical chairs. Place pictures of different nuts on chairs and have the children tell the names of the nuts on their chairs when they sit down. Pictures of nuts should be laminated before using.

Food Experiences: Coconut Tasting

Have a whole coconut in the shell. Crack open and cut into pieces. Shred some into a bowl. Let the children discover what this kind of nut tastes like.

Theme Activities: Finger Play

"Whisky, Frisky" (Traditional)
Whisky, frisky, hippity hop. *(Hold up one finger.)*
Up he goes to the treetop, *(Finger climbs up opposite arm.)*
Whirly, twirly, round and round, *(Finger goes in a circle motion.)*
Down he scampers to the ground. *(Finger runs down arm.)*
Furly, curly, what a tail, *(Wiggle finger.)*
Tall as a feather, broad as a sail. *(Hand goes up and then out wide.)*
Where's his supper? In the shell. *(Make a circle with fingers.)*
Snappy, cracky, out it fell. *(Open hand wide.)*

Thursday

Sharing Time: Colors of The Season

Talk about the colors of the season. When do leaves turn colors? Do all leaves change color? Share different leaves with the children.

Art: Leaf Rubbings

Give children leaves, a sheet of white paper, and crayons. Have them place the leaves under the paper. Rub the crayon on the paper over the leaves to create a leaf rubbing.

Story Time: Poem

Read "Harvest Home" by Arthur Guiterman from *The Random House Book of Poetry for Children*. Talk about the animals mentioned in the poem. Ask why the bee is called a "hummer."

Circle Time: Falling Leaves

Pretend to be falling leaves. Play some soothing music for the children. Encourage them to be fall leaves dropping off of trees. Have them lazily drift down to the ground as the music plays.

Food Experiences: Honey

Let the children taste two types of honey (like that which the bee in "Harvest Home" produces). Spread the honey on crackers. Can the children tell the difference? Do they like the taste?

Theme Activities: Adopt a Tree

Take the children for a walk and find a tree. See what it looks like now. Notice if it has leaves and what colors they are. Come back to visit the tree throughout the year and observe the changes.

50

Friday

Sharing Time: Fall Weather

Talk about the colors of fall. What colors do the children see in nature? Hold up several crayons and let them choose the colors that they feel represent fall. Help them to name colors.

Art: A Fall Tree

Give children red, green, gold, yellow, and orange crayons and a piece of white paper. Let them use the colors to draw a fall tree.

Story Time: Book

Read *The Cinnamon Hen's Autumn Day* by Sandra Dutton.

Circle Time: Experiences

What experiences do children enjoy most in the fall? Discuss these with the children and then let each child fill in the sentence: What I like best about fall is....

Food Experiences: Squash

Squashes are common fall foods. Choose one and open it for the children. Steam, microwave, or bake and let the children taste it.

Theme Activities: Crunching Leaves

If a large pile of fall leaves is accessible, let the children walk on them and experience the "crunching" sound they will produce. If leaves aren't accessible, scrunch newspapers or left over butcher paper into grocery bags, put them on the floor, and allow children to walk on them. This will produce a simulated crunching experience.

Classroom Additions

Center Ideas

Here are some suggestions of materials that can be placed in the learning centers in addition to your regular materials.

- Housekeeping: toy rakes, baskets, nuts in shells
- Circle: laminated pictures of nuts
- Books: books on fall, squirrels, nuts, leaves
- Music: tapes of nature sounds, soft music
- Table Activities: file folder activities listed, puzzles
- Blocks: trees, clean wood to build with
- Art: construction paper in fall colors, craft sticks, paper, red paint
- Puppets: bird, squirrel, nut, and leaf puppets
- Science: different types of nuts, leaves, and trees

Teachers' Aids

File Folder Activities: Choose which skills you wish to emphasize this week. See directions on pages 5-6.

- Leaf Wallpaper Matching
- Squirrel Matching Nuts

Bulletin Board Ideas:

- Trees in fall colors
- Squirrels and nuts
- Different types of nuts
- Forest Animals

For Parents

- Walk through the woods, collect nuts, and listen to the sounds of the woods.
- Take a leaf walk with your child. Look for different colored leaves.
- Discuss the colors of the leaves. Let your child find other items that are the same colors.
- Collect leaves for crayon rubbings.
- Dry leaves in an old book.
- Iron leaves between two sheets of wax paper. Frame with construction paper and hang in a window.

Bibliography

Children's Books

dePaola, Tomie. *Tomie dePaola's Mother Goose.* G.P. Putnam's, 1985
Dutton, Sandra. *The Cinnamon Hen's Autumn Day.* Macmillan, 1988
Lionni, Leo. *Frederick.* Pantheon, 1967
Prelutsky, Jack, selected by. *The Random House Book of Poetry for Children.* Random House, 1983
Testa, Fulvio. *Leaves.* Peter Bedrick, 1980
Wildsmith, Brian. *Squirrels.* Franklin Watts, 1975

Patterns

Weekly Theme: *Community Places and People #1*   Week of: _____

	Monday	Tuesday	Wednesday	Thursday	Friday
Date					
Sharing Time	Book: *My Doctor*	Book: *I Know a Dentist*	Book: *Mail and How It Moves*	Fingerplay: Policeman	Song/Activity: The Bus Song
Art	Stethoscope	Face Masks	Mailbag	Badges	Sailboat
Story Time	Fingerplay: Miss Polly	Fingerplay: Dentist	Fingerplay: Any Mail for Me?	Fingerplay: Traffic Lights	Fingerplay: Choo Choo Train
Circle Time	Activity: Name Your Body Parts	Activity: Pretend to Be Dentists	Activity: Field Trip to the Post Office	Poem: Police Officer	Activity: Vehicle Charades
Food Experiences	Discuss Healthy Eating	Soft Foods	Graham Crackers in White Envelopes	Peanut Butter Badges	Transportation Cookies
Theme Activities	Book: *Dr. Doctor*	Book: *My Dentist*	Book: *Where Does the Mail Go?*	Book: *Police*	Book: *Boat Book*

Monday

Materials Needed For The Week:

surgical gowns and discarded x-rays from your local hospital, cotton balls, pillow, blanket, pen light, band-aids, junk mail, stickers, paper towels, envelopes, foam egg cartons, toothpicks, ball of clay, cardboard boxes, shoe boxes, large paper bags, instant pudding or gelatin, graham crackers, peanut butter, raisins, honey, coconut, non-fat dry milk, refrigerated cookie dough, vehicle shaped cookie cutters

Sharing Time: Book

Read the book My *Doctor* by Harlow Rockwell.

Discuss doctors with the children. Ask who has been to the doctor before. Why? Explain that a doctor is someone who helps us remain well and takes care of us when we get sick.

Art: Stethoscope

Cut out stethoscope shapes from construction paper. (See pattern on page 61.) Cover the round part with aluminum foil. Let children take turns playing with them.

Story Time: Finger Play

"Miss Polly"

Miss Polly had a dolly
Who was sick, sick, sick. *(Rock the baby.)*
She called for the doctor *(Imitate calling on the telephone.)*
To come quick, quick, quick.
He came in a hurry
With his bag and his hat. *(Imitate putting on hat.)*
He knocked on the door *(Knock.)*
With a rat-a-tat-tat.
He looked at the baby *(Cradle arms.)*
And he shook his head. *(Shake head)*
He said to Miss Polly
"Put her right to bed." *(Point and shake finger.)*
He wrote on a paper *(Imitate writing.)*
For a pill, pill, pill.
I'll be back in the morning *(Point to self.)*
With my bill, bill, bill. *(Pretend to wave a piece of paper.)*

This can also be done by using the appropriate props mentioned in the Finger Play.

Circle Time: Where Is My!!!?

Play a game where the children name different body parts. Ask the children, "Where is my!!!?" as you point to a body part and have the children call it out.

Food Experiences: Discuss Healthy Eating

Explain that if we eat nutritious food, we will be healthy and that nutritious food is also good for our teeth. Let children name some healthy foods.

Theme Activities: Book

Read the book *Dr. Doctor* by Richard Scarry.

Tuesday

Sharing Time: Book

Discuss dentists with the children. Ask questions. Why do we go to the dentist? Read I *Know a Dentist* by Naomi Barnett.

Art: Surgical Face Masks

Many dentists wear surgical face masks while working with patients. Let children make their own. Use thick paper towels and fold into thirds lengthwise. Poke holes into the middle of both ends. Attach yarn and tie.

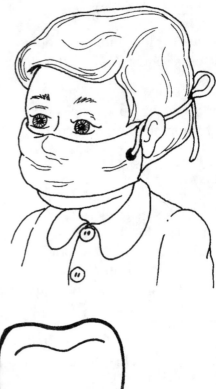

Story Time: Finger Play

"Dentist" (Traditional)
If I were a dentist, *(Point to yourself.)*
I know what I would do.
I'd tell all the children, "Brush your teeth."
(Imitate brushing.)
"Keep a smile like new." (Smile.)
And if a tiny hole should show, *(Make circle with fingers.)*
I'd say, "Climb into my chair."
I'd make my little drill go buzzzzzzzzz,
(Make bzzzz sound.)
And put a filling there! *(Point to teeth.)*

Circle Time: Pretend to be Dentists

Wearing the face masks made during art, let the children pretend to be dentists and look into each other's mouths.

Food Experiences: Soft Foods

Explain that sometimes we have to eat soft foods after visiting the dentist. Serve pudding or gelatin.

Theme Activities: Book

Read the book *My Dentist* by Harlow Rockwell.

Wednesday

Sharing Time: Book

Ask questions about the post office. What do we do at the post office? Then read *Mail And How It Moves* by Gail Gibbons.

Art: Mailbag

Make a mailbag for each child. Use a large paper grocery bag cut in half. Use the top to cut out a wide shoulder strap. Adjust and staple to each side of the bag. Let the children decorate the bags.

Story Time: Finger Play

"Any Mail For Me?" (Traditional)
Five little letters lying on a tray, *(Hold up five fingers.)*
Mommy came in and took the first away. *(Take away a finger.)*
Then Daddy said, "This big one is for me." *(Take away another.)*
I counted them twice; now there were three. *(Count fingers.)*
Brother Bill asked, "Did I get any mail?"
He found one and cried, "A letter from Gale!" *(Take away finger.)*
My sister Jane took the next to the last *(Take away finger.)*
And ran upstairs to open it fast.
As I can't read, I'm not able to see
Whom the last one's for, but I hope it's for me! *(Remove thumb.)*

Circle Time: Field Trip to the Post Office

Ask parents to send in self-addressed, stamped envelopes. Have each child draw a picture and put it into his or her envelope. Take a field trip to the post office. Have children carry their mail bags and mail their "letters" to their parents.

Food Experiences: Graham Crackers in White Envelopes

Give each child a "special delivery" by placing a graham crackers in a white envelope. Let them open the envelope and taste the treat.

Theme Activities: Book

Read *Where Does The Mail Go?* by Tim and Julie Nyberg. Discuss the trip of a letter.

Thursday

Sharing Time: Finger Play

"Policeman"

This is a car driving down the street. *(Hand goes right to left.)*
Here's a policeman walking his beat. *(Hold up one finger.)*
Now he is checking the stores at night.
To see that doors are locked up tight. *(Pretend to turn doorknob.)*
And this is a friendly traffic cop. *(Hold up opposite finger.)*
Who tells when to go or stop. *(Motion go, then stop.)*
When cars get in a traffic jam,
He helps them better than anyone can. *(Nod finger.)*
Discuss the police and how they help us.

Art: Badges

Make badges out of aluminum foil using the pattern at the bottom of the page. Tape a safety pin onto the back. Pin onto each child's shirt.

Story Time: Finger Play

"Traffic Lights" (Author Unknown)

"Stop," says the red light. *(Hold up hand.)*
"Go," says the green. *(Point finger.)*
"Wait," says the yellow light,
Blinking in between. *(Open and shut hand.)*
That's what they say and
That's what they mean.
We all must obey them, *(Point to children.)*
Even the Queen. *(Form hands into a crown and place on head.)*

Circle Time: Poem

"Police Officer" (Traditional)
Police officers are helpers wherever they may stand.
They tell us when to stop and go by holding up their hands.

Food Experiences: Peanut Butter Badges

Mix the following ingredients: ½ cup (118 mL) peanut butter, 2½ Tbsp. (37.5 mL) nonfat dry milk, 2 Tbsp. (30 mL) raisins, 2 Tbsp. (30 mL) honey, ¼ cup (59 mL) coconut.
Children can form the mixture into a ball, then flatten and shape into a badge shape and eat. (You may use the pattern at the right as a template and have children cut around it.)

Theme Activities: Book

Read the book *Police* by Ray Broekel.

Friday

Sharing Time: Song/Activity

Sing "The Bus Song" (see page 14). Act out the motions as you sing the song. Discuss what we ride in. Ask the children questions about different types of transportation.

Art: Sailboat

Use foam egg cartons, plastic clay, round toothpicks, tape, and paper triangles. Cut the egg cartons into individual egg cups. Cut small paper triangles. Let each child color a triangle. Tape it to the toothpick to make a sail. Press plastic clay into the egg cup. Push the sail into the clay and float the boats.

Story Time: Finger Play

"Choo-Choo Train" (Traditional)
This is a choo-choo train, *(Move right hand and arm along.)*
Puffing down the track. *(Make puffing sound.)*
Now it's going forward, *(Go forward.)*
Now it's going back. *(Go backward.)*
Now the bell is ringing, *(Pretend to ring bell with left hand.)*
Now the whistle blows. *(Whistle.)*
What a lot of noise it makes *(Cover ears.)*
Everywhere it goes! *(Move right hand and arm along.)*

Circle Time: Vehicle Charades

Play vehicle charades. Ask children to pretend to be a vehicle and make sounds. Ask them questions about the type of vehicle they are supposed to be.

Food Experiences: Transportation Cookies

Use a basic refrigerated cookie dough and cut out cookies with transportation shaped cookie cutters.

Theme Activities: Story and Poem

Read the *Boat Book* by Gail Gibbons. Then share the poem "Auto.

"Auto"
Auto, auto may I have a ride?
Yes sir, yes sir, step right inside.
Pour on the water,
Turn on the gasoline
Chug-a-way, chug-a-way to the country green.

Center Ideas

Here are some suggestions of materials that can be placed in the learning centers in addition to your regular materials.

- Housekeeping: dolls, band-aids, surgical gowns and masks, telephone, pillow, blankets, tissues, cotton balls, stethoscope, doctor's kit, old X-rays, small pen light
- Circle: posters of people in different professions
- Books: books about doctors, nurses, dentists, policemen, mailmen
- *Music: ABC's In Bubbaville* record or any songs about community helpers
- Table Activities: mailbox made from a shoe box, envelopes, junk mail, stickers, pencils, paper
- Science: toothbrush, teeth model, photos of doctors and dentists, toy vehicles
- Blocks: vehicles made from cardboard boxes, traffic signs, police officer's hat, mail carrier's hat, mailbag
- Art: stamp pads, stickers, pencils, note pads, x-rays
- Puppets: puppets of different professions

Teachers' Aids

File Folder Activities: Choose the skills you wish to emphasize this week. See directions on pages 5-6.

- Car Matching
- Boat Matching

Bulletin Board Ideas:
- Construct a community that will also be used with the lesson on Community Places and People #2.

    Use sandpaper for roads. Include some of the following community helpers:
- Police Officer
- Firefighter
- Mail Carriers
- Nurses
- Dentists
- Doctors

For Parents

- Discuss what happens when you go to the doctor or dentist.
- Discuss what police officers do and how they help us.
- Let your child write a letter or drawing. Take a trip together to the post office, purchase a stamp, and mail it to someone
- Discuss different types of transportation.

Bibliography

Children's Books

Barnett, Naomi. *I Know A Dentist. G.1P, Putnam's Sons, 1977*
Broekel, Ray. *Police.* Childrens Press, 1981
Gibbons, Gail, *Boat Book.* Holiday, 1983
Gibbons, Gail. *Post Office Book: Mail and How It Moves.* Harper, 1982
Nyberg, Tim and Julie. *Where Does The Mail Go?* Lonameadow Press, 1989
Rockwell, Harlow. *My Dentist.* Greenwillow, 1975
Rockwell, Harlow. *My Doctor.* Mactmillan, 1973
Scarry, Richard. *Dr. Doctor.* Western, 1988

Records

Libby Core Bearden, Cafnille. Core Gift, Kathleen Patrick. *ABC's In Bubbaville.* Upbeat Basics, 1986.

Patterns

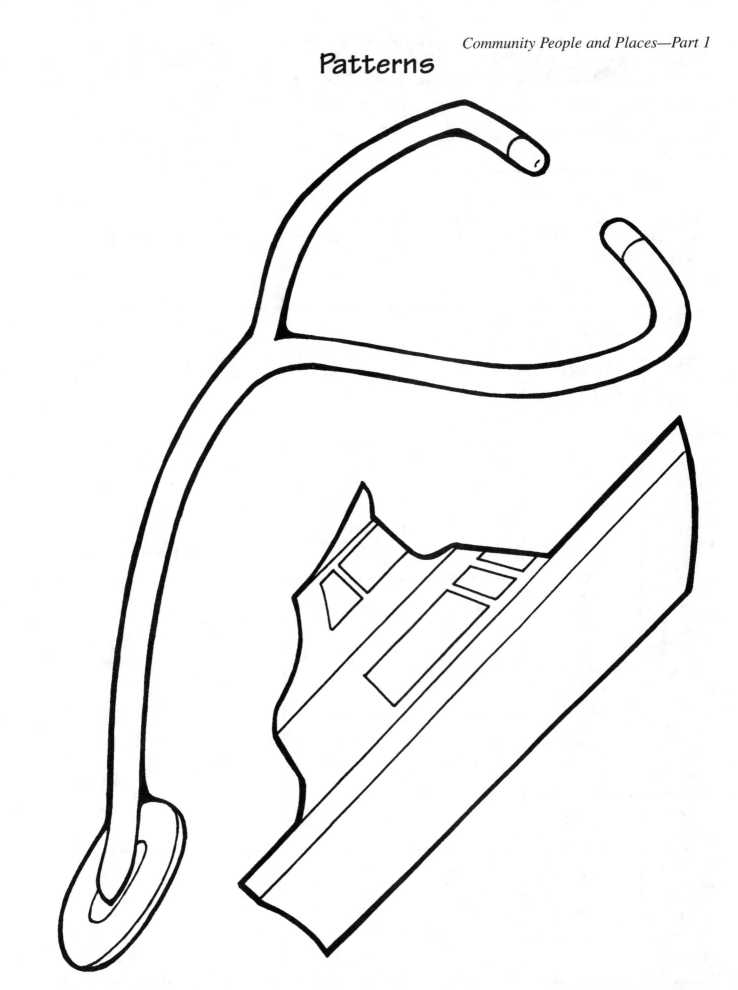

Weekly Theme: *Community Places and People #2*   Week of: _____

	Monday	Tuesday	Wednesday	Thursday	Friday
Date					
Sharing Time	Discussion about Supermarkets	Discussion about Gas Stations	Discussion about Laundromats	Discussion on Libraries	Discussion about Barber and Beauty Shops
Art	Grocery Store Collage	Painting Cars	Painting with Soap Bubbles	Make a Book	Hair Design
Story Time	Book: *The Supermarket*	Book: *Trucks*	Poem: The Little Wash Bench	Book: *Check It Out*	Song: Hippity Hop to the Barber Shop
Circle Time	Field Trip to the Supermarket	Song: I'm a Little Gas Pump	Activity: Washing Doll Clothes	Activity: Field Trip to the Library	Activity: Good Grooming Session
Food Experiences	From the Supermarket	Pineapple Rings	Pie Crust Shirts	Cheese Books	Heads with Cheese Hair
Theme Activities	Book: *Supermarket Magic*	Activity: Washing Cars	Book: *Corduroy*	Classroom Library	Rhyme: Barber Book: *My Barber*

Monday

Materials Needed For The Week:

square and round crackers, sliced and spray cheese, pineapple rings, dishwashing liquid, old magazines, coupons, play money, large brown grocery bags, supermarket circulars, clip clothespins, clothesline, small dish pans, old hair dryer without cord, disposable combs, laundry basket, empty food containers, detergent box, large cardboard boxes, round pasta, yarn

Sharing Time: Discussion about Supermarkets

Discuss with the children what they can see in a supermarket. Tell the children where the supermarkets are located in your community.

Art: Grocery Store Collage

Have the children cut pictures of groceries from a magazine. Cut large brown grocery sacks into various sizes. Let the children choose their own and glue their pictures onto them to create a grocery store collage.

Story Time: Book

Read *The Supermarket* by Anne and Harlow Rockwell.

Circle Time: Field Trip to the Supermarket

Take a field trip to the local supermarket or grocery store. Discuss the different foods you see. Purchase a food item for a food experience. With the children go through the checkout line and watch how the food is checked out of the market.

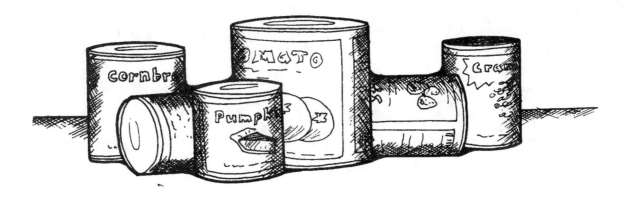

Food Experiences: From the Supermarket

Share the snack you bought at the market. Before children eat it, ask them what they think it cost. Discuss the price with them.

Theme Activities: Book

Read *Supermarket Magic* by J. Kent.

Tuesday

Sharing Time: Discuss Gas Stations

Discuss with the children what happens at the gas station. What do we buy at a gas station? Tell the children where the gas stations are located in your community.

Art: Painting Cars

Have children paint pictures of cars and trucks. Give them round pasta to glue on to their cars and trucks to create the wheels.

Story Time: Book

Read *Trucks* by Donald Crews.

Circle Time: Song

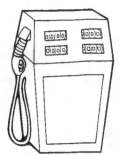

"I'm a Little Gas Pump" (To the tune of "I'm a Little Tea Pot.")
I'm a little gas pump, short and stout.
Here is my handle; here is my spout.
When I fill a car up, hear me shout.
Just squeeze my handle and pour me out.

Food Experiences: Pineapple Rings

Serve pineapple rings. Discuss what they look like. See how many children say tires and how many say steering wheels. Have them name other things that are round.

Theme Activities: Washing Cars

Provide water and sponges for the children to wash small cars and trucks. They can also wash large outside toys such as tricycles. This is a good outdoor activity.

Wednesday

Sharing Time: Discuss Laundromats

Discuss with the children what one does at the laundromat. Ask if they wash their clothes at home or take them out. Where are the laundromats located in your community? What items do we need to take with us to the laundromat?

Art: Soap Bubble Painting

Mix dish washing liquid with water to make the soap bubbles. Use wide paintbrushes and buckets and let the children paint objects that can be easily washed such as plastic plates.

Story Time: Poem

"The Little Wash Bench"
Here's a little wash bench,
Here's a little tub,
Here's a little scrubbing board.
And here's the way to rub.
Here's a little cake of soap.
Here's a dipper new.
Here's a basket wide and deep,
And here's our clothespins, too.
Here's the line away up high,
Here are the clothes all drying.
Here's the sun so warm and bright,
And now the wash is drying.

If possible hold up items mentioned in the poem.

Circle Time: Washing Doll Clothes

Have the children gather a few pieces of doll's clothing from the housekeeping area. Provide two pans of water and detergent. After children wash and rinse the clothing let them hang it up on a clothesline. Use clip on clothespins.

Food Experiences: Pie Crust Shirts

Mix up pie crust dough or use canned biscuits. Using craft sticks, have the children cut them into shirt shapes.

Theme Activities: Book

Read the classic story, *Corduroy*, by Don Freeman. Ask children to pretend they are in a box of detergent. How does it feel?

Thursday

Sharing Time: Discuss Libraries

Discuss with the children what you do at a library. Why would they go to the library? Discuss getting a library card and the proper way of caring for the books you check out.

Art: Make A Book

Cut several 9" x 12" (23 cm x 30 cm) sheets of construction paper in half. Use a hole punch to make holes down the left side of the pages. Have children make a wordless book by drawing a story on each page. Use yarn to tie several pieces of paper together.

Share the stories with the class.

Story Time: Book

Read the book, *Check It Out* by Gail Gibbons

Circle Time: Field Trip to the Library

Take a field trip to the library. Sign the children up for their own library cards. Have the librarian read the class a story.

Food Experiences: Cheese Books

Make books that are edible. Cut cheese into small squares. Stack up two squares of crackers. They look like books.

Theme Activities: Classroom Library

Set up a classroom library where the children can check out books every week. Make each child an individual library card. Let children take turns being the class librarian. This can be as simple as passing books out or stamping each card for checking out the books.

Friday

Sharing Time: Discuss Barber Shops/ Beauty Salons

Discuss with the children why we go to a barber shop or beauty salon. Ask who has been to a beauty salon or the barber. Have volunteers describe their experiences. Read *Mop Top* by Don Freeman.

Art: Hair Design

Have the children draw a face on construction paper. Hair can be designed out of yarn, cotton, or other materials and glued onto the head. Make sure they use a lot of material for the hair and leave some hanging. After the picture dries the children can use scissors to cut the hair.

Story Time: Song

"Hippity Hop To The Barber Shop" (English Traditional Song)

Hippity hop to the barber shop,
To buy a stick of candy.
One for you and one for me
And one for sister Annie.

Circle Time: Good Grooming Session

Have children pretend to be a barber or beautician. Provide an old hair dryer that has the cord removed. Talk about why it is important to keep hair clean and not share brushes and combs with other people.

Food Experiences: Heads with Cheese Hair

Use round crackers. Let the children use spray cheese and form hair.

Theme Activities: Rhyme

"Barber" (Mother Goose Rhyme)

Barber, barber, shave a pig.
How many hairs will make a wig?
Four and twenty; that's enough.
Give the barber a pinch of snuff.

Share the book, *My Barber*, by Anne and Harlow Rockwell.

Classroom Additions

Center Ideas

Here are some suggestions of materials that can be placed in the learning centers in addition to your regular materials.

- Housekeeping: supermarket ads, plastic shopping cart, food containers, plastic fruits and vegetables, play money, coupons, play cash register. In another area set up small dish pans, clip clothespins, clothesline, doll clothes, small detergent box, small laundry basket
- Circle: pictures of people in each profession
- Books: books about supermarkets, laundromats, libraries, gas stations, and beauty or barber shops
- Music: the record *ABC's In Bubbaville* or any songs about community helpers
- Table Activities: file folder activities listed, puzzles, games
- Blocks: two large cardboard boxes, one decorated like a gas pump and the other a car
- Art: dishwashing liquid, paint, paper, yarn, pencils, old magazines, cotton balls
- Puppets: puppets of each profession
- Science: pictures of gas stations and vehicles, pan of water, soap flakes
- Science Activity: Potatoes with Hair
  - Make this by cutting off the top of a potato and scooping out a small amount of the inside. Pour a small amount of grass seed inside the potato. Water and watch it grow. When grass grows long, you can trim the hair (grass).

Teachers' Aids

- File Folder Activities: Choose the skills you wish to emphasize this week. See directions on pages 5-6.
- Food Matching   • Car and Truck   • Grooming Objects   • Books
- Continue bulletin board from Community Helpers-Part 1. Add grocery store, gas station, laundromat, library, and beauty/barber shop.

For Parents

- Take child to the grocery store and let them help you shop.
- Let your child help you put gas in your car at the gas station.
- Discuss getting your hair cut.
- Set a day for library visits and take your child.
- Go to the laundromat.

Bibliography

Children's Books

Crews, Donald. *Truck.* Greenwillow, 1980

Freeman, Don. *Dandelion.* Puffin, 1989

Freeman, Don. *Mop Top.* Viking, 1955

Gibbons, Gail. *Check It Out.* Harcourt Brace Jovanovich, 1985

Kent, J. *Supermarket Magic.* Random House, 1978

Nyberg, Tim and Julie. *Where Does The Laundry Chute Go?* Longmeadow Press, 1989

Rockwell, Anne and Harlow. *My Barber.* Macmillan, 1981

Rockwell, Anne and Harlow. *The Supermarket.* Macmillan, 1979

Records

Libby Core Beardon, Camille Core Gift, Kathleen Patrick. *ABCs in Bubbaville.* Upbeat Basics, 1986

Patterns

Patterns

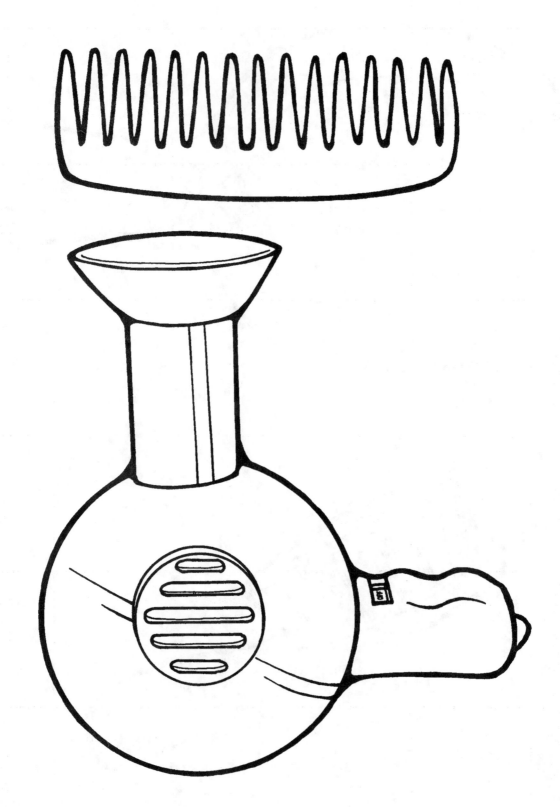

Weekly Theme: _Senses_ Week of: _____

	Monday	Tuesday	Wednesday	Thursday	Friday
Date					
Sharing Time	Book: _My Five Senses_	Book: _A Button In Her Ear_	Book: _The Quilt Story_	Book: _The Sniff and Tell Riddle Book_	Book: _Gregory the Terrible Eater_
Art	Binoculars	Elephant Ears	Gooey Mixture	Smelly Play Dough	Food Collage
Story Time	Flannel Story: Wee Red Shoes	Song: Do Your Ears Hang Low?	Song/Activity: This Old Man	Book: _Little Bunny Follows His Nose_	Book: _Growing Vegetable Soup_
Circle Time	Activity: Charades	Activity: Using Tape Recorders	Activity: Feelie Box	Activity: Take a Smell Walk	Song: The Muffin Man
Food Experiences	Healthy Mixture	Popcorn	Pudding in a Bag	Onions	Lemons and Pears
Theme Activities	Song: Popcorn	Poem: Pound Goes the Hammer	Poem: Warm Hands	Song/Activity: Who's Got the Bean Bag?	How Does the Food Taste?

Monday

Materials Needed For The Week:

small bottles, cotton balls, toilet paper tubes, cornstarch, salt, alum, fruit flavored drink mix, old magazines, tape recorder, blank cassettes, empty shoe box, popcorn, lemon, pear, nuts, raisins, dried fruit, instant pudding, onion

Sharing Time: Book

Read *My Five Senses* by Aliki. Discuss eyes. What do they let us do? What if we were blind? Discuss wearing eye glasses.

Art: Binoculars

Let each child decorate two toilet paper tubes. Glue them together and tie yarn so they can be placed around each child's neck.

Story Time: Flannel Story

"Wee Red Shoes" (See patterns on pages 79-80)

Once there were some Wee Red Shoes. They lived in a shoe shop. They lived there a long time. "This is no fun," said one Wee Red Shoe. "I want to run," said the other Wee Red Shoe. So they ran out of the shoe shop. They ran down the street-patter, patter, patter. They saw a speckled hen.

"Stop!" called Speckled Hen. "I want to wear you." She jumped into Wee Red Shoes. "Now scratch!" said Speckled Hen. "We cannot scratch," said Wee Red Shoes. "Then I cannot wear you," said Speckled Hen. "Run along!" Wee Red Shoes ran on. They ran and ran-patter, patter, patter.

They saw brown duck. "Stop!" called Brown Duck. "I want to wear you." She jumped into Wee Red Shoes. "Now swim!" said Brown Duck. "We cannot swim," said Wee Red Shoes. "Then I cannot wear you," said Brown Duck. "Run along!" Wee Red Shoes ran on. They ran and ran-patter, patter, patter.

They saw Dog Nero. "Stop!" called the dog. "I want to wear you." He jumped into Wee Red Shoes. "Now run!" said the dog.

Monday (cont.)

"There are only two of us," said Wee Red Shoes. "You need four shoes." "Then I cannot wear you," said the dog. "Run along!!" So Wee Red Shoes ran on. They ran and ran— patter, patter, patter.

They saw a wee girl. She was barefoot. She was crying. Wee Red Shoes jumped on wee girl. She saw the Wee Red Shoes. She stopped crying.

"Will you wear us?" asked Wee Red Shoes. "We will run for you."

"Will you run to school?" asked the wee girl.

"Yes," answered the Wee Red Shoes. "We will run to school every day."

"Oh, thank you, thank you!" said the wee girl. "Now I can go to school."

Then the Wee Red Shoes were happy. The wee girl was happy. Away they all ran to school—patter, patter, patter.

Circle Time: Charades

Have the children take turns acting out an animal, emphasizing that they cannot make any sounds. Tell the rest of the children to use their eyes to guess the animal. Take a sight walk around the room or outside. Ask the children what they see.

Food Experiences: Healthy Mixture

Mix together nuts, raisins, and dried fruits. Ask the children questions such as, "What color are the raisins?" "Are the nuts soft or crunchy?"

Theme Activities: Song

Play "Popcorn" from the record *We All Live Together,* Vol. 2.

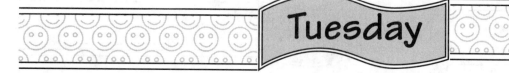

Tuesday

Sharing Time: Book

Read A *Button In Her Ear* by Ada B. Litchfield. Discuss sound. What would happen if we could not hear? Discuss wearing hearing aids.

Art: Elephant Ears

Have the children cut out elephant ears from gray construction paper. (See pattern on page 390.) Attach to a band that fits each child's head.

Story Time: Song

"Do Your Ears Hang Low?" (American Revolutionary Folk Song)

Do your ears hang low,
Do they wobble to and fro?
Can you tie them in a knot,
Can you tie them in a bow?
Can you fling them over your shoulder,
Like a continental soldier?
Do your ears hang low?

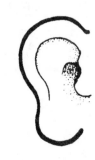

Circle Time: Using Tape Recorders

Have the children speak into a tape recorder, one at a time, and then play it back. See if each child can pick out his or her own voice. You may also tape everyday household noises and then play them back for the children. Have children guess what sound they are hearing. Take a sound walk around the playground or through the hallways at school. Ask children what sounds they hear.

Food Experiences: Popcorn

Show unpopped popcorn and then pop it. Ask questions about what the unpopped kernels look like, what the popped corn looks like, and what the difference is between them.

Theme Activities: Poem

"Pound Goes The Hammer"

Pound pound pound pound
goes the hammer,
pound pound pound pound pound pound pound.
Bzz bzz bzz bzz bzz
goes the big saw,
Bzz bzz bzz bzz bzz bzz bzz.
Chop chop chop chop chop goes the big axe, Chop chop
chop chop chop chop chop.

Wednesday

Sharing Time: Book

Read *The Quilt Story* by Tony Johnston. Discuss touch. Discuss different textures of items. Let the children close their eyes and feel objects. Discuss how people who are blind use their hands.

Art: Gooey Mixture

See recipe on page 7. Ask children how it feels. Is it soft? Is it hard?

Story Time: Song/Activity

(Follow the motions in the song. After each verse repeat chorus.)

"This Old Man" (Traditional)

This old man, he played one, *(Hold up appropriate number of fingers.)*
He played knick-knack on his thumb.
(Tap thumbs together.)
With a knick-knack, paddy-whack, give a dog a bone *(Make right hand into fist, point thumb over shoulder.)*
This old man came rolling home. *(Roll hands over each other)*
This old man, he played two,
He played knick-knack on his shoe
This old man, he played three,
He played knick-knack on his knee
This old man, he played four,
He played knick-knack on the door.

This old man, he played five,
He played knick-knack on his hive.
This old man, he played six,
He played knick-knack on his sticks.
This old man, he played seven,
He played knick-knack up to heaven.
This old man, he played eight,
He played knick-knack on his plate.
This old man, he played nine,
He played knick-knack on his spine.
This old man, he played ten,
He played knick-knack now and then.
With a knick-knack, paddy-whack, give a dog a bone
This old man came rolling home.

Circle Time: Feelie Box

Prepare a feelie box. (See directions on page 7.) Have the children take turns placing their hands in the box and guessing if the object is soft, hard, etc., then naming the object.

Food Experiences: Pudding In A Bag

In a self-sealing sandwich bag, put ½ cup (118 ml) of milk and 2 tablespoons (30 ml) of instant pudding. Have children shake and knead the bag until thick. Cut a small hole in one corner to eat. Discuss what the ingredients looked like when you put them in the bag and what they looked like after the children shook the bag. Ask the children how the bag of pudding feels and tastes.

Theme Activities: Poem

"Warm hands" (Traditional)
Do you know how?
If you want to
Warm your hands,
Warm your hands now.

Thursday

Sharing Time: Book

Read *The Sniff and Tell Riddle Book* by R. McKie. Discuss smell. Introduce the children to different smells. Make smell containers. Use small bottles with lids, and put cotton balls in the bottles and saturate with a scent. Possible scents to use include perfume, vanilla extract, and shaving lotion. You may also chop up small bits of garlic and onion. Use your imagination on different smells to use.

Art: Smelly Play Dough

Play with smelly play dough. See directions on page 6.

Story Time: Book

Read *Little Bunny Follows His Nose* by K. Howard.

Circle Time: Take a Smell Walk

Take a walk inside or outside and tell the children they are hunting for smells. Have them tell you when they smell something. Ask questions about each particular smell.

Food Experiences: Onions

Have the children smell a whole onion that has the skin on it. Ask them questions. Next, peel the onion and have the children smell again. Ask them how it smells. Finally, cut the onion into pieces. Have the children smell again. Ask them which smell is strongest. Why do they think this is so? Caution: Hold the onion and do not let the children touch it as they may touch their eyes and make them water.

Theme Activities: Song/Activity

Do "Who's Got The Bean Bag" from the record *Bean Bag Activities and Coordination Skills* or choose a song and toss a bean bag for children to catch.

Friday

Sharing Time: Book

Read *Gregory, The Terrible Eater* by Mitchell Sharmat.

Discuss taste. Why do foods taste different? Do the children know the different types of taste, salty, sour, sweet, or bitter. Ask questions about the book.

Art: Food Collage

Have the children cut food pictures from magazines and paste on construction paper. Ask the children: What do you eat? What did Gregory the goat eat? Include these pictures in the collage.

Story Time: Book

Read *Growing Vegetable Soup* by Lois Ehlert.

Circle Time: Song

"The Muffin Man" (Nursery Rhyme)

Oh, do you know the muffin man, the muffin man, the muffin man?

Oh, do you know the muffin man who lives on Drury Lane?

Oh, yes I know the muffin man, the muffin man, the muffin man.

Oh, yes I know the muffin man who lives on Drury Lane.

Food Experiences: Lemons And Pears

Give children a lemon slice and a pear slice. Have them compare the sour taste of the lemon with the sweet taste of the pears.

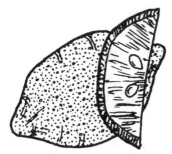

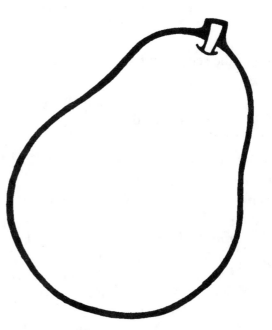

Theme Activities: How Does the Food Taste?

Hold up pictures of different foods, and ask the children how each food tastes. Is it tart, sweet, sour, etc.? Now ask the children to name their favorite foods. What do they taste like? Write the sentence, "My favorite food is _____ and it tastes like _____ . Let the children take turns filling in the blanks.

Classroom Additions

Center Ideas

Here are some suggestions of materials that can be placed in the learning centers in addition to your regular materials.

- Housekeeping: soft and hard items, plastic fruits and vegetables, baby powder
- Circle: posters of the five senses
- Books: books on the five senses, tape recorder, cassettes
- Music: tape recorder, cassettes, records, musical instruments
- Table Activities: Me folder activities listed, gooey mixture, smell containers, feelie box
- Blocks: various blocks of different sizes
- Art: old magazines, paper, paste, yarn, gooey mixture, play dough, paints, especially fingerpaints
- Puppets: puppets made from various textured materials
- Science: infrared light, bells, large rubber bands, sandpaper, piece of tile, cotton balls, perfume, smell bottles, feelie box

Teacher' Aids

File Folder Activities: Choose the skills you wish to emphasize this week. See directions on pages 5-6.

- Different Foods
- Feelie Box Shaker Canisters
- Hard/Soft Objects
- Sorting Texture Feelings
- Smell Stickers

Bulletin Board Ideas:
- Divide board into five sense areas. Add pictures and items under each area.

For Parents

- Discuss each of the senses with your child.
- Try a new food.
- Take walks with your child. Discuss what you see, hear, smell, and touch.
- Let your child feel talcum powder.

Bibliography

Children's Books

Aliki. *My Five Senses.* Harper Collins, 1989

Ehlert, Lois. *Growing Vegetable Soup.* Harcourt Brace Jovanovich, 1987

Howard, K. *Little Bunny Follows His Nose.* Golden Press and Western, 1971

Johnston, Tony. *The Quilt Story.* G.P. Putnam's Sons, 1985

Litchfield, Ada B. *A Button In Her Ear.* Whitman, 1976

Martin, Bill, Jr. and John Archambault. *Here Are My Hands.* Henry Holt, 1987

McKie, R. *The Sniff and Tell Riddle Book.* Random House, 1978

Sharmat, Mitchell. *Gregory, The Terrible Eater.* Scholastic, 1980

Showers, Paul. *The Listening Walk.* Crowell, 1961

Records

Steve Millang and Greg Scelsa. *We All Live Together, Vol. 2.* Youngheart Records, 1978

Georgiana Liccione Stewart. *Bean Bag Activities and Coordination Skills.* Kimbo, 1977

Patterns

Patterns

Weekly Theme: *Halloween*   Week of: _____

	Monday	Tuesday	Wednesday	Thursday	Friday
Date					
Sharing Time	Fingerplays: One, Two, Three Little Witches or A Little Witch	Fingerplay: The Ghost	Activity: Scarecrow, Scarecrow	Fingerplay: Itsy Bitsy Spider	Fingerplay: Five Little Pumpkins
Art	Black Funny Putty	Tissue Paper Ghosts	Scarecrow Collage	Hand-Print Spiders	Sponge Painting Orange Pumpkins
Story Time	Flannel Story: Teeny Tiny	Book: *Popcorn*	Flannel Story: The Scarecrow	Poem: Spider Web	Fingerplay: Very Nice Jack-O-Lantern
Circle Time	Activity: Halloween Fishing	Activity: Pin the Nose on Ghost	Activity: Dress Like a Scarecrow	Activity: Spider	Activity: Carve a Jack-O-Lantern
Food Experiences	Witches Brew	Ghost Snacks	Shredded White Type Cereal	Prune and Pretzel Spiders	Toasted Pumpkin Seeds
Theme Activities	Poem: Witch's Cat	Poem: Scary Eyes	Chant: A Goblin Lives in our House	Rhyme: Bat, Bat	Poem: My Pumpkin

Monday

Materials Needed For The Week:

liquid starch, black tempera paint, box of tissues, yarn, straw, scrap material, sponges, foam trays, Halloween cutouts, white poster board, blindfold, old clothes to make a scarecrow, pumpkin to carve, red juices, shredded wheat type cereal, prunes, stick pretzels

Sharing Time: Two Finger Plays

"One, Two, Three Little Witches" (Traditional)

One little, two little, three little witches *(Hold up one, two, three fingers.)*
Fly over haystacks, fly over ditches, *(Let three fingers fly.)*
Slide down moonbeams without any hitches, *(Slide fingers down.)*
Heigh-ho! Halloween's here!

"A Little Witch"

A little witch in a pointed cap, *(Make hands into a point over head.)*
On my door went rap, rap, rap. *(Pretend to knock on door.)*
When I went to open it, *(Pretend to open door.)*
She was not there; *(Hold hands outward.)*
She was riding a broomstick, *(Fork two fingers over the pointer finger of left hand.)*
High up in the air. *(Raise fingers into the air.)*

Art: Black Funny Putty

See directions on page 6. Add black tempera paint for coloring.

Story Time: Flannel Story

Do this story in a teeny-tiny voice, until the last line. See patterns on page 90.

"Teeny Tiny" (English Folk Tale)

Once upon a time there was a teeny-tiny woman who lived in a teeny-tiny house in a teeny-tiny village.

Now, one day, this teeny-tiny woman put on her teeny-tiny bonnet, and went out of her teeny-tiny house to take a teeny-tiny walk.

And when this teeny-tiny woman had gone a teeny-tiny way, she came to a teeny-tiny gate; so the teeny-tiny woman opened the teeny-tiny gate, and went into a teeny-tiny garden.

And when this teeny-tiny woman had got into the teeny-tiny garden, she saw a teeny-tiny scarecrow, and the teeny-tiny scarecrow wore a teeny-tiny bonnet and a teeny-tiny dress. And the teeny-tiny woman said: "That teeny-tiny bonnet and that teeny-tiny dress will fit my teeny-tiny self."

Monday (cont.)

So the teeny-tiny woman hung the teeny-tiny dress and the teeny-tiny bonnet over her teeny-tiny arm, and then she went home to her teeny-tiny house.

Now when the teeny-tiny woman got home to her teeny-tiny house, she was a teeny-tiny bit tired; so she went up her teeny-tiny stairs to her teeny-tiny bed, and put the teeny-tiny dress and the teeny-tiny bonnet into a teeny-tiny closet. And when this teeny-tiny woman had been asleep a teeny-tiny time, she was awakened by a teeny-tiny voice from the teeny-tiny closet which said: "Give me my clothes."

At this, the teeny-tiny woman was a teeny-tiny bit flustered; so she hid her teeny-tiny head under the teeny-tiny bed clothes and went to sleep again.

And when she had been asleep again a teeny-tiny time, the teeny-tiny voice cried out from the teeny-tiny closet a teeny-tiny bit louder:

"Give me my clothes."

This made the teeny-tiny woman a teeny-tiny bit more flustered; so she hid her teeny-tiny head a teeny-tiny bit farther under the teeny-tiny bed clothes. And when the teeny-tiny woman had been asleep again a teeny-tiny time, the teeny-tiny voice from the teeny-tiny closet said again a teeny-tiny bit louder:

"Give me my clothes."

Then the teeny-tiny woman put her teeny-tiny head out of the teeny-tiny bed clothes and said in her loudest teeny-tiny voice:

"TAKE'EM!"

Circle Time: Halloween Fishing

Directions for the fishing poles are on page 7. Use fishing poles and construction paper cutouts of bats, jack-o-lanterns, and ghosts. Have the children try to catch a specific cutout you name.

Food Experience: Witches' Brew

Mix cranberry juice or other red mixtures for a witches' brew.

Theme Activities: Poem

"Witch's Cat"
I am the witch's cat.
Miaow, miaow.
My fur is black as darkest night.
My eyes are glowing green and bright.
I am the witch's cat.

Tuesday

Sharing Time: Finger Play

> ***"The Ghost"*** (Traditional)
> See my great big scary eyes. *(Circle fingers around eyes.)*
> Look out now for a big surprise. *(Raise hands in surprise.)*
> Oo-oo-oo *(Make sound.)*
> I'm looking right at you. *(Point to children.)*
> Boo! (Say Boo!)

Art: Tissue Paper Ghosts

Ball up one tissue. Take another and lay it out flat. Put the ball in the middle of the flat tissue. Fold over and tie a piece of yarn around the ball to form a head. Put eyes on with a black marker. Hang from ceiling.

Story Time: Book

Read *Popcorn* by Frank Asch.
Discuss left and right with your group of children at this time. See who knows their left and right.

Circle Time: Pin the Nose on the Ghost

On a poster board, draw a large picture of a ghost. Cut noses out of black construction paper. If children are willing, blindfold them. Give them the nose with tape on it and see who gets closest. Have children give directions to the child who is blindfolded, emphasizing left and right.

Food Experiences: Ghost Shakes

Make vanilla milk shakes by mixing one gallon (4.5 mL) of vanilla ice cream and a gallon of milk in a blender. Add ice cream as needed to thicken.

Theme Activities: Poem

> ***"Scary Eyes"***
> See my big and scary eyes.
> Look out now
> A big surprise -BOO!

Read *Georgie's Halloween* by Robert Bright.

Wednesday

Sharing Time: Rhyme

"Scarecrow, Scarecrow"

Use the rhyme "Teddy Bear, Teddy Bear," substituting the word "scarecrow" for "teddy bear."
("Teddy Bear, Teddy Bear" can be found on pages 194 and 199.)

Art: Scarecrow Collage

Use the pattern on page 92. Give the children pieces of material and bits of straw. Let the children glue the pieces onto the scarecrow.

Story Time: Flannel Story

Use the patterns on pages 92–93.

"The Scarecrow" (Source Unknown)

Once upon a time, a grandmother who lived in the country had a large cherry tree. It was loaded with ripe red cherries. Now this grandmother was not so spry as she used to be. She could not climb to the top of the tree to pick the ripe red cherries to put in a pie. She had to wait until her grandson, Jack, came from the city. Jack's father had promised to bring him the next Saturday. But now it was Wednesday.

Grandmother didn't know what to do. She wanted to wait for Jack to pick the cherries, but how could she? Something was taking them and it was the blackbirds. If something were not done about it at once, the cherries would be all gone. So she thought and thought of some way to frighten the birds away. Finally she had an idea. Do you know what she did?

Grandmother took a stick and stuck it in the ground. She hung an old shirt on it. She tied a bundle of straw on it for a head. She tied on some old ragged overalls. She fastened old gloves for hands. When the wind blew, it made him flop just like a man, and the birds didn't dare go near to steal any more cherries.

Now, Grandmother's funny scarecrow could move his head. I'll show you how and you can move your head that way, too.

The old scarecrow is such a funny man.
He flops in the wind as hard as he can.
He flops to the right,
He flops to the left,
He flops back and forth,
Till he's most out of breath.
His arms swing out; his legs swing, too.
He nods his head in a How-do-you-do?
See him flippity flop when the wind blows hard,
The funny scarecrow in our back yard.

Wednesday (cont.)

Circle Time: Dress Like a Scarecrow

Have one child be the scarecrow. Let the other children dress that child in baggy clothes and accessories. Let all the children take turns being the scarecrow, if they so desire.

Food Experiences: Shredded Wheat Type Cereal

Scarecrows are stuffed with straw. Let the children feel some shredded wheat type cereal that is similar to the feel of straw. Let them taste it without milk. Ask if they would like to be stuffed with straw.

Theme Activities: Chant

"A Goblin Lives In Our House" (French Folk Rhyme)

A goblin lives in our house, in our house, in our house.
A goblin lives in our house all the year round.
He BUMPS! And he JUMPS! And he THUMPS! And he STUMPS!
He KNOCKS! And he ROCKS! And he raffles at the locks.
A goblin lives in our house, in our house, in our house.
A goblin lives in our house all the year round.

Thursday

Sharing Time: "Itsy Bitsy Spider"

Make a glove puppet to use with as you say the rhyme. The directions for making a glove puppet are on page 7. Use the patterns at the bottom of the page.

"Itsy Bitsy Spider" (Traditional)

The itsy, bitsy spider went up the water spout.
Down came the rain and washed the spider out.
Out came the sun and dried up all the rain.
And the itsy, bitsy spider went up the spout again.

Art: Hand Print Spiders

Trace around the children's hands. Use their hand prints to create spiders. This may be done by having the children draw spider features on their hand prints.

Story Time: Poem

Spider Web (Author Unknown)

I'm a big spider,
I spin, I spin,
I spin big webs,
To catch little flies in.

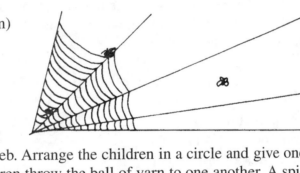

Circle Time: Spider Web

Let children make a spider web. Arrange the children in a circle and give one child a large ball of yarn or string. Have the children throw the ball of yarn to one another. A spider web will be made.

Food Experiences: Prune & Pretzel Spiders

Using stick pretzels, have children push them into prunes to form spider shapes.

Theme Activities:

"Bat, Bat" (Mother Goose)

Bat, bat,
Come under my hat,
And I'll give you a slice of bacon;
And when I bake
I'll give you a cake
If I am not mistaken.

Friday

Sharing Time: Finger Play

"Five Little Pumpkins" (Traditional)

Five little pumpkins sifting on a gate, *(Hold up five fingers.)*
The first one said, "Oh my, it's getting late." *(Point to first finger.)*
The second one said, "There are witches in the air." *(Hold up second finger.)*
The third one said, I don't care." *(Hold up third finger.)*
The fourth one said, "Let's run, run, run." *(Hold up fourth finger.)*
The fifth one said, "It's Halloween fun." *(Hold up fifth finger.)*
Then wooooooooooooo went the wind, *(Let five fingers swoosh through the air.)*
And out went the light! *(Fold five fingers under.)*
Five little pumpkins rolled out of sight. *(Roll hands.)*

Art: Sponge Painting

Sponge paint orange pumpkins. Cut an old sponge into the shape of a pumpkin. Put orange tempera paint into a foam tray. Let the children stamp the design onto construction paper. They may add features of a jack-o-lantern after the paint dries.

Story Time: Finger Play

"Very Nice Jack- O-Lantern"

This is a very nice jack-o-lantern,
These are the eyes of the jack-o-lantern.
This is the nose of the jack-o-lantern.
This is the mouth of the jack-o-lantern.
And this is where the candle goes.
(This can also be told as a chalkboard story or a flannel story.)

Circle Time: Carve a Jack-O-Lantem

Carve a jack-o-lantern. Save the seeds for today's food experience.

Food Experiences: Toasted Pumpkin Seeds

Clean and wash the pumpkin seeds saved when carving the jack-o-lantern. Place seeds in a baking pan and bake in a 350 degree (approx. 177°C) oven until browned. Add salt if desired. If toasting your own seeds is not possible, purchase some at your grocery store and explain to the children how they were prepared.

Theme Activities: Poem

"My Pumpkin"

See my pumpkin round and fat.
See my pumpkin yellow.
Watch him grin on Halloween.
He's a very funny fellow.

Read *Joey Jack-O-Lantern* by Janet Craig.

Classroom Additions

Learning Centers

Here are some suggestions of materials that can be placed in the learning centers in addition to your regular materials.

• Housekeeping: dress up clothes for boys and girls
• Circle: flannel board and flannel pieces
• Books: books about Halloween, witches, ghosts, bats, spiders jack-o-lanterns, and scarecrows
• Music: spooky sounds of Halloween
• Table Activities: file folder activities listed, puzzles, lacing cards
• Blocks: cardboard boxes, fishing activity, make and stuff a scarecrow
• Art: gooey mixture, play dough, orange, black, white, and brown paint; construction paper
• Puppets: bat glove puppet, simple ghost, bat, jack-o-lantern, and witch stick puppets
• Science: pumpkin, pumpkin seeds, spider in a jar, straws

Teachers' Aids

File Folder Activities: Choose the skills you wish to emphasize this week. See directions on pages 5-6.

• Ghost Matching   • Jack-O-Lantem Matching   • Bat Matching
• Lacing Cards: See directions on page 6.
• Ghost   • Bat   • Jack-O-Lantern
• Puzzles: See directions on page 6.
• Ghost   • Bat   • Jack-O-Lantern

Bulletin Board Ideas:
• Halloween Scene   • Haunted Houses
• Bats   • Jack-O-Lanterns
• Black Cats   • Ghosts
• Witches   • Scarecrows
• Spiders   • Children's Art Projects

For Parents

• Discuss Halloween activities. Explain that Halloween is a fun time, not a scary time.
• Have a Halloween party for your child.
• Go to the library and check out books about Halloween.
• Tell children what to expect when they go trick or treating. Make sure your child wears reflective clothing, discuss street safety and check your child's treats.

Bibliography

Children's Books

Asch, Frank. *Popcorn.* Parents, 1979

Bright, Robert. *Georgie's Halloween.* Doubleday, 1958

Craig, Janet. *Joey Jack-O-Lantern.* Troll Associates, 1988

Prelutsky, Jack, selected by. *Read-Aloud Rhymes for the Very Young.* Knopf, 1986

Patterns

Patterns

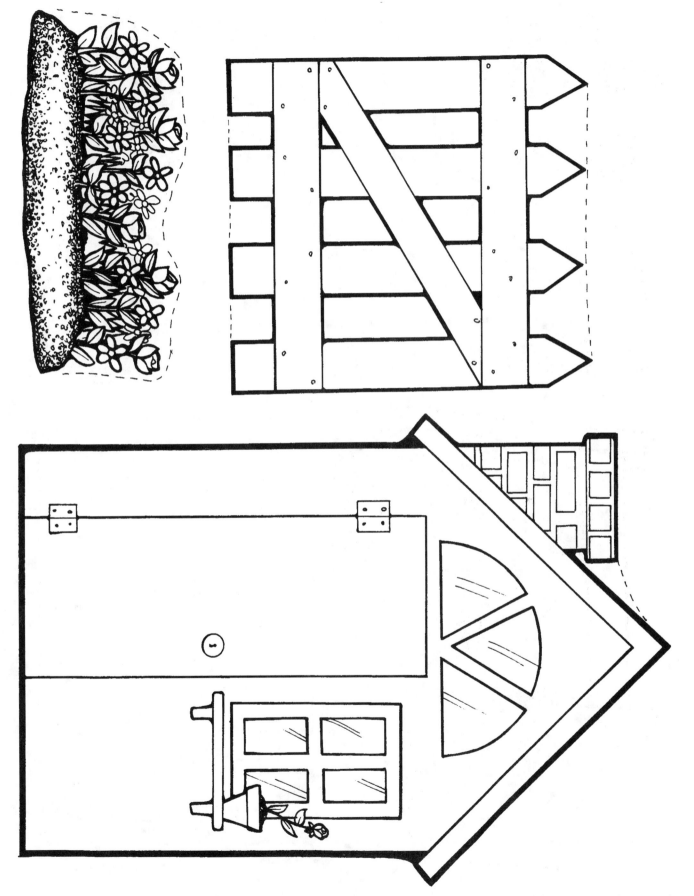

Patterns

Patterns

Weekly Theme: *Colors*   Week of: _____

	Monday	**Tuesday**	**Wednesday**	**Thursday**	**Friday**
Date					
Sharing Time	Book: *Purple Is Part of the Rainbow*	Poem: Five Red Pegs	Poem: Rain on the Green Grass	Book: *Blue Bug's Vegetable Garden*	Song: The World is a Rainbow
Art	Purple Shaving Cream	Fingerpaint with Red	Easel Paint with Green	Straw Paint with Blue	Sponge Paint with Yellow
Story Time	Book: *A Picture for Harold's Room*	Flannel Story: The Little Red Hen and the Grain of Wheat	Song: The Green Grass Grew All Around	Song: Little Boy Blue	Poem: Traffic Lights
Circle Time	Activity: Lollipop Game	Activity: Musical Colors	Activity: Fishing for Colors	Activity: Hop On Colors	Activity: Crayon Pass
Food Experiences	Purple Grapes	Red Apples	Green Broccoli	Blueberries	Yellow Bananas
Theme Activities	Book: *Harold and the Purple Crayon*	Flannel Story: Wee Red Shoes	Rhyme: Rock-a-Bye Baby, Thy Cradle is Green	Activity: Blue Hunt	Activity: Color Sorting

Monday

Materials Needed For The Week:
shaving cream, plain white sheet, crayons, five cardboard boxes, small drinking straws, various items of each color, sponges, flashlight, prism, food coloring, color cut-outs, purple grapes, yellow bananas, broccoli, blueberries, red apples

Sharing Time: Book
Read *Purple is Part of the Rainbow* by Carolyn Kowaczyk.

Art: Purple Shaving Cream
Spray shaving cream on a table. Sprinkle purple powdered tempera paint over shaving cream. Let children mix in the color as they create with the shaving cream.

Story Time: Book
Read *A Picture for Harold's Room* by Crockett Johnson.

Circle Time: Lollipop Game
Cut circles of five different colors out and tape them onto craft sticks. Give one to each child. Then call out the name of a color, and have the children with this same color stand or sit. Continue with the other colors.

Food Experiences: Purple Grapes
Let children taste purple grapes. Have them bite into them. Ask if they are they purple on the inside too.

Theme Activities: Book
Read *Harold and the Purple Crayon* by Crockett Johnson.

Tuesday

Sharing Time: Poem

"Five Red Pegs"

Five red pegs standing in a row,
Watch out, watch out, here they go.
Down goes one peg—
Down goes two pegs—
Down goes three pegs—
Down goes four pegs—
Down goes five pegs—
All five pegs lying just so.

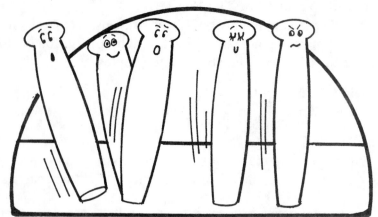

Art: Fingerpaint with Red

Using red fingerpaint encourage the children to create red pictures.

Story Time: Flannel Story

"The Little Red Hen and the Grain of Wheat" (English Folk Tale)

Once upon a time a Little Red Hen was in the farm yard with her chicks, looking for something to eat, when she came upon a grain of wheat. That gave her an idea.

"Now who will help me plant this wheat?" she called.

"Not I," said the Duck.

"Not I," said the Mouse.

"Not I," said the Pig.

"Then I will plant it myself," said the Little Red Hen. And she did. The grain of wheat sprouted, and it grew until it was tall and golden and ripe.

"Now who will help me cut the wheat?" called the Little Red Hen.

"Not I," said the Duck.

"Not I," said the Mouse.

"Not I," said the Pig.

"Then I'll cut it myself," said the Little Red Hen. And she did. When the wheat was cut, she called, "Now who will help me thresh the wheat?

"Not I," said the Duck.

"Not I," said the Mouse.

"Not I," said the Pig.

"Then I'll thresh it myself,' said the Little Red Hen. And she did. When the wheat was ready to be ground into flour, the Little Red Hen called, "Now who will help me take the wheat to the mill?"

Tuesday (cont.)

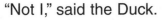

"Not I," said the Duck.

"Not I," said the Mouse.

"Not I," said the Pig.

"Very well, I'll take it myself," said the Little Red Hen. And she did. When the wheat was ground, the Little Red Hen called, "Who will help me bake the bread?"

"Not I," said the Duck.

"Not I," said the Mouse.

"Not I," said the Pig.

"Then I'll bake it myself," said the Little Red Hen. And she did. When the bread was baked, the Little Red Hen called, "Now who will help me eat the bread?"

"I will!" quacked the Duck.

"I will!" squeaked the Mouse.

"I will!" grunted the Pig.

"No you won't!" said the Little Red Hen. "I'll do it myself. Cluck! Cluck! My chicks! I earned this bread for you. Eat it up! Eat it up!"

And they did.

Circle Time: Musical Colors

Play this like musical chairs but place a piece of color on the back of each chair. Determine which color remaining will be the winner.

Food Experiences: Red Apples

Give children slices of red apples to eat.

Theme Activities: Flannel Story

Do the "Wee Red Shoes" as a flannel story. The story and patterns can be found on pages 72-73, and 79-80, Senses Week.

Wednesday

Sharing Time: Poem

> ***"Rain On The Green Grass"*** (Anonymous)
>
> Rain on the green grass,
> And rain on the tree,
> And rain on the housetop,
> But not upon me!

Art: Easel Paint with Green

Give children large pieces of paper, paint brushes, and green paint. Let them color green pictures.

Story Time: Song

Have children repeat the words in parentheses. This can also be done as a flannel story using the patterns on pages 105-106.

> ***"The Green Grass Grew All Around"*** (Traditional)
>
> There was a hole *(There was a hole)*.
> All in the ground *(All in the ground)*.
> The prettiest hole *(The prettiest hole)*.
> That you ever did see *(That you ever did see)*.
> Oh, the hole in the ground
> And the green grass grew all around, all around.
> And the green grass grew all around.
> Now in that hole *(Now in that hole)*.
> There was a root *(There was a root)*.
> The prettiest root *(The prettiest root)*.
> That you ever did see *(That you ever did see)*.
> Root in the hole and the hole in the ground
> And the green grass grew all around, all around.
> And the green grass grew all around.
> Now on the root *(Now on the root)*.
> There was a tree *(There was a tree)*.
> The prettiest tree *(The prettiest tree)*.
> That you ever did see *(That you ever did see)*.
> Tree on the root and the root in the hole and the hole in the ground.
> And the green grass grew all around, all around.
> And the green grass grew all around.
> Now on that tree there was a branch, etc.
> Now on that branch there was a nest, etc.
> Now in that nest there was an egg, etc.
> Now on that egg there was a bird, etc.
> Now on that bird there was a wing, etc.
> Now on that wing there was a feather, etc.
> Now on that feather there was a bug, etc.

Wednesday (cont.)

Bug on the feather, and the feather on the wing, and the wing on the bird, and the bird in the egg, and the egg in the nest, and the nest on the branch, and the branch on the tree, and the tree on the root, and the root in the hole and the hole in the ground, and the green grass grew all around, all around, and the green grass grew all around.

Circle Time: Fishing for Colors

Use fishing pole and cut outs of different colors. See directions on page 7.

Food Experiences: Green Broccoli

Give each child a small broccoli floret. Let them taste it raw. Let them name some other green vegetables they have tried.

Theme Activities: Rhyme

"Rock-a-bye Baby, Thy Cradle Is Green"

Rock-a-bye baby, thy cradle is green,
Father's a nobleman, mother's a queen;
And Betty's a lady and wears a gold ring,
And Johnnie's a drummer and drums for the King.

Thursday

Sharing Time: Book

Read *Blue Bug's Vegetable Garden* by V. Poulet

Art: Straw Paint with Blue

Place blobs of blue paint onto paper. Give each child a straw to blow on the paint. Let them mix it into different formations by blowing on it.

Story Time: Song

"Little Boy Blue" Mother Goose
Little Boy Blue, come blow your horn
The sheep's in the meadow,
The cow's in the corn.
Where is the boy who looks after the sheep?
He's under the haystack fast asleep.
Will you wake him?
No not I,
For if I do
He's sure to cry.

This may also be done by using flannel pieces on page 104.

Circle Time: Hop On Colors

Paint shapes of different colors onto an old white sheet. Then as you call out one of the colors, have the children hop on it. Do this with small groups of children at a time, or call children's names to hop on a certain color.

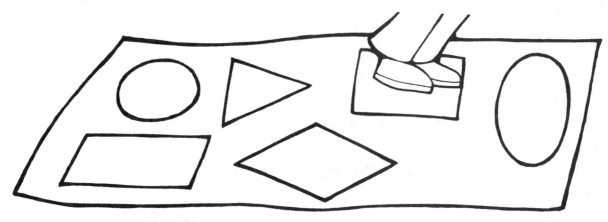

Food Experiences: Blueberries

Give children some blueberries to eat. Ask them if they are really blue. Ask them what other name they would give them.

Theme Activities: Blue Hunt

Have children hunt for blue items in the classroom or outside. Count how many blue items they find.

Friday

Sharing Time: Song

Share "The World is a Rainbow" from the record *We All Live Together, Vol. 2.*

Art: Sponge Paint with Yellow

Cut sponges into various shapes. Give children trays with yellow paint, paper, and the sponges. Let them create a yellow picture.

Story Time: Traffic

As a flannel activity do the poem below. Emphasize the colors of each object. (Use patterns in Community Places and Helpers).

"Traffic Lights" (Traditional)
"Stop," says the red light.
"Go," says the green.
"Wait," says the yellow light,
Blinking in between.

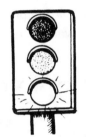

Circle Time: Crayon Pass

Take red, blue, yellow, green, and purple crayons and give them to five children who are in a circle. Play music as children pass crayons. When the music stops, ask the children holding the crayons what colors they have. Continue until all the children have had a turn.

Food Experiences: Yellow Bananas

Show children an unpeeled banana. Ask them what color it is. Slowly peel it, then ask what color the inside of a banana is. Slice the banana and let each child have some to taste.

Theme Activities: Color Sorting

Prepare color boxes, one of each color. An easy way to do this is to cover a shoe box or other box with colored construction paper of the color you wish to teach. Write the color name on the box. Put out items of several different colors. Have children drop items of different colors into the correct boxes.

Classroom Additions

Here are some suggestions of materials that can be placed in the learning centers in addition to your regular materials.

• Housekeeping: colored plates, cups, spoons, knives, and forks
• Circle: posters of the different colors, flannel board and patterns
• Books: books about the different colors, colored stuffed animals
• Music: records with a color theme
• Table Activities: teddy bear bingo and colored plates to match, puzzles, color boxes, color games
• Blocks: blocks of various colors, color sheet, color boxes, fishing poles and cutouts
• Art: paints, construction paper, play dough, and crayons of the colors used each day
• Puppets: colored stick puppets made from small paper plates; give each color puppet a name
• Science: colored plastic containers of clear water, food coloring, prism, kaleidoscope, flashlight

Teachers' Aids

File Folder Activities: Choose the skills you wish to emphasize this week. See directions on pages 5-6.

• Crayon Color Matching
• Paintbrushes with Paint Cans
• Three Little Kittens with Mittens (See patterns, page 31, Pets)
• Colored Lollipops

Bulletin Board Ideas:
• Divide your bulletin board into five sections and display items of the five colors.

For Parents

• Play color games with your child.
• Look for colored items at home.
• Visit the library and check out books on colors.
• Try food coloring experiments at home with your child.

Bibliography

Children's Books
Goulet, V. *Blue Bug's Vegetable Garden.* Childrens Press, 1973
Kowalczyk, Carolyn. *Purple is Part of the Rainbow.* Childrens Press, 1985
Johnson, Crockett. *A Picture for Harold's Room.* Harper and Row, 1960
Johnson, Crockett. *Harold and the Purple Crayon.* Harper and Row, 1955
Martin, Bill. Jr. *Brown Bear, Brown Bear, What Do You See?* Henry Holt, 1983

Record
Steve Millang and Greg Scelsa. *We All Live Together, Vol 2.* Youngheart Records, 1978

Resources
Levin, Ina Massler and Mary Ellen Sterling. *TCM 177 Readiness Manipulatives: Colors.* Teacher Created Resources, 1990

Patterns

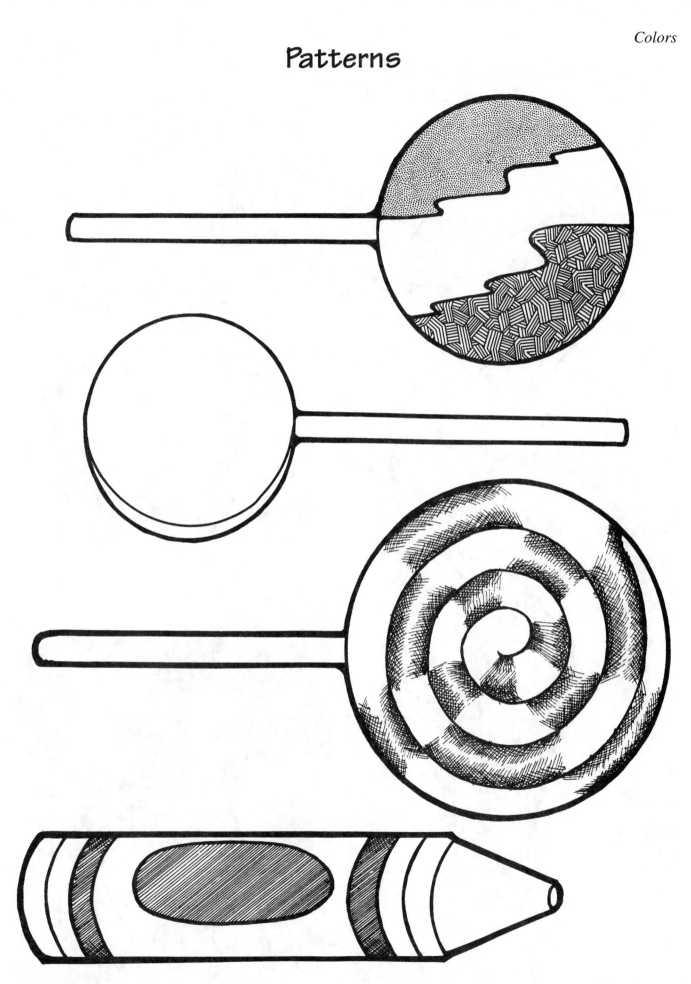

103

Patterns

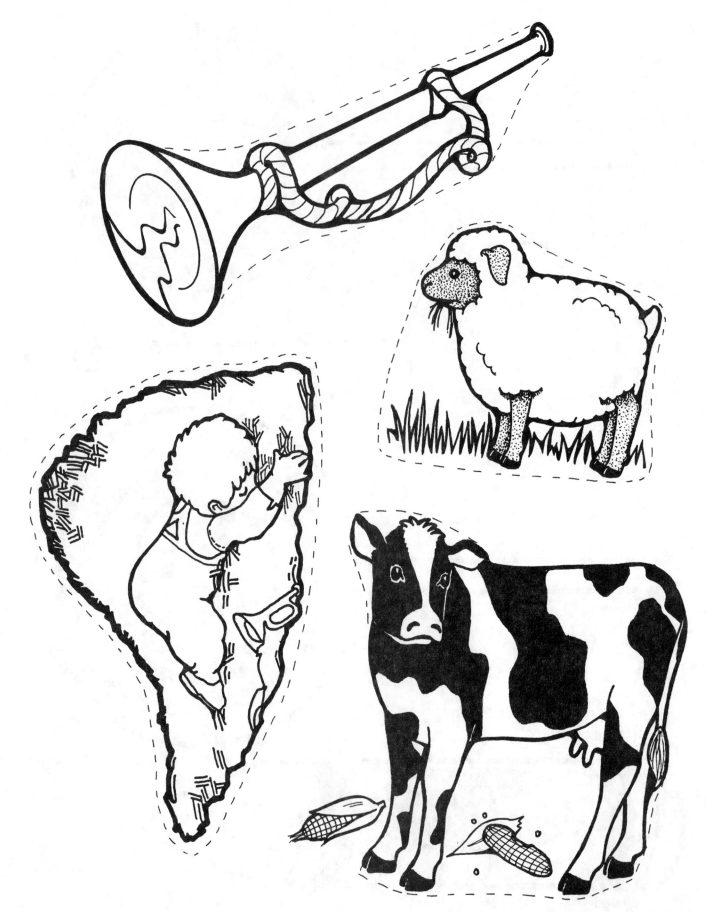

Patterns

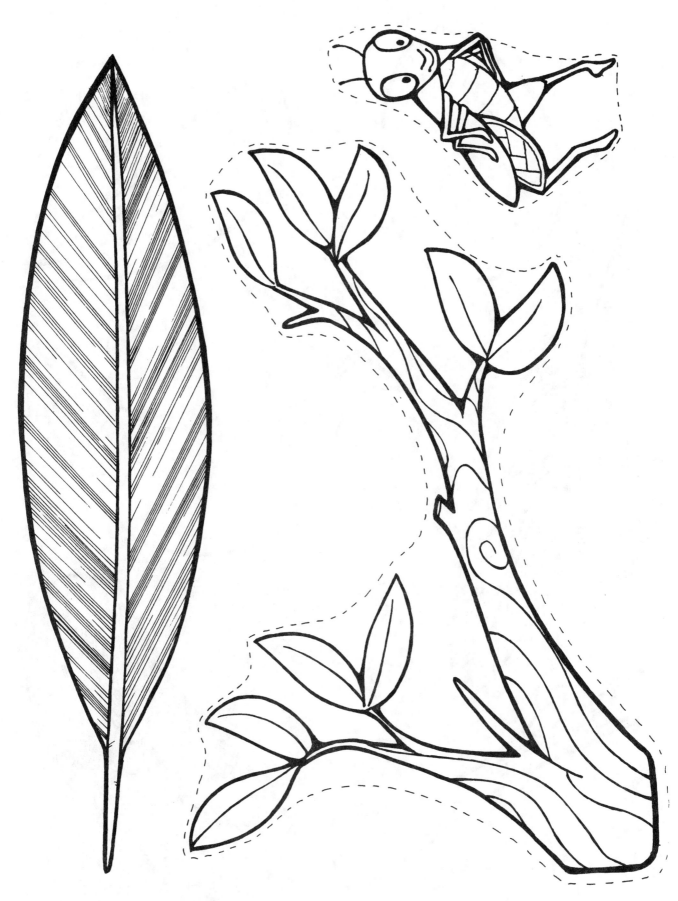

Patterns

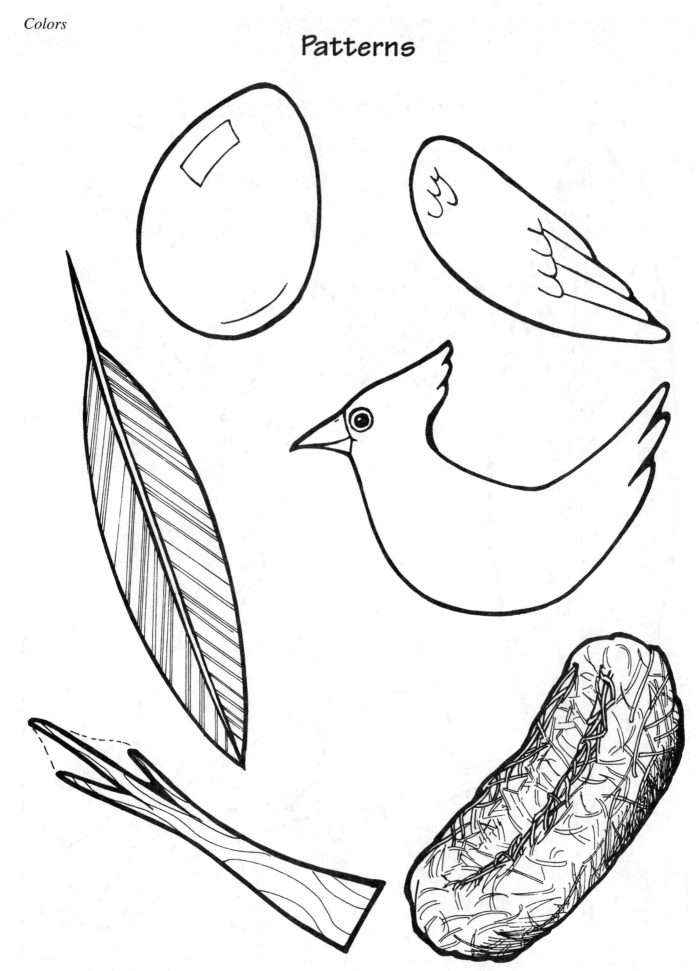

Weekly Theme: *Self-Concepts*   Week of: _____

	Monday	Tuesday	Wednesday	Thursday	Friday
Date					
Sharing Time	Activity: Hands On Shoulders	Fingerplay: Here's a Little Washboard	Fingerplay: Two Little Hands So Clean and Bright	Song: If You're Happy and You Know It	Book: *I Thought I Saw*
Art	Drawing Children's Bodies	Material Collage	Bars of Soap	Feeling Puppet	Yarn Collage
Story Time	Flannel Story: The Stone in the Road	Fingerplay: Shiny Shoes	Book: *Meanies*	Song: It Didn't Frighten Me	Flannel Story: The Three Wishes
Circle Time	Song/Activity: Heads, Shoulders, Knees, Toes	Song: Mary Wore Her Red Dress	Song: The Body Care Song	Song: Who Feels Happy	Song: What A Miracle
Food Experiences	Gingerbread People	Healthy Person	Fingerpaint Pudding Clean It Up!	Apple Smiles	Friendship Sandwich
Theme Activities	Book: *Simon Says*	Flannel Story: Three Little Kittens	Book: *The House That Had Enough*	Book: *She Was Scared Silly*	Book: *It Looked Like Spilt Milk*

Monday

Materials Needed For The Week:

butcher paper, soap flakes, small paper plates, yarn, craft sticks, stencils of a dress, shirt and pants, material, thread, burlap, large plastic blunt-end needles, clothesline, clothespins, balance beam, pineapple rings, cheese strips, celery, raisins, bread, sandwich fillings, cream cheese

Sharing Time: Activity

Have children perform actions as mentioned in the poem.

"Hands On Shoulders" (Traditional)

Hands on shoulders, hands on knees,
Hands behind you if you please.
Touch your shoulders, now your nose,
Now your chin and now your toes.
Hands up high in the air,
Down at your sides and touch your hair.
Hands up high as before,
Now clap your hands—one, two, three, four.

Art: Drawing Children's Bodies

Have the children lie down on butcher paper. Trace around their bodies. Children can then draw in their facial features, hair, and clothing.

Story Time: Flannel Story

See patterns on page 116.

"The Stone in the Road"

A certain country was ruled by a kindhearted king, who would do anything for his subjects. But at last he noticed that they were growing lazy and seldom did anything for themselves or for each other. The king wondered if there was anyone left in his kingdom who would go out of his way to help his neighbors. So he concocted a plan.

Late one night the king went to the main road of the kingdom and rolled a huge stone right smack into the middle of it. Then he secretly placed a bag of gold under the stone. The next morning he hid near the road to watch.

First, a woman came by on her way to market. Because of the stone, she had to walk in the mud at the side of the road. "Someone should really move that stone," she snapped angrily.

Next, two students passed by on their way to school. "What a nuisance!" they cried. "Why doesn't the king move that rock out of our road?"

Monday (cont.)

And so it continued all day long: some people blamed the king, some blamed the stone, and some even hit the stone as they walked around it.

As the sun was about to set, a young girl passed by. When she saw the stone, she stopped. "I'd better get this out of the road," she said. "Someone might pass by here after dark and not see the stone and bump into it." The girl pushed and pushed the stone.

A man walking by said, "Let the king take care of that." But the girl kept pushing until at last the stone began to roll, and it rolled over the edge of the road and down a hill.

It was then that she saw the bag of gold the king had left there.

Everyone agreed that the girl deserved the gold. And everyone was more than a little bit ashamed that they had not thought of moving the stone. After that, they began helping each other instead of waiting for the king to do things for them.

Circle Time: Song/Activity

"Head, Shoulders, Knees, Toes" (Traditional)

Head, shoulders, knees, and toes,
Knees and toes.
Head, shoulders, knees, and toes,
Knees and toes,
And eyes and ears,
And mouth and nose.
Head, shoulders, knees, and toes,
Knees and toes.
(Children touch body parts as you sing or say the words.)

Food Experiences: Gingerbread People

Give children already prepared gingerbread people cookies. Provide frosting and raisins to decorate the cookies. Have them decorate the cookies to look like themselves.

Theme Activities: Song/Activity:

Play "Simon Says" body parts, from the record: *We All Live Together, Vol.* 3. or create your own game of "Simon Says."

Tuesday

Sharing Time: Fingerplay
"Here's a Little Washboard"

Here's a little washboard; *(Hold up palm of left hand.)*
Here's a little tub; *(Make a circle with fingers on right hand.)*
Here's a little cake of soap, *(Make oval with fingers on right hand)*
And here's the way we scrub; *(Have fingers go up and down on left hand)*
Here's a line away up high; *(Draw an imaginary line in the air.)*
Now the clothes are drying; *(Wave fingers back and forth.)*
Hear the wind come whistling by; *(Cup hand to ear.)*
See! The clothes are flying. *(Wave hand harder.)*

Art: Material Collage
Prepare stencils of large dress, shirt, and pants. Have available different textured materials, buttons, rick rack, and lace. Children can cut out materials to glue onto their construction paper piece of clothing.

Story Time: Finger Play
"Shiny Shoes"

First I loosen mud and dirt, *(Use one hand to brush the other.)*
My shoes I then rub clean, *(Rub one hand.)*
For shoes in such a dreadful sight *(Hide hand behind back.)*
Never should be seen.
And then I spread the polish on, *(Rub one hand)*
And then I let it dry. *(Make fist and brush.)*
I brush and brush, and brush and brush,
How those shoes shine! Oh, my! *(Extend hand and admire.)*

Circle Time: Song
"Mary Wore Her Red Dress" Folk Song

Mary wore her red dress, red dress, red dress.
Mary wore her red dress all day long.
Mary wore her black hat, black hat, black hat.
Mary wore her black hat all day long.
Mary wore her blue shoes, blue shoes, blue shoes.
Mary wore her blue shoes all day long.
Mary wore her green socks, green socks, green socks.
Mary wore her green socks all day long.

Food Experiences: A Healthy Person
Give children pineapple rings for a head, celery for a body, cheese strips for arms and legs, and raisins for eyes, nose, and mouth. Give each a paper plate and let them arrange the items to make a person.

Theme Activities: Flannel Story
"Three Little Kittens"
See page 31 for patterns.

Wednesday

Sharing Time: Fingerplay

"Two Little Hands So Clean And Bright" (Traditional)

Two little hands so clean and bright. *(Hold up hands.)*
This is my left and this is my right. *(Point to each.)*

Read *No Bath Tonight* by Jane Yolen.

Art: Bars of Soap

Mix soap flakes and water until you have a thick mixture. Then have the children mold their own bar of soap. Let them try using it. Ask them how it feels.

Story Time: Book

Read *Meanies* by Joy Cowley. Discuss keeping our bodies clean and why it is important to do so.

Circle Time: Song

Sing "The Body Care Song" from the record *It's Fun To Clap*.

Food Experiences: Fingerpaint Pudding—Clean it Up!

Make some instant pudding following package directions. Give each child a piece of wax paper and a few spoonfuls of the pudding. Let them finger paint in it. When they are finished, have them clean up their painting by throwing out the wax paper with the pudding and washing their hands very carefully, perhaps using the soap they made.

Theme Activities: Book

Read *The House That Had Enough* by P.E. King.

Thursday

Sharing Time: Song

"If You're Happy And You Know It" (Traditional)

If you're happy and you know it, clap your hands.
If you're happy and you know it, clap your hands.
If you're happy and you know it, then your face will surely show it.
If you're happy and you know it, clap your hands.
(You may add "stomp your feet," "snap your fingers," etc.)

Art: Feeling Puppet

Use paper plates and let children draw facial features that reflect how they are feeling at that moment. Attach craft stick. Discuss the different feelings.

Story Time: Book

Read *It Didn't Frighten Me* by Janet L. Gross and Jerome C. Harste. Discuss being frightened sometimes.

Circle Time: Song

"Who Feels Happy" (Traditional)

Who feels happy? Who feels glad today?
All who do clap their hands this way.
Who feels happy? Who feels glad today?
All who do nod their heads this way.

(Continue adding other body parts such as "stomp their feet this way" or "with your mouth, shout hurray!")

Food Experiences: Apple Smiles

Cut an apple into wedges. Spread on cream cheese. Use colored miniature marshmallows for teeth.

Theme Activities: Books

Read *She Was Scared Silly* by Ellen H. Goins and *I Was So Mad* by Mercer Mayer.

Friday

Sharing Time: Book

Read *I Thought I Saw* by Pam Adams and Ceri Jones.

Art: Yarn Collage

Give children yarn, glue and paper. Have them use their imagination along with the yarn and glue to make a picture. Discuss each picture.

Story Time: Flannel Story

Use pattern on pages 117-118.

"The Three Wishes" (Folk Tale)

Once, many years ago, there was a poor woodcutter and his wife who lived from day to day in a humble cottage near the edge of the woods. Every day the man would go into the forest to chop wood and return in time for supper. Then, they usually talked about the good things that their neighbors owned and wished that they, too, might have such good things.

One day while the woodcutter was in the forest, he said aloud as he had often said before, "Oh, it is a hard life! I have to work so hard all day long, and yet I am still poor. There are so many things I would like to have—if only I could ever hope to get them!"

As he uttered these words, a beautiful fairy appeared before him. "I have heard your complaints," she said, "and so I shall grant you three wishes. Choose them wisely, because you may have no more than three." Then she faded from view as mysteriously as she had appeared.

When the woodcutter went home that evening, he told his wife what had happened, and they were both so excited they could hardly eat. "Imagine!" said the wife. "We can ask for anything we like—anything! Oh, I'm so happy!"

"Yes, it is wonderful," agreed the man, "Just think—we can have great wealth!"

"Or a fine house," said his wife.

"Even a mansion—or a palace," added the husband, his eyes shining brightly.

They went on talking in this way, thinking of all the things they could possibly wish for, but they could not agree on any one wish right away, so they decided to put it off until the next day. Then they sat down to the table to eat.

The man looked at the bowl of soup that was before him and sighed. "Oh, dear, soup again!" he said. "How I wish for once that I could have a nice fat sausage!"

Wonder of wonders, at that very instant a plump sausage appeared magically on the table!

The wife was the first to realize what had happened. "Now look what you have done!" she cried. "You have wasted a wish on a silly old sausage. Now we have only two wishes left!"

"Oh, well, there is still much to be wished for," said the man.

"Is that all you have to say for yourself?" scolded the woman. "Here you have wasted a perfectly good wish for all time. How could you have been so foolish?" And she went on like that, complaining loudly.

Soon the man lost his patience and exclaimed, "I am tired of hearing about the sausage! I am tired of hearing you speak! I wish that the sausage were stuck to your nose!"

No sooner were the words out of his mouth then the sausage was hanging at the end of his wife's nose!

"Now see what you have done!" cried the wife. "You have wasted another wish by your foolish tongue!" And she tried desperately to remove the sausage from the end of her nose, but it would not come off.

"We still have one wish left," said the husband. "We can still wish for great wealth."

"What good is money or riches," the woman asked, "if I must go through life with a sausage on the end of my nose? Everyone would laugh at me and I could not abide that! No, there is only one thing to do, and that is to wish it off."

"But then we will be left as poor as we were before," said the husband.

"That is all that I wish for," said the wife. And in a flash the sausage was gone.

The three wishes had been granted, and for all of their plans, the woodcutter and his wife were no better off. In fact, sad to say, they could not even have sausage for dinner.

Circle Time: Song
    Sing "What a Miracle" from the record Walter *The Waltzing Worm.*

Food Experiences: Friendship Sandwich
    Let children make friendship sandwiches by taking turns putting the sandwich together. When the sandwich is assembled, the teacher cuts it for children share. (You may wish to have children wear plastic gloves.)

Theme Activities: Book
    Read *It Looked Like Spilt Milk* by Charles G. Shaw. After reading the story take a walk outside and look at the clouds. Ask the children what they see.

Classroom Additions

Here are some materials that can be placed in the learning centers in addition to your regular materials.

- Housekeeping: doll clothes, clothesline, clothespins, towels, soap, wash cloths, small pan of water
- Circle: posters of body, clothing, feelings, and cleanliness; posters that provoke imagination
- Books: books on each of the five areas discussed
- Music: records on exercise and body movement
- Table Activities: sewing cards, body puzzles, games
- Blocks: balance beam, large blocks, cardboard boxes
- Art: play dough, small paper plates, crayons, markers, paints
- Puppets: puppets representing body, clothing, cleanliness, feelings, and imagination
- Science: thread, large plastic needles, burlap, dancing dolls

Teachers' Aids
- Paper Dolls and Clothing
  File Folder Activities: Choose the skills you wish to emphasize this week. See directions on pages 5-6.
  - Hat Matching
  - Beach Towel Matching
  - Sock Matching
  - Body Parts Puzzle

  Bulletin Board Ideas:
  - Feelings Posters
  - Feeling Faces
  - Grooming Items
  - Children with Different Expressions
  - Clothing For Different Seasons

For Parents
- Discuss different feelings with your child.
- Tell him or her it is all right to feel mad, sad, etc.
- Play imagination games with your child.
- Talk about clothing while your child gets dressed for school.
- Let your child use the bar of soap made at school in the bath.
- Discuss the importance of cleanliness.

Bibliography

Children's Books
Adams, Pam and Ceri Jones. *I Thought I Saw.* Child's Play, 1974
Cowley, Joy. *Meanies.* Shortland Publications, 1988
Goins, Ellen H. *She was Scared Silly.* Steck-Vaughn, 1971
Gross, Janet L. and Jerome C. *It Didn't Frighten Me.* Willowisp Press, 1985
King, P. E. *The House That Had Enough.* Western, 1986
Mayer, Mercer. *I Was So Mad.* Western, 1983
Shaw, Charles G. *It Looked Like Spilt Milk.* Harper, 1947
Slobodkina, Ephyr. *Caps For Sale.* Harper and Row, 1940
Yolen, Jane. *No Bath Tonight.* Harper and Row, 1978
Records
Steve Millang and Greg Scelsa. *We All Live Together, Vol. 3.* Youngheart Records, 1979
Hap Palmer. *Walter The Waltzing Worm.* Educational Activities, Inc., 1982

Patterns

Patterns

Patterns

Patterns

Patterns

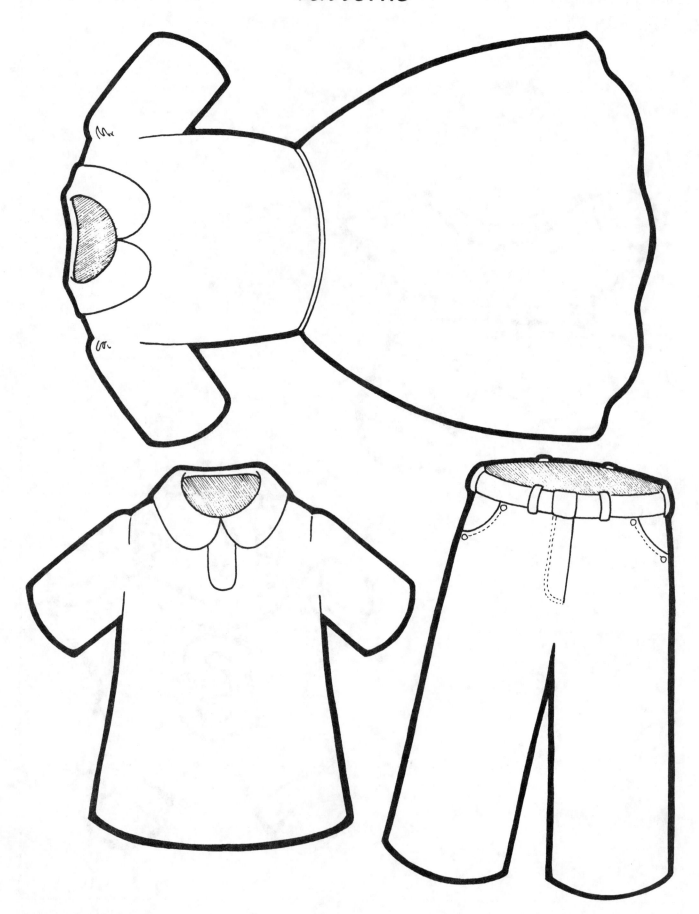

Weekly Theme: _Children of the World_   Week of: _____

	Monday	Tuesday	Wednesday	Thursday	Friday
Date					
Sharing Time	Discuss Children of Africa	Discuss Eskimo Children	Discuss Children of Mexico	Discuss Children of Asia	Discuss American Cowboys and Pioneers
Art	Headdresses Masks Necklaces	Mukluks, Eskimo Village	Mexican Sashes, Bolas	Lanterns, Fans, Rubbings	Cowboy Vests and Brands
Story Time	Book: _Jambo Means Hello_ and _Ashanti to Zulu_	Book: _Ootah's Lucky Day_	Song: Mexican Counting Song	Flannel Story: The Tale of the Clever Deer	Book: _Thunderhoof_
Circle Time	Activity: Limbo	Activity: Story Telling	Activity: Dancing	Activity: Music	Activity: Pioneer Games
Food Experiences	Fried Bananas	Eskimo Foods	Mexican Foods	Rice and Vegetables	Food on the Range
Theme Activities	Activity: Balancing Skills	Rub Noses	Activity: Bull Fighting	Book: _The Emperor and the Kite_	Activity: Sit Around the Campfire

Monday

Materials Needed For The Week:

paper plates, large buttons, styrofoarn packing pellets, egg cartons, brown lunch bags, cotton balls, soap flakes, white material, liquid embroidery paints or markers, styrofoarn cups, craft sticks, large grocery bags, popcorn, cactus, bananas, honey, peanut butter, canning jar lids, buttons, coffee cans

Sharing Time: Discuss Children of Africa.

Introduce the continent of Africa. Locate Africa on a map or a globe. Talk about the children who live there. Explain some of their ways of life, what they wear, eat, and play.

Introduce some new words: MAMA (mother), BABA (father), JAMBO (hello). Write the new words on cards and post in the classroom.

Use these words in your conversations and encourage the children to use them, too.

Art: Native African Headdresses, Masks, and Necklaces

To make a headdress, use a 9" x 12" (22.5 cm. x 30 cm) piece of construction paper cut in half lengthwise. Staple two halves together to fit child's head. Cut one inch (25mm) slits all around and curl them outward.

To make an African mask, cut a mask shape out of construction paper or use paper plates. Children can use crayons or paint to decorate them. Punch a hole in each side and tie two pieces of yarn so it can be fastened to the child's head.

To make African necklaces, use canning jar lid rings or large buttons. Thread rings or buttons with yarn.

Story Time: Books

Read *Ashanti To Zulu* by Margaret Musgrove and *Jambo Means Hello* by Muriel Feelings.

Circle Time: Play Limbo

Two adults hold up a jump rope, and the children take turns going under the rope. Every time all the children have gone through, lower the rope. Children try not to touch the rope.

Let children play drums. Make these from empty coffee cans. Let some of the children beat them while others are doing the limbo.

Listen to the record *Rhythms of Childhood* by Ella Jenkins.

Food Experiences: Fried Bananas

Slice bananas lengthwise, and sprinkle on lemon juice and cinnamon. Fry in butter.

Serve a milk and honey beverage. Mix ½ gallon (1.9 L) milk and one cup (236 mL) honey.

Let children make peanut butter. Combine ½ (354mL) cups salted roasted peanuts, 1 Tbsp. (15 mL) oil. Blend in a blender. You may add honey. Spread on crackers.

Theme Activities: Balancing Skills

Let children try to balance and carry objects on their heads. Soft covered books or empty baskets are good objects to try.

Tuesday

Sharing Time: Discuss Eskimo Children.

Discuss Eskimo children and their way of life. Locate Alaska on a map or globe. Introduce new words: IGLOO (house), MUKLUKS (boots).

Write the new words on cards and post in the classroom. Use these new words in your conversations. Encourage the children to use them, too.

Art: Mukluks and Eskimo Village

To make mukluks, take brown lunch bags and let the children decorate them with crayons. Glue cotton balls or batting around the tops of the bags. Put them on over their shoes.

To make an Eskimo village, take egg cartons and cut out one section for each child. Cover a large piece of cardboard with blue construction paper for water. Mix up two cups (472 ml) Ivory Snow Washing Power® and ½ cup (118 ml) water. Let each child cover his section of the egg carton with the mixture. Place them on the covered cardboard.

Story Time: Book

Read *Ootah's Luck Day* by Peggy Parish.

Circle Time: Story Telling

Let children take turns acting out pulling a sled through the snow. Use cardboard boxes for sleds. Then let the children pretend to be crawling through a tunnel.

Food Experiences: Eskimo Foods

Let children try some Eskimo foods. These would include boiled eggs, tea, sardines or salmon (pretend to be raw fish), and ice cream (AUGUTUK).

Theme Activities: Rub Noses

Eskimos have a different way of kissing. They rub noses. Let children try this. Also do a fishing activity for color and shape recognition and for counting. See directions for fishing on page 7.

Wednesday

Sharing Time: Discuss the Children of Mexico.

Discuss children in Mexico and their way of life. Locate Mexico on a map or globe. Introduce new words in Spanish: SIESTA (nap time). NIÑA (girl), SÎ (yes), ADIOS (good-bye). Write the new words on cards and post in the classroom. Use these new words in your conversations and encourage the children to use them.

Art: Mexican Sashes and Bolas

To make sashes, cut three-inch (75mm) strips out of white material long enough to fit around children's waists. Use liquid embroidery or markers to write the child's name and also write the Spanish words and their meanings on the sashes.

To make a Mexican bola, attach a craft stick to the bottom of a styrofoam cup. Tie yarn to the edge of the cup rim and attach a button or small ball. Child tries to get the button or ball in the cup.

Story Time: Books

Read *The Story of Ferdinand* by Munro Leaf and *Amigo Means Friend* by Louis Everett. Also sing the "Mexican Counting Song."

"Mexican Counting Song" (Folk Song)

Uno, dos, tres, cuatro, cinco, seis,
Siete, ocho, nueve, I can count to diez.
La la la la
La la la la la
La la la la la la!
La la la!

The numbers are:
Uno - one
Dos - two
Tres - three
Cuatro - four
Cinco - five
Seis - six
Siete - seven
Ocho - eight
Nueve - nine
Diez - ten

Circle Time: Dancing

Give children an opportunity to dance. First let them pretend to be jumping beans. Then try the Mexican Hat Dance. Get a straw hat and place it on the floor. Play some Mexican music and let the children dance around the hat.

Food Experiences: Mexican Foods

There are several types of foods that children can taste. They include tacos, nachos and cheese dip, papaya, bananas, orange, and avocados. Use those that are the easiest for you.

Theme Activities: Bull Fighting

Pretend to have bull fights. Provide children with a "cape". An old towel will work and have one pretend to be the bullfighter and one pretend to be the bull. Have the child who is the bull put his/her fingers at the side of his/her head as he/she charges the cape.

Thursday

Sharing Time: Discuss the Children of Asia

Find the continent of Asia on the map or globe. Point out Japan and China. Talk about children in Asia and their way of life. Introduce new words YEW (fish), DOZO (please), NA (name), GAKKO (school). Write the new words on cards and post in the classroom. Use these new words in your conversation and encourage the children to use them, too.

Art: Japanese Lanterns and Fans; Chinese Rubbing

To make Japanese lanterns, use brightly colored 9" x 12" (22.5 cm x 30 cm) construction paper. Fold paper lengthwise and cut slits almost all the way across, leaving about one or two inches uncut. Fold widthwise and staple. Attach a handle on top. To make Japanese fans, cut a 9" x 12" (22.5 cm x 30 cm) piece of construction paper in half. Fold each half in an accordion fashion, and staple the bottom. To make Chinese rubbing, take a piece of cardboard. Cut out Chinese figures or letters. Glue them onto another 9" x 12" (22.5 cm x 30 cm) piece of cardboard. Take manila paper and lay it on top of the pattern. Use sides of crayons and rub.

Story Time: Flannel Story

Share this old Chinese folk tale as a flannel story.

"The Tale of the Clever Deer"

A little deer was quietly nibbling some grass, when suddenly a tiger jumped out of the bushes. At the sight of the fierce tiger, the little deer's heart stood still with fear. But since there was no way to escape, he bravely stood his ground.

Now, ordinarily, the tiger would have eaten so small and tender an animal, but this tiger had never seen a deer before.

"What are those things growing out of your head?" asked the tiger.

"Those are horns," said the little deer.

"Of what use are horns?" asked the tiger.

"Why, they are used especially to fork tigers," said the clever little deer.

"Really?" replied the tiger. "And what are all those white spots on your body for?"

"Don't you know?" said the little deer. "I thought everybody knew that. Every time I eat a tiger, a spot appears on my body. As you can see, I've eaten so many tigers that I'm practically covered with spots."

When the tiger heard this, he was so frightened that he bounded into the forest.

Thursday (cont.)

Pretty soon he met a fox. He told the fox of the fearsome animal he had just met—the animal who forked tigers with his horns and who had eaten so many tigers.

"A little deer forking and eating tigers!" laughed the fox. "Oh, what a trick he has played on you!"

The tiger couldn't believe that the little deer had fooled him so completely. But the fox said, "If you don't believe me, I'll show you myself. Just let me ride on your back and lead me to the deer. You'll soon see."

So they set out. When the little deer saw the tiger returning with the fox on his back, he knew at once that the fox had told the tiger the truth. He had to think fast to save himself, and think fast he did.

"Ho, there, friend fox!" he called. "I see you have kept your promise. You told me that you would bring a fine tiger for me to eat, and that surely is a beauty you're bringing me now!"

When the tiger heard this, he needed no more convincing. He darted back into the forest —with the fox in his mouth! And the clever little deer was saved!

Circle Time: Music

Let children experience the music of Asia. Use wooden blocks, drums, and cymbals to create music.

Food Experiences: Rice and Vegetables

Rice is a food served quite often in Asia. Make rice with your class and add some water chestnuts, bamboo shoots, or Chinese pea pods. Serve tea and tangerines.

Theme Activities: Book

Read *The Emperor and The Kite* by Jane Yolen.

Explain "bonsai," which is the art of growing miniature trees in containers. With the group, plant a very small tree or plant in a container.

Friday

Sharing Time: Discuss American Cowboys and Pioneers.

Discuss cowboys and pioneers in the United States. Ask children if there are still cowboys and pioneers today. How did they live? Introduce some new words: LICK (molasses), SPUDS (potatoes), SHIVERING LIZ (jello). Write the new words on cards and post in the classroom. Use these words in your conversations and encourage the children to use them, too.

Art: Cowboy Vests and Brands

To make cowboy vests, use large grocery bags and cut a neck hole and arm holes in the bottom of the bag. Fringe the bottom and let children decorate them.

To make a branding iron, cut branding symbols out of a sponge and attach to a clothespin. Dip the sponge in paint and decorate a vest or make a picture.

Story Time: Book

Read *Thunderhoof* by Sid Hoff.

Circle Time: Games and Songs

Play some games that pioneers and cowboys might have played. These include:

• Ring toss—You can set up objects for the children to toss rings over.

• Sack race—Give children pillow cases to race in.

• Cards—Play "Old Maid" and "Go Fish."

Food Experiences: Food on the Range

Try some foods that pioneers and cowboys might have eaten. These include popcorn, molasses, potatoes, and beans.

Theme Activities: Pretend Campfire

Sit around a pretend campfire, eat popcorn, and have children tell stories or sing songs. Make up tall tales or tell some classic ones such as Pecos Bill or John Henry. Play guitars or harmonicas.

Sing this cowboy song.

"Home On The Range" (Traditional Cowboy)

Oh, give me a home where the buffalo roam, And the deer and the antelope play, Where seldom is heard a discouraging word, And the skies are not cloudy all day. Home, home on the range, where the deer and the antelope play, Where seldom is heard a discouraging word, And the skies are not cloudy all day.

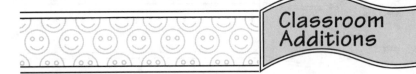

Classroom Additions

Here are some materials that can be placed in the learning centers in addition to your regular materials.

- Housekeeping: clothing from various countries including jewelry, mittens, parkas, boots, sandals, ponchos, kimonos
- Circle: piñata, fans, hobby horses, Chinese jump rope
- Books: books about different people and countries
- Music: drums, maraca, guitar Table Activities: lacing cards, file folder games, cards with words from the week on them
- Blocks: straw baskets, kayak and igloo made from cardboard
- Art: wooden beads and yarn for stringing, materials to make paper rattlesnakes
- Puppets: puppets and dolls representing various countries
- Science: drinking gourds, toy harpoon, chopsticks, Mexican jumping beans, cactus, crickets, dried gourds, hay, horns, cactus, driftwood
- Science Activities: Try these activities as they fit into your weekly plan.
  - Ice Fishing
  - Cut a piece of yarn about six inches (15cm) long for each child. Get a shallow pan and fill it up with cold water. Place an ice cube for each child in the pan. Have children place one end of their yarn on top of an ice cube. Sprinkle salt on top of the yarn and the ice cubes. Wait a couple of seconds and have the children lift the yarn.

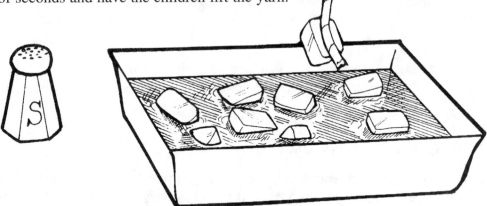

  - Salt Water vs. Fresh Water: Have a container of ice so children can see it melt. Add some salt. Compare the taste of salt water with plain water.

Teachers' Aids

File Folder Activities: Choose the skills you wish to emphasize this week. See directions on pages 5 and 6.

- Bananas
- Fish
- African Drums
- Cowboy Hats

Lacing Cards: Use shape of bears, whales, igloos, drums, bananas, and fans.

Classroom Additions (cont.)

Bulletin Board Ideas:

- Start at the beginning of the week and keep adding to your bulletin board. By the end of the week you will have a room filled with examples of different cultures. Post the new words learned from each culture each day.

- Use photographs and pictures of each culture.

For Parents

- Talk with your child about children of other lands. Discuss the types of clothing they wear, foods they eat, and houses in which they live.

- Your child will be exposed to simple words of different cultures. Ask your child what new words he/she learned today.

- Visit the library and check out books about different cultures.

- Make a recipe of some type of food that originates in a foreign country.

- Volunteer in the classroom this week.

Bibliography

Children's Books

Everett, Louise. *Amigo Means Friend.* Troll Associates, 1988
Feelings, Muriel. *Jambo Means Hello.* Dial Books, 1974
Flack, Marjorie and Kurt Wiese. *The Story About Ping.* Viking, 1933
Hoff, Sid. *Thunderhoof.* Harper and Row, 1971
Leaf, Munro. *The Story of Ferdinand.* Viking, 1936
Musgrove, Margaret. *Ashanti To Zulu.* Dial Books, 1976
Parish, Peggy. *Ootahs' Lucky Day.* Harper and Row, 1970
Yashirna, Taro. *Crow Boy.* Viking Press, 1955
Yolen, Jane. *The Emperor and The Kite.* Philomel Books, 1988

Records

Jenkins, Ella. *Rhythms of Childhood.* Folkways Records.

Patterns

© Teacher Created Resources, Inc.

Weekly Theme: *Thanksgiving*   Week of: _____

	Monday	Tuesday	Wednesday	Thursday	Friday
Date					
Sharing Time	Discuss Native Americans	Discuss Pilgrims	Discuss Turkeys	Fingerplay: Five Wild Turkeys	Book: *Squash Pie*
Art	Native American Projects	Pilgrim Hats	Hand Turkey	Corn on the Cob	Sand Painting
Story Time	Books: *Snapping Turtle's All Wrong Day; Granny and the Indians*	Fingerplay: Five Little Pilgrims	Fingerplay: Five Little Turkeys	Flannel Story: Why the Bear Has a Short Tail	Book: *Little Bear's Thanksgiving*
Circle Time	Game: Hide and Seek	Book: *The First Thanksgiving*	Fingerplay: Ten Fat Turkeys	Poem: Mr. Turkey and Mr. Duck	Poem: Wake Up Little Pilgrims
Food Experiences	Popcorn	Cranberries	Sweet Potatoes	Corn on the Cob	Canned Pumpkin
Theme Activities	Poem: Our Table	Poem: The Turkey	Poem: Creeping Indians	Book: *Autumn Harvest*	Book: *Bring in the Pumpkins*

Monday

Materials Needed For The Week:
> feathers, rocks, sand, popcorn, pumpkins, sweet potatoes, cranberries, ornamental corn, baskets, squash, gourds, packing peanuts

Sharing Time: Discuss Native Americans and Their Customs
> Discuss Native Americans and their customs. Give each child a Native American name for the day and use the names in your daily conversations. Introduce Native American rebus symbols. Write a few simple ones on cards and post for the day.

Art: Native American Projects
> Bead Necklaces: Let the children paint packing peanuts different colors with tempera paint. When the paint is dry, let the children string them on yarn.

> Headbands: Use different colored construction paper to cut out feathers. Use a two inch (50 mm) wide band of paper cut to fit each child's head. Staple together and attach several feathers to each headband.

> Feather Painting: Collect feathers. Use them to dip into paint and draw Native American designs on paper.

> Rock Painting: Collect smooth, round rocks. Wash them and let dry. Have children draw designs on them.

Story Time: Books
> Read *Snapping Turtle's All Wrong Day* and *Granny and the Indians* by Peggy Parish.

Circle Time: Game
> Play Hide and Seek. Encourage children to be very quiet and go on tiptoe as they hide.

Food Experiences: Popcorn
> Popcorn is a food served at the first Thanksgiving feast. Make some and share it with your class.

Theme Activities: Poem

> *"Our Table"*
> Every day when we eat our dinner
> Our table is very small.
> There's room for father, mother, brother,
> Sister, and me—that's all.
> But when Thanksgiving Day, and the company comes,
> You'd scarcely believe your eyes;
> For that very same table stretches
> until it is just this size.

Tuesday

Sharing Time: Discuss Pilgrims

Discuss Pilgrims, why they came to America, the first feast, and why we give thanks. Introduce new words: TONIC (soda pop); COBBLER (shoe repairman). Write the new words on cards and post in the classroom. Use these words in your conversations and encourage the children to use them also.

Art: Pilgrim Hats

Use black and white construction paper. For the boy's hat cut a two inch (50 mm) strip sized to fit child's head from black paper. Cut a three by four inch (75 mm x 100 mm) piece of black paper to attach to the front of band. Cut a buckle from white paper and glue it onto the black front.

For the girl's hat, fold a 9" x 12" (22.5 cm x 30 cm) sheet of white paper in half, and turn one side up for brim of hat. Fold and staple other side of hat to form back. Attach yarn to each side of hat to tie.

Story Time: Finger Play

"Five Little Pilgrims" (Author Unknown)

Five little Pilgrims on Thanksgiving Day *(Hold up 5 fingers.)*
The first one said, "I'll have cake if I may." *(Wiggle thumb.)*
The second one said, "I'll have turkey roasted." *(Wiggle next finger.)*
The third one said, "I'll have chestnuts toasted." *(Wiggle next.)*
The fourth one said, "I'll have pumpkin pie." *(Wiggle next.)*
The fifth one said, "Oh, cranberries I spy." *(Wiggle next.)*
But before the Pilgrims ate their turkey dressing,
They bowed their heads and said a Thanksgiving blessing. *(Bow head.)*

Circle Time: Book

Read *The First Thanksgiving* by Maude Burnham.

Food Experiences: Cranberries

Let children taste some prepared cranberries.

Theme Activities: Poem:

"The Turkey" (Traditional)

The turkey is a funny bird.
His head goes wobble, wobble.
All he says is just one word,
"Gobble, gobble, gobble!"

Wednesday

Sharing Time: Discuss Turkeys

Visit a turkey farm if you can. Introduce new words: HENS (female turkey), TOMS (male turkey).

Art: Hand Turkey

Trace children's hand prints onto paper. Fingers can be colored for the feathers. Also, mouth, eyes, wattles, and legs can be drawn.

Story Time: Finger Play

"Five Little Turkeys" (Author Unknown)

Five little turkeys standing in a row, *(Hole up five fingers.)*
First little turkey said, "I don't want to grow." *(Wiggle thumb.)*
Second little turkey said, "Why do you say that?" *(Wiggle next.)*
Third little turkey said, "I want to get fat." *(Wiggle next.)*
Fourth little turkey said, "Thanksgiving is near." *(Wiggle next.)*
Fifth little turkey said, "Yes, that's what I hear." *(Wiggle next.)*
Then the five little turkeys that were standing in a row,
All said together, "Come on, let's GO!" *(Run fingers away.)*

Circle Time: Finger Play

"Ten Fat Turkeys" (Author Unknown)

Ten fat turkeys standing in a row, *(Hole up ten fingers.)*
They spread their wings and tails just so. *(Fan fingers out.)*
They strut to the left. *(Fingers go left.)*
They strut to the right. *(Fingers go right.)*
They all stand up ready to fight. *(Fingers are still and straight.)*
Along comes a man with a great big gun—
Bang! You should see those turkeys run! *(Say bang and make fingers run.)*

Food Experiences: Sweet Potatoes

Serve children some cooked sweet potatoes. Show them both raw and cooked potatoes.

Theme Activities: Poem

"Creeping Indians" (Traditional)

The Indians are creeping, shhhhhh.
The Indians are creeping, shhhhhh.
They do not make a sound as their feet touch the ground.
The Indians are creeping, shhhhhh!

Thursday

Sharing Time: Poem

"Five Wild Turkeys"

A farmer and his wife caught five wild turkeys and put them inside a tall pen. They wanted to eat the turkeys for Thanksgiving. They were going to invite their family and their friends. But they forgot that wild turkeys can fly very well. When the turkeys saw the ax, they just flew away.

1. Five wild turkeys,
Locked in a pen.
They can't fly out,
But they tried again.

2. Five wild turkeys,
Pushed on the door.
One flew out,
Then there were four.

3. Four wild turkeys,
Sad as can be.
One flew out,
Then there were three.

4. Three wild turkeys,
Don't know what to do.
One flew out,
Then there were two.

5. Two wild turkeys,
This is no fun.
One flew out.
Then there was one.

6. One wild turkey,
That's not many.
He flew out,
Then there weren't any.

7. They flew to a tree,
And slept all night.
The cook couldn't find them,
And that's all right.

Art: Corn On The Cob

Have children cut out yellow corn shapes from construction paper. Next, have them cut two shucks out of green paper. Glue popcorn and the shucks onto the cob.

Story Time: Flannel Story

"Why the Bear Has a Short Tail" (American Folk Tale)

One cold morning when the fox was coming up the road with some fish, he met a bear.

"Good morning, Mr. Fox," said the bear.

"Good morning, Mr. Bear," said the fox. "The morning is brighter because I have met you."

Thursday (cont.)

"Those are very good fish, Mr. Fox," said the bear. "I have not eaten such fish for many a day. Where do you find them?"

"I have been fishing, Mr. Bear," answered the fox.

"If I could catch such fish as those, I should like to go fishing, but I do not know how to fish."

"It would be very easy for you to learn, Mr. Bear," said the fox. "You are so big and strong that you can do anything."

"Will you teach me, Mr. Fox?" asked the bear.

"I would not tell everybody, but you are such a good friend that I will teach you. Come to this pond, and I will show you how to fish through the ice." So the fox and the bear went to the frozen pond, and the fox showed the bear how to make a hole in the ice.

"That is easy for you," said the fox, "but many an animal could not have made that hole. Now comes the secret. You must put your tail down into the water and keep it there. That is not easy, and not every animal could do it, for the water is very cold, but you are a learned animal, Mr. Bear, and you know that the secret of catching fish is to keep your tail in the water a long time. Then when you pull it up, you will pull with it as many fish as I have."

The bear put his tail down into the water, and the fox went away. The sun rose high in the heavens, and still the bear sat with his tail through the hole in the ice. Sunset came but still the bear sat with his tail through the hole in the ice, for he thought, "When an animal is really learned, he will not fear a little cold."

It began to get dark, and the bear said, "Now I will pull the fish out of the water. How good they will be!" He pulled and pulled, but not a fish came out. Worse than that, when he finally broke himself loose, not all of his tail came out, for the end of it was frozen fast to the ice.

He went slowly down the road, growling angrily, "I wish I could find that fox." But the cunning fox was curled up in his warm nest, and whenever he thought of the bear, he laughed.

Circle Time: Poem

"Mr. Turkey and Mr. Duck"

Mr. Turkey took a walk one day,
In the very best of weather.
Along came Mr. Duck,
And they both talked together.

Gobble, gobble, gobble,
Quack, quack, quack,
Good-bye, good-bye,
And they both walked back.

Food Experiences: Corn On The Cob

Cook corn on the cob and let children try it. Serve it with butter if you wish.

Theme Activities: Book

Read *Autumn Harvest* by Alvin Tresselt.

Friday

Sharing Time: Book

Read Squash Pie by W. Gage. Bring in a squash for the children to look at. Discuss how it feels. Is it rough or smooth? Tell them how squash is grown.

Art: Sand Painting

Put sand into tempera paint and mix. Children can paint Thanksgiving pictures.

Story Time: Book

Read *Little Bear's Thanksgiving* by Janice.

Circle Time: Poem

"Wake Up Little Pilgrims"

Wake up little pilgrims,
The sun's in the East.
Today is the day for our Thanksgiving Feast.
Come jump out of bed,
See how tall you can stand.
My, my, but you are wide awake.
Wash your hands, wash your faces,
So that you'll look neat.
Then come to the table; say prayers before you eat

Food Experiences: Canned Pumpkin

Have children each taste some canned pumpkin without adding anything to it. Ask if they like it. If not, what would they add to it?

Theme Activities: Book

Read *Bring in the Pumpkins* by D. Ipcar.

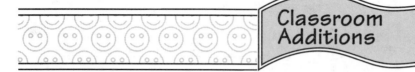

Here are some materials that can be placed in the learning centers in addition to your regular materials.

- Housekeeping: cradleboards made from cardboard for carrying dolls, bonnets, baskets, Native American dolls, long dresses, Native American beads, head dresses
- Circle: flannel board and patterns, pictures of Native Americans
- Books: books about Native Americans, pilgrims, Thanksgiving
- Music: records of traditional Thanksgiving songs, musical instruments
- Table Activities: file folder activities listed, puzzles, lacing cards
- Block: canoe made from a large cardboard box
- Art: feathers, packing material, sand, smooth clean rocks
- Puppets: puppets of Indians, pilgrims, pumpkins, turkeys
- Science: dried ornamental corn, arrowheads, Native American beads, feathers, pumpkins, gourds, baskets, squash

Teachers' Aids

File Folder Activities: Choose the skills you wish to emphasize this week. See directions on pages 5 and 6.

- Arrowheads
- Matching Pies
- Turkey/Matching Feathers
- Pumpkin Match

Bulletin Board Ideas:

- Native American Symbols
- Photographs
- Pictures From Magazines
- Native American Figures
- Pilgrim Figures
- Pumpkins
- Corn
- Cornucopia
- The First Feast
- Turkeys
- Farm Yard

For Parents

- Discuss the meaning of Thanksgiving with your child.
- Name the things you are thankful for and then let your child do the same.
- Let your child help you prepare Thanksgiving dinner.
- Visit the library and check out books about Thanksgiving.
- Visit a turkey farm with your child. New words will be introduced this week, so ask your child daily what new word he/she has learned. Use these new words at home with your child.

Bibliography

Children's Books

Gage, W. *Squash Pie.* Greenwillow, 1976
Ipcar, D. *Bring in the Pumpkins.* Scholastic, 1976
Janice. *Little Bear's Thanksgiving.* Lothrop, Lee, Shepard, 1967
Parish, Peggy. *Granny and the Indians.* Macmillan, 1969
Parish, Peggy. *Snapping Turtle Is All Wrong Day.* Simon and Schuster, 1970
Tresselt, Alvin. *Autumn Harvest.* Lothrop, Lee, Shepard, 1951

Patterns

Patterns

Patterns

Weekly Theme: *Mother Goose*   Week of: _____

	Monday	Tuesday	Wednesday	Thursday	Friday
Date					
Sharing Time	Song: Baa Baa Black Sheep	Rhyme: Little Miss Muffet	Glove Puppet: Itsy Bitsy Spider	Rhyme: Hickory Dickory Dock	Rhyme: Hey Diddle Diddle
Art	Easel Painting	Fill a Pie	Straw Painting	Humpty Dumpty	Play Dough
Story Time	Flannel Story: Poor Old Lady	Flannel Story: Five Hungry Chickens	Flannel Story: The Three Little Kittens	Rhyme: Humpty Dumpty	Flannel Story: There Was a Crooked Man
Circle Time	Rhyme: Peter, Peter	Play: Sing a Song of Sixpence	Activity: London Bridge	Activity: Jumping Over a Candle	Song: Over in the Meadow
Food Experiences	Cooked Pumpkin	Cottage Cheese	Pies	Hard Boiled Eggs	Fish Crackers
Theme Activities	Book: *There Was an Old Lady Who Swallowed a Fly*	Activity: Pat-a-Cake	Rhyme: Mary, Mary Quite Contrary	Rhyme: Little Boy Blue	Flannel Story: Old Mother Hubbard

Monday

Materials Needed For The Week

small drinking straws, styrofoam cups, large buttons, pumpkin seeds, wool, magnets, clock, sheet, patchwork quilt, weather chart, stuffed animals, blue napkins, fish crackers, eggs, canned pumpkin

Sharing Time: Song

"Baa, Baa, Black Sheep" (Nursery Rhyme)

Baa, baa, black sheep, have you any wool?
Yes sir, yes sir, three bags full.
One for my master, one for my dame,
And one for the little boy who lives down the lane.

Art: Easel Painting

Let children easel paint. Encourage them to paint a picture about "Baa, Baa, Black Sheep."

Story Time: Flannel Story

Use the patterns that are found on this page and page 144.

"Poor Old Lady" (Mother Goose)

Poor old lady, she swallowed a fly.
I don't know why she swallowed a fly.
Poor old lady, I think she'll die.
Poor old lady, she swallowed a spider.
It squirmed and wriggled and turned inside her.
She swallowed the spider to catch the fly.
I don't know why she swallowed a fly.
Poor old lady, I think she'll die.
Poor old lady, she swallowed a bird.
How absurd! She swallowed a bird.
She swallowed the bird to catch the spider.
She swallowed the spider to catch the fly.
I don't know why she swallowed a fly.
Poor old lady, I think she'll die.

Poor old lady, she swallowed a cat.
Think of that! She swallowed a cat.
She swallowed the cat to catch the bird.
She swallowed the bird to catch the spider.
She swallowed the spider to catch the fly.
I don't know why she swallowed a fly.
Poor old lady, I think she'll die.
Poor old lady, she swallowed a dog.
She went the whole hog when she swallowed the dog.
She swallowed the dog to catch the cat.
She swallowed the cat to catch the bird.
She swallowed the bird to catch the spider.
She swallowed the spider to catch the fly.
I don't know why she swallowed a fly.
Poor old lady, I think she'll die.
Poor old lady, she swallowed a cow.
I don't know how she swallowed a cow.
She swallowed the cow to catch the dog.
She swallowed the dog to catch the cat.
She swallowed the cat to catch the bird.
She swallowed the bird to catch the spider.
She swallowed the spider to catch the fly.
I don't know why she swallowed a fly.
Poor old lady, I think she'll die.
Poor old lady, She swallowed a horse.
She died, of course.

Circle Time: Rhyme Activity

   "Peter, Peter" (Traditional)

   Peter, Peter, Pumpkin eater,
   Had a wife and couldn't keep her.
   He put her in a pumpkin shell,
   And there he kept her very well.

Food Experiences: Cooked Pumpkin
   Let children taste pumpkin that has been
   cooked. Does it taste like any other foods
   they have experienced?

Theme Activities: Book
   Share the book, *There Was An Old Lady Who Swallowed
   A Fly,* by Child's Play International. Let children compare it
   to the traditional version of the poem.

Tuesday

Sharing Time: Rhyme

"Little Miss Muffet" (Nursery Rhyme)

Little Miss Muffet sat on a tuffet, eating her curds and whey.
Along came a spider and sat down beside her,
And frightened Miss Muffet away.

Art: Fill a Pie

Give children an outline of a pie crust. Have them "fill" (color) it in with whatever they choose.

Story Time: Flannel Story

"Five Hungry Chickens" (Mother Goose Rhyme)

Said the first little chicken,
With a queer little squirm,
"I wish I could find a fat little worm."
Said the second little chicken,
With an odd little shrug,
"I wish I could find a fat little bug."
Said the third little chicken,
With a sharp little squeal,
"I wish I could find some nice yellow meal."

Said the fourth little chicken,
With a sign of grief,
"I wish I could find a green little leaf."
Said the fifth little chicken,
With a faint little moan,
"I wish I could find a wee gravel stone."
"Now, see here," said the mother,
From the green garden patch,
"If you want any breakfast, just come here and scratch!"

Circle Time: Rhyme/Activity

Children can act out the words.

"Sing A Song of Sixpence: (Nursery Rhyme)

Sing a song of sixpence, a pocket full of rye,
Four and twenty blackbirds baked in a pie;
When the pie was opened, the birds began to sing.
Wasn't that a dainty dish to set before the king?
The king was in his counting house counting out his money.
The queen was in the parlor eating bread and honey.
The maid was in the garden hanging out the clothes.
Along came a blackbird and snipped off her nose!

Food Experiences: Curds and Whey

Cottage cheese is a type of curds and whey. Let children taste some to see what Miss Muffet was eating.

Theme Activities: Rhyme/Activity

"Pat-A-Cake" (Nursery Rhyme)

Pat-a-cake, pat-a-cake, baker's man,
Bake me a cake just as fast as you can.
Pat it and shape it and mark it with a B,
And put it in the oven for baby and me.

Wednesday

Sharing Time: Spider Glove Puppet

Glue a large black pom-pom to the top of a glove. Use with finger play. (See page 7 for directions.)

"Itsy, Bitsy Spider" (Traditional)

The itsy, bitsy spider went up the water spout.
Down came the rain and washed the spider out.
Out came the sun and dried up all the rain.
And the itsy, bitsy spider went up the spout again.

Art: Straw Painting

Using drinking straws and black paint, have children straw paint spiders. Put a blob of black paint on a piece of paper. Let children use the straws to gently blow the paint around and create a spider.

Story Time: Flannel Story

"The Three Little Kittens"

See the story on page 20 and the patterns on page 31.

Circle Time: Rhyme/Activity

"London Bridge" (Nursery Rhyme)

London Bridge is falling down, falling down, falling down.
London Bridge is falling down, my fair lady.
Take the keys and lock her up, lock her up, lock her up.
Take the keys and lock her up, my fair lady.

Food Experiences: Pies

Let children try a piece of pie like Little Jack Horner. Ask them if they think they could "stick in their thumb and pull out a plum."

Theme Activities: Rhyme

"Mary, Mary, Quite Contrary" (Mother Goose)
Mary, Mary, quite contrary,
How does your garden grow?
Silver bells and cockle shells,
And pretty maids all in a row.

Thursday

Sharing Time: Rhyme

"Hickory, Dickory Dock" (Nursery Rhyme)

Hickory, dickory, dock.
The mouse ran up the clock.
The clock struck one.
The mouse ran down.
Hickory, dickory, dock. Tick, Tock!

Art: Humpty Dumpty

Give children paper with an egg shape drawn on it. Let them use crayons to decorate it to look like Humpty Dumpty.

Story Time: Dramatization

"Humpty Dumpty" (Mother Goose Rhyme)

Humpty Dumpty sat on a wall,
Humpty Dumpty had a great fall.
All the King's horses and all the King's men,
Couldn't put Humpty together again.

Let one child be Humpty Dumpty while the rest of the children are the King's horses and men. Act out the rhyme.

Circle Time: Activity

Have children pretend to be Jack-be-Nimble. Let them take turns jumping over an object representing a small candle or a real unlit candle.

Food Experiences: Hard Boiled Eggs

Give children hard boiled eggs and crayons. Let them color Humpty Dumpty on the eggs. Before eating, you may wish to let them drop their eggs to see Humpty Dumpty fall.

Theme Activities: Rhyme

"Little Boy Blue" (Mother Goose)

Little Boy Blue, come blow your horn.
The sheep's in the meadow,
And the cow's in the corn.
Where's the little boy who looks after the sheep?
Under the haystack, fast asleep!

You may wish to do this as a flannel activity. See patterns on page 104.

Mother Goose

Sharing Time: Rhyme

"Hey Diddle, Diddle" (Nursery Rhyme)

Hey diddle, diddle, the cat and the fiddle,
The cow jumped over the moon.
The little dog laughed to see such a sport,
And the dish ran away with the spoon.

Art: Play Dough

Let children create a blue figure using blue play dough.

Story Time: Flannel Story

"There Was A Crooked Man" (Mother Goose Rhyme)

There was a crooked man, and he went a crooked mile,
He found a crooked sixpence beside a crooked stile;
He bought a crooked cat, which caught a crooked mouse,
And they all lived together in a little crooked house.

See pattern on page 150.

Circle Time: Song

"Over in The Meadow" (Traditional)

Over in the meadow, in the sand, in the sun,
Lived an old mother frog and her little froggie one.
"Croak," said the mother. "I croak," said the one,
So they croaked and they croaked in the sand in the sun.
Over in the meadow, in the stream so blue,
Lived an old mother fish and her little fished two.
"Swim," said the mother. "We swim," said the two.
So they swam and they swam in the stream so blue.
Over in the meadow, in the stream so blue,
Lived an old mother bird and her little birdies three.
"Sing," said the mother. "We sing," said the three.
So they sang and they sang on a branch of the tree.

Food Experiences: Fish Crackers

Let children make the fish swim down the stream by lining up three fish crackers—one as the mother and two as the babies—on a blue napkin or paper plat.

Theme Activities: Flannel Story.

See patterns on page 151.

"Mother Hubbard" (Traditional)

Old Mother Hubbard,
Went to the cupboard,
To get her poor dog a bone;
But when she got there,
Her cupboard was bare,
And so the poor dog had none.

The dame made a curtesy,
The dog made a bow;
The dame said, "Your servant,"
The dog said, "Bow-wow!"

You may wish to do additional verses of Mother Hubbard as they are appropriate with your class.

Classroom Additions

Center Ideas

Here are some materials that can be placed in the learning centers in addition to your regular materials.

- Housekeeping: patchwork quilt, candlestick, candle, clock, sheet
- Circle: weather chart, flannel board and flannel pieces
- Books: books of Mother Goose rhymes, stuffed animals to read to
- Music: songs of Mother Goose rhymes
- Table Activities: file folder activities listed, sequence stories, puzzles, games Blocks: blocks, sheet
- Art: paints, play dough, paper plates, yarn, cotton balls
- Puppets: different types of puppets
- Science: magnets, wool, wind-up clock
- Science Activities:
  - Keep a daily weather chart with the children. Determine if it is a sunny, cloudy, rainy, or windy day. Mark it on a calendar. Discuss the changes in the weather.
  - Grow pumpkin seeds.

Teachers' Aids

- Make sequence stories for table activities. Take the lines from "Hey Diddle, Diddle" and "Humpty Dumpty" and write them on large sentence strips. Let children take turns putting them into the proper sequence of the poem.
- File Folder Activities: Choose the skills you wish to emphasize this week. See directions on pages 5 and 6.
- Matching Kittens and Colored Mittens
- Humpty Dumpty and Matching Eggs Humpty Dumpty Puzzle Bulletin Board Ideas
- Mother Goose Characters

For Parents

- Read a nursery rhyme with your child every night.
- Take your child to visit his/her grandparents or other older people and have them talk about when they were young.
- Have child bring his/her grandparents to class.
- Share old quilts with the class.
- Have cottage cheese for a nutritious snack.
- Let child help you bake a pie.
- Have boiled eggs for breakfast.
- Let your child play with shaving cream or play dough.

Bibliography

Children's Books

Adams, Pam. ***There Was An Old Lady Who Swallowed A Fly.*** illus. (1973), Child's Play International.

Patterns

Patterns

Weekly Theme: *Shapes*   Week of: _____

	Monday	Tuesday	Wednesday	Thursday	Friday
Date					
Sharing Time	Poem: Great Big Ball	Book: *Boxes! Boxes!*	Book: *Magic Monsters Look for Shapes*	Book: *Wilbur Worm*	Book: *Wing On A Flea; A Book About Shapes*
Art	My Circle	Drawing Shapes	Yarn Shapes	Shape Stick Puppets	Easel Paint Shapes
Story Time	Song: The Green Grass Grew All Around	Poem: Three Cornered Hat	Book: *Shapes*	Book: *Shopping Spree Identifying Shapes*	Book: *Circles, Triangles, and Squares*
Circle Time	Activity: Shape Bean Bag Toss	Activity: Monster Shape Mask	Activity: Shape Lotto	Activity: Lollipop Game	Activity: Footprints
Food Experiences	Egg In a Circle	Square Toast	Triangle Cheese and Crackers	Rectangle Graham Crackers	Assorted Shape Crackers
Theme Activities	Book: *Spence Makes Circles*	Activity: Body Shapes	Activity: Musical Shapes	Activity: Jump Rope Shapes	Activity: Hide and Seek Shapes

Monday

Materials Needed For The Week:
yarn, craft sticks, paper plates, bean bags, shape sheet, saltines, graham crackers, assorted crackers, shape cutouts of various sizes and colors, jump ropes, eggs, bread, butter, skillet

Sharing Time: Poem

"Great Big Ball"

A great big ball,
A middle-sized ball,
A little ball I see.
Let's see if we can count them:
One, two, three.

Discuss items in the classroom that are round.

Art: My Circle
Let children practice drawing circles. Let them choose the one they like the best and decorate it.

Story Time: Song
Sing "The Green Grass Grew All Around". (See page 98, Colors Week, for the words to this song.)

Circle Time: Shape Bean Bag Toss
Use an old sheet or a large piece of butcher paper. Draw several shapes on it. Then give children bean bags. Call out the shapes and let them take turns tossing bean bags on the shapes you call out.

Food Experiences: Egg In a Circle
Tear a hole in the center of a piece of bread. Place in a skillet that has been coated with butter. Put a egg in the hole and fry. Have the children look at the bread and tell you what shapes they see.

Theme Activities: Book
Read *Spence Makes Circles* by Christa Chevalier. Take a shape walk. Ask children what shapes they see.

Tuesday

Sharing Time: Book

Read *Boxes! Boxes!* by Leonard Everett Fisher. Discuss items in the classroom that are square.

Art: Drawing Shapes

Give children plenty of paper and crayons. Let them draw any shapes they wish.

Story Time: Poem

"Three Cornered Hat"

(Traditional)

My hat, it has three corners,
Three corners has my hat.
A hat without three corners,
Could never be my hat.

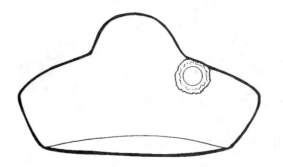

Circle Time: Monster Shape Mask

Give the children some masks. Let them wear them as they act out the song from the record *Monsters and Monstrous Things.* If the record is unavailable, let them pretend to be monsters. Use masking tape and make a large square, circle, and a triangle on the floor. Let them march around the shapes to music.

Food Experiences: Square Toast

Give each child a piece of toast. Let them identify the shape. Have them each take a bite. Ask them if all the shapes now look the same.

Theme Activities: Body Shapes

Have children make shapes by moving their bodies. Encourage them to curl up into balls or move their arms to make squares.

154

Wednesday

Sharing Time: Book

Read *Magic Monsters Look For Shapes* by Jane Belk Moncure. Discuss items in the classroom that are shaped like triangles.

Art: Yarn Shapes

Give each child several pieces of yarn. Have them practice with it to make many shapes. Then give them glue and have them glue the shapes down. Help them to identify the shapes.

Story Time: Book

Read *Shapes* by John Reiss.

Circle Time: Shape Lotto

Put different colored shapes made of construction paper on the floor. Have children name the shapes as they step on them.

Food Experiences: Triangle Cheese and Crackers

Serve children triangle-shaped crackers with cheese. Have them identify the shapes before they eat them.

Theme Activities: Musical Shapes

Play this like musical chairs. Choose a shape to put on the chairs. Put the shapes on each chair for children to sit on. Each time you play this game change the shapes on the chairs so that you alternate between playing Square Musical Chairs, or Circle Musical Chairs, Triangle Musical Chairs, etc.

Thursday

Sharing Time: Book
   Read *Wilbur Worm* by Richard and Nicky Hale and Andre Amstutz. Discuss items in the classroom that are shaped like rectangles.

Art: Shape Stick Puppets
   Have children cut out a circle, square, triangle, and rectangle. Have them draw faces on each one. Tape the shapes to craft sticks. Write the name of each shape on the back.

Story Time: Book
   Read *Shopping Spree Identifying Shapes* by Monica Weiss.

Circle Time: Lollipop Game
   Cut several large circles out of colored construction paper. Attach them to crafts sticks. Cut several different small shapes out of contrasting construction paper. Glue them onto different colored circles creating "shape lollipops." Give each child a lollipop, and as you call out a name of a shape, each child holding that shape should stand up.

Food Experiences: Rectangle Graham Crackers
   Give each child a rectangle graham cracker. Let the children spread peanut butter on them as they identify the shape.

Theme Activities: Jump Rope Shapes
   Let children use jump ropes to create different shapes. Put them on the floor and have them take turns arranging the jump ropes into different shapes. Have them take turns identifying the shapes.

Friday

Sharing Time: Book

Read *A Wing On A Flea: A Book About Shapes* by Ed Emberley. Discuss all of the shapes that you have talked about this week. Review the items they have identified as different shapes.

Art: Easel Paint Shapes

Let children use contrasting colors of paint to make shapes.

Story Time: Book

Read *Circles, Triangles, and Squares* by Tana Hoban.

Circle Time: Footprints

Explain that not all shapes are recognizable as a circle, square, rectangle, or triangle. Show them the shape of a footprint. Make large footprints out of different colors. Tape them to the floor. Have children move on footprints taped to the floor while listening to the record *Monsters and Monstrous Things.*

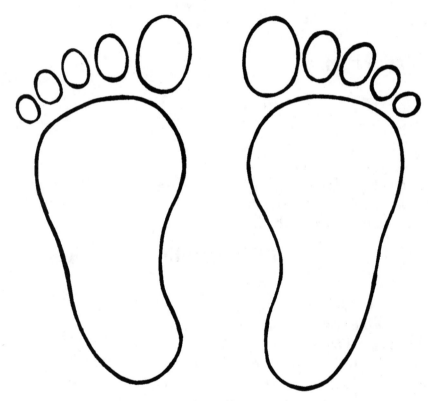

Food Experiences: Assorted Shape Crackers

Serve crackers in various shapes. See if children can sort them into circles, squares, rectangles, and triangles before they eat them.

Theme Activities: Hide and Seek Shapes

Cut various shapes out of construction paper. Hide the cut-out shapes around the classroom. Let the children search for them. As they find them, see if they can identify the shape of each cut-out they find.

Classroom Additions

Here are some suggestions of materials that can be placed in the learning centers in addition to your regular materials.
- Housekeeping: jack-in-a-box, shape sheet
- Circle: flannel board with felt shapes
- Books: books about different shapes
- Music: musical triangles, drums
- Table Activities: file folder activities listed, puzzles, small colored blocks
- Science: items of different shapes, rectangle card, square box, musical triangle, round circle
- Blocks: blocks of different sizes, shapes, and colors
- Art: paint, paper, play dough
- Puppets: various shape puppets

Teachers' Aids

File Folders: Choose which skills you wish to emphasize this week. See directions on pages 5-6.
- Match Shapes To Shapes
- Match Big Shapes To Small Shapes

Bulletin Board Ideas:
- Display shapes
- Display children's art work

For Parents
- Go over shapes with your child.
- Look around the house for different shapes.
- Serve foods with different shapes.
- Visit the library and check out books about shapes.
- Play shape games with your child.
- Let your child draw shapes and tell you the name of each one.
- Make shapes out of yarn with your child.

Bibliography

Children's Books

Chevalier, Christa. *Spence Makes Circles.* Whitman, 1982

Emberley, Ed. *A Wing on a Flea: A Book About Shapes.*

Fisher, Leonard Everett. *Boxes! Boxes!* Viking, 1984

Hale, Richard and Nicky, Andre Amstutz. *Wilbur Worm. Willowisp,* 1986

Hoban, Tana. *Circles, Triangles, and Squares.* Macmillan, 1974

Moncure, Jane Belk. *Magic Monsters Look For Shapes.* Child's World, 1979

Reiss, John. *Shapes.* Bradbury Press, 1974

Weiss, Monica. *Shopping Spree Identifying Shapes.* Troll Associates, 1992

Records

Kathleen Patrick, Camille Core Gift, Libby Core Bearden. *Monsters and Monstrous Things.* Upbeat Basics, 1983

Resources

Levin, Ina Massler and Mary Ellen Sterling. *TCM 180 Readiness Manipulatives: Shapes.* Teacher Created Resources, 1992

Patterns

Weekly Theme: *Winter Holidays* Week of: _____

	Monday	Tuesday	Wednesday	Thursday	Friday
Date					
Sharing Time	Discuss Hanukkah	Introduce Dreidels	Discuss Kwanzaa	Discuss Famous African-Americans	Discuss New Year's Day
Art	Marshmallow Menorahs	Making Dreidels	Bookmarks	Placemats	Noise Makers
Story Time	Book: *Latkes and Applesauce*	Book: *Hershel and the Hanukkah Goblins*	Book: *Kwanzaa*	Book: *My First Kwanzaa*	Book: *Happy New Year*
Circle Time	Song: "One Little, Two Little"	Song: The Dreidel Song	Pass the Kwanzaa Gifts	Concepts of Kwanzaa	What's New?
Food Experiences	Potato Latkes	Doughnuts	Peanuts/Peanut Butter	Kwanzaa	New Foods
Theme Activities	Song: Act out "One Little, Two Little"	Spin Like A Dreidel	African Musical Instruments	Celebrate Kwanzaa	New Year's Party

Monday

Materials Needed For The Week:

marshmallows, frosting, birthday candles, potatoes, oil, onions, eggs, flour, applesauce, dreidel, small homemade gifts, plastic soda bottles, rice, beans, pie tins

Sharing Time: What is Hanukkah?

Discuss Hanukkah with the children. Explain that it is the Jewish "Festival of Lights." It celebrates the finding of oil to light a special lamp in ancient times after a battle with the Syrians. The lamp was in the holy temple, and the oil was expected to last only one day, but it lasted for eight. That is why a menorah is lit for eight nights.

Art: Marshmallow Menorahs

Let children make a menorah using frosting and marshmallows. Give each child a piece of tagboard 11" x 4" (28cm x 10cm), ten marshmallows, and nine candles. Have the children spread some white frosting on the bottom of each marshmallow and then put them onto the tagboard. With the frosting, "glue" a second marshmallow on top of the middle marshmallow to create the shammash or "servant." Poke birthday candles into each marshmallow to create a menorah.

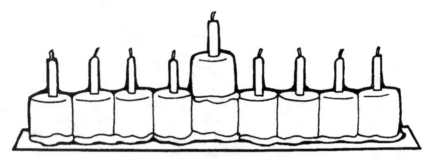

Story Time: Book

Read *Latkes and Applesauce: A Hanukkah Story* by Fran Manushkin.

Circle Time: Song

"One Little, Two Little, Three Little Candles"
(Sing this song to the tune of "One Little, Two Little, Three Little Indians.
One little, two little, three little candles,
Four little, five little, six little candles,
Seven little, eight little, nine little candles,
In my Hanukkah lamp.
The first night, one little candle,
The second night, two little candles,
The third night, three little candles in my Hanukkah lamp.
The fourth night, four little candles,
The fifth night, five little candles,
The sixth night, six little candles in my Hanukkah lamp.
The seventh night, seven little candles,
The eighth night, eight little candles,
The shammash makes nine little candles in my Hanukkah lamp.
Repeat first verse.

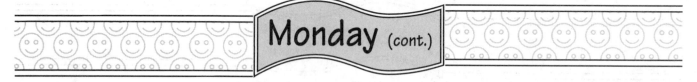

Monday (cont.)

Food Experiences: Potato Latkes (Pancakes)

To remember the oil that lit the lamp, fried foods are served at Hanukkah time. Potato pancakes, called latkes, are one of the traditional foods. Try these with your class, using an electric skillet, but remember to use caution around the hot oil.

- 2 cups (475 mL) peeled and grated potatoes

- 2 teaspoons (10 mL) grated onion

- 1 egg

- 6 Tablespoons (90 mL) flour

- 4 Tablespoons (60 mL) oil

Mix together all ingredients except oil. Heat oil in a pan. Drop a tablespoon (15 mL) of the mixture into oil. Cook and turn once until brown on both sides. Serve with applesauce.

Theme Activities: Song/Activity

Sing "One Little, Two Little, Three Little Candles" again. This time line up eight children and have them all curl over or squat down. Choose another child to be the shammash. As the song is sung, the shammash lightly taps each "candle," who then rises.

Repeat, letting all children have a turn to be a candle.

Tuesday

Sharing Time: Discuss Dreidels.

Dreidels are spinning tops used in ancient times as a game to distract enemy soldiers. Locate a dreidel to share with your class. (Inexpensive plastic and wooden ones can be found in toy stores and card shops.) Explain that the letters in Hebrew on the dreidel mean "A Great Miracle Happened There" and refer to the oil that lasted the eight days. Let children take turns spinning the top.

Art: Making Dreidels

Using the pattern on page 168, let children cut out and decorate their own dreidel.

Story Time: Book

Read *Hershel and the Hanukkah Goblins* by Eric Kimmel.

Circle Time: Song

Sing or recite the poem, ***"The Dreidel Song."***

I have a little dreidel.
I made it out of clay.
And when it's dry and ready
Oh dreidel I shall play.
Dreidel, dreidel, dreidel.
I made it out of clay.
When it's dry and ready,
Oh dreidel I shall play.

Food Experiences: Doughnuts

Doughnuts, another food prepared in oil, are served during Hanukkah in parts of the world. Serve this treat to your children. Doughnut holes work especially well for young children.

Theme Activities: Spin Like A Dreidel

Let children spin around as if they were dreidels. One child can start out in a crouching position, and another can pretend to be turning him or her. As the top spins faster, the child gets to spin more. Play some music such as "My Dreidel" from *Kindergarten Songs.*

Wednesday

Sharing Time: Discuss Kwanzaa .

Locate Africa and the United States on a globe. Explain to the children that Kwanzaa begins on December 26th and lasts until January Ist. Kwanzaa concludes with a harvest feast. Gifts are usually homemade or homegrown, and they are given each of the seven days of Kwanzaa. It is a cultural holiday.

Art: Bookmarks

Let children make book marks to give as Kwanzaa gifts to classmates. Give each child a 1" x 5" (2.54 cm x 13 cm) piece of construction paper to decorate.

Story Time: Book

Read *Kwanzaa* by A.P. Porter. Discuss the book with the children.

Circle Time: Pass The Kwanzaa Gifts

Ahead of time, let children make small gifts such as bookmarks. Wrap one small gift for each child (homemade, if possible). Play African music as the children sit in a circle and pass the gifts. Then say, "Kwanzaa" and have everyone open the gift in his/her hands. Then have each child show his/her gift and tell about it.

Food Experiences: Peanuts/Peanut Butter

Peanuts grow in Africa and are used in many dishes. An African-American scientist, George Washington Carver, experimented with peanuts and discovered all kinds of uses for them. He used them to make instant coffee, salad oil, and ink, for instance. Let children try some peanuts in shells or make some peanut butter by blending peanuts in a blender. Serve it on crackers.

Theme Activities: African Musical Instruments

Play a recording of African music for your students. Bring in a variety of instruments such as flutes and drums. Enjoy the music.

Thursday

Sharing Time: Discuss Famous African-Americans.

Discuss African-American history with your children. Mention some famous African Americans such as Martin Luther King Jr., Harriet Tubman, and George Washington Carver. Tell children what these people did to help the United States.

Art: Placemats

Let each child decorate a large mkeka (placemat). Use these later during your celebration.

Story Time: Book

Read *My First Kwanzaa Book* by Deborah M. Newton Chocolate.

Circle Time: Concepts Of Kwanzaa The concepts of Kwanzaa are as follows:

- **Umoja**-We help each other.

- **Kujichagulia**-We decide things for ourselves.

- **Ujima**-We work together to make life better.

- **Uajamaa**-We build and support our own business.

- **Nia**-We have a reason for living.

- **Kuumba**-We use our minds and hands to make things.

- **Imani**-We believe in ourselves, our ancestors, and our future.

Choose one of these and ask children what they think it might mean. Then explain it to them.

Food Experiences: Kwanzaa Foods

Foods such as apples, potatoes, bananas, and oranges are served throughout Kwanzaa. Let children help arrange these foods on platters to serve at the celebration during.theme activities.

Theme Activities: Celebrate Kwanzaa

Have a feast (karamu). Place a large **Mkeka** (placemat) on the floor. Put a **Kikombe** (a large cup) on the mkeka. Put the **Mazao** (fruits and vegetables) onto the mkeka. Make a **Kinara** (See page 170.), a candle holder for seven candles, in the center of the mkeka. Enjoy your feast.

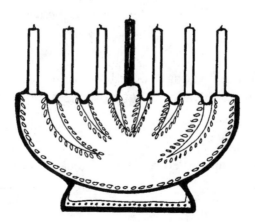

Friday

Sharing Time: Discuss New Year's Day.

Discuss some of the ways people celebrate the New Year. Ask children if they watch parades or have special gatherings. Look at the calendar and note how it will change. Explain to the children that noise making began as a way to drive out evil spirits. Sing "Auld Lang Syne."

Art: Noise Makers

Make various noise makers. Fill small plastic soda bottles with rice or beans. Hot-glue the lids on the bottles. Decorate aluminum pie tins for banging.

Story Time: Book

Read *Happy New Year* by Emily Kelley.

Circle Time: What's New?

Bring in some new items to your classroom. These could include small toys, new pencils or books, balls, jewelry, or anything else that hasn't been in the classroom before. Hide them around the room. Ask children "What's new?" and let them search the room for only those things they haven't seen before.

Food Experiences: New Foods

What foods might your children not yet have tasted? Give them the opportunity to try several new foods. Some suggestions include avocados, Roquefort cheese, matzo crackers, turnips, and pita bread.

Theme Activities: New Year's Party

Have a New Year's Party. At the appointed time set a clock to almost 12:00. Let the children count down backwards from 10 to 1 with you and then turn the clock to 12. (If you are using an alarm clock, be sure to set it to ring.) Have the children use the noisemakers they made earlier. Play some music and let them march in a parade or dance.

Classroom Additions

Here are some materials that can be placed in the learning centers in addition to your regular materials.

- Housekeeping: new clothes, menorah and candles
- Circle: calendar, clock, globe,
- Books: books about Kwanzaa, Hanukkah, New Years
- Music: drums, noise makers
- Table Activities: file folder activities listed, puzzles, dreidels
- Blocks: flags from each country,
- Art: black, red, green, blue, and gold crayons
- Science: peanuts, candles of various colors, clock
- Science Activities:
  - Grow a peanut plant.
  - Show children a real poinsettia plant. (CAUTION: Do not let the children touch.)
  - Take apart a clock.

Teachers' Aids

File Folder Activities: Choose the skills you wish to emphasize this week. See directions on pages 5 and 6.
- candles
- noisemakers

Bulletin Board Ideas:
- Kinara
- Menorah
- Bendera
- Clock striking midnight
- Children's art work

For Parents

- Go to the library and read some books about the holidays.
- Create a family tradition for New Year's.
- Let your child mark the dates for the holidays on a calendar.

Bibliography

Children's Books

Kelley, Emily. *Happy New Year.* Carolrhoda/Lerner, 1986

Kimmel, Eric. *Hershel and the Hanukkah Goblins.* Holiday House, 1985

Manushkin, Fran. *Latkes and Applesauce: A Hanukkah Story.* Scholastic, 1989

Newton Chocolate, Deborah M. *My First Kwanzaa Book.* Scholastic, 1992

Porter, A.P. *Kwanzaa.* Carolrhoda/Lerner, 1991

Sharmat, Marjorie W. *Griselda's New Year.* Aladdin, 1979

Records

Kindergarten Songs. I. Bowmar

Patterns

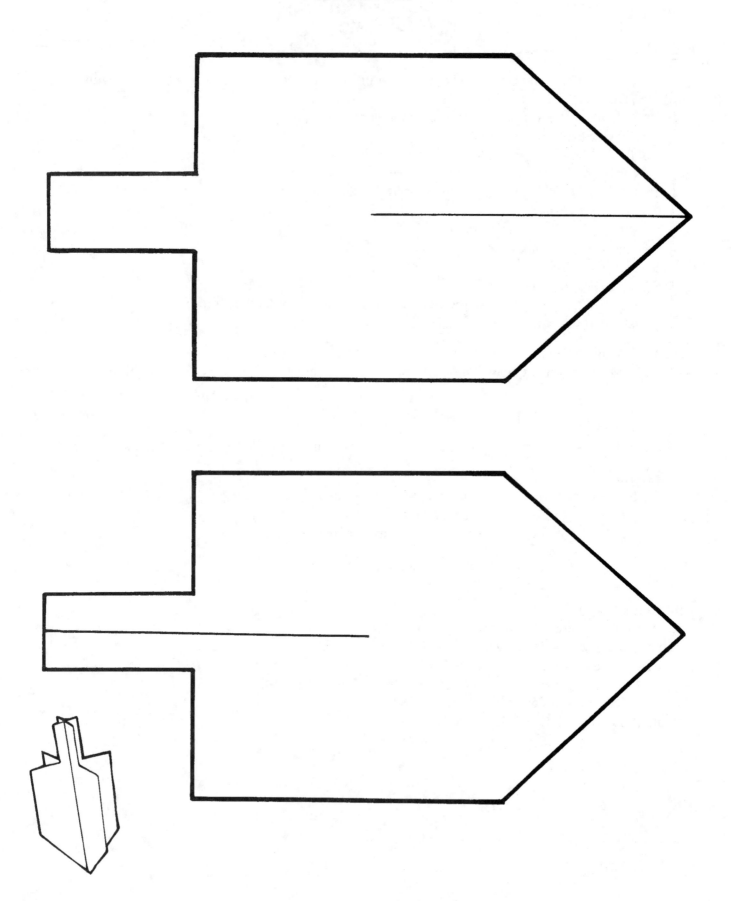

Patterns

Patterns

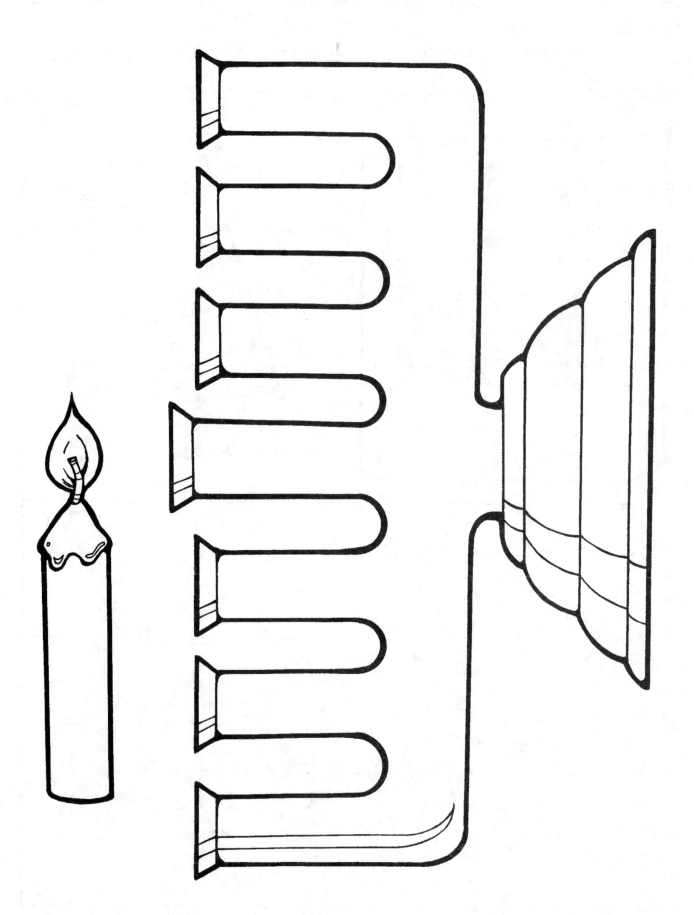

Weekly Theme: *Christmas Around the World*   Week of: _____

	Monday	Tuesday	Wednesday	Thursday	Friday
Date					
Sharing Time	Discuss Germany	Discuss England	Discuss Mexico	Fingerplay: Five Little Reindeer	Fingerplay: Five Little Bells
Art	Wreaths	Christmas Cards	Paper Lanterns	Christmas Tree Stick Puppet	Bells
Story Time	Book: *The Cobweb Christmas*	Book: *Friendly Beasts: An Old English Christmas Carol*	Flannel Story: Pedro's Christmas Flower	Book: *The Biggest Most Beautiful Christmas Tree*	Book: *Christmas Time*
Circle Time	Decorate a Tree	Song: Christmas Bells	Break a Piñata	Song: Rudolph the Red-Nosed Reindeer	Ringing Bells
Food Experiences	Ginerbread Cookies	Fruit Cake	Buñuelos	Rudolph Sandwiches	Cheese Ball Bells
Theme Activities	Song: O Tannenbaum	Book: *A Christmas Carol*	Book: *The Christmas Piñata*	Flannel Activity: Christmas Tree	Chain of Children

Monday

Materials Needed For The Week:

wooden toys, wreath, holly, ivy, small Christmas trees, gingerbread cookie cutters, ingredients for cookies, candle, nuts, Christmas cards, Yule log, fruitcake, Spanish moss, evergreen branches, piñata, stick, scarf, advent calendar, stockings, bells, red and gold ribbons, poinsettia, globe, small gift for each child

Sharing Time: Discuss Christmas in Germany.

Locate Germany on the globe and then locate your city. Ask children questions such as, "Is Germany near or far away?" Explain that Germany had the very first Christmas tree and wreaths. Tell the children that the Christmas tree is called "Tannenbaum" in Germany. Also, Santa is sometimes called "Kris Kringle" in Germany.

Art: Wreaths

Cut the centers from paper plates. Tear green tissue paper into small pieces. Glue tissue paper onto the paper plate rim until it is covered. Punch a hole in the top and lace yarn through it for hanging. Decorations may then be added.

Story Time: Book

Read *The Cobweb Christmas* by Shirley Climo.

Circle Time: Decorate a Tree.

Decorate a small Christmas tree with German ornaments such as stockings, candy canes, wooden toys, and gingerbread cookies.

Food Experiences: Gingerbread Cookies

Use this recipe and make gingerbread cookies. Let children cut out and decorate before baking.

- 1½ cups (350 mL) molasses
- 1 cup (250 mL) packed brown sugar
- 6½ cups (1.5 L) self rising flour
- 2 teaspoons (10 mL) ginger
- 1 teaspoon (5 mL) cinnamon
- ⅓ cup (80 mL) shortening
- ⅔ cups (160 mL) cold water
- 1 teaspoon (5 mL) allspice
- 1 teaspoon (5 mL) cloves

Mix together molasses, brown sugar, water, and shortening. Then add all the other ingredients. Cover for approximately 2 hours. Heat oven to 350°F (180°C). On a floured surface, roll out dough until it is ¼ inch (.6 cm) thick. Cut with gingerbread cookie cutters and place on cookie sheet. Bake approximately 10 minute and then cool. Add frosting if desired.

Theme Activities: German Folk Song

"O Tannenbaum" (O Christmas Tree)

O Tannenbaum, O Tannenbaum,
How evergreen your branches.
(Repeat)
You never change the whole year 'round,
You brighten up the snowy ground.
O Tannenbaum, O Tannenbaum,
How evergreen your branches.

Tuesday

Sharing Time: Discuss Christmas In England.

Locate England on a globe. Explain that England had the first Christmas cards, Yule logs, and fruitcakes. Santa is called "Father Christmas."

Art: Christmas Cards

Provide children with various materials for making Christmas cards. Old cards they have received at home are good for cutting up and creating new cards. Let them exchange them with each other.

Story Time: Book

Read *Friendly Beasts: An Old English Christmas Carol* by Tomie dePaola.

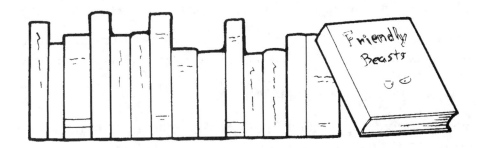

Circle Time: Song

Before singing or reciting this song, pass out bells. Let the children ring them as the song is sung.

"Christmas Bells" (Old English Tune)

The bells in the steeple are ringing today.
I listen and wonder, oh, what do they say?
Come, Mother, come, Father, how sweetly they chime.
They tell all the people it's glad Christmas Time.

After singing the song, have the children use musical bells.
Which bell is the loudest? Which bell is the quietest?

Food Experiences: Fruitcake

Buy a fruitcake. Before tasting, discuss the colors, texture, and different fruits and nuts used in the cake.

Theme Activities: Book

Read *A Christmas Carol* by I.M. Richardson.

Wednesday

Sharing Time: Discuss Christmas In Mexico.

Locate Mexico on a globe. "Las Posadas" begins nine days before Christmas Day. Explain that in Mexico there are "The Three Kings" instead of Santa; and, instead of hanging stockings, the children leave out their shoes. Children in Mexico receive candies and trinkets on Christmas Eve. On January 6th (Epiphany), the children receive gifts. Tell children that "Feliz Navidad" means Merry Christmas in Mexico.

Art: Paper Lanterns

In Mexico children carry paper lanterns during Las Posadas.

Use 9" x 12" (23 cm. x 30 cm) sheets of brightly colored construction paper. Fold paper in half lengthwise. Cut slits almost to the edge. Unfold and staple together. Attach a paper handle.

Story Time: Flannel Story

See patterns on page 180.

"Pedro's Christmas Flower" (Mexican Folk Tale)

"How are you this morning, Mama?" Pedro spoke softly as he bent over the thin-faced woman who lay on the cot.

"Better maybe-a little better, Pedro," she whispered.

"Perhaps I can get up soon-maybe mañana, Pedro."

But Pedro knew that it was not so. Each day his tired little mother grew thinner and paler. If only he could have a good doctor come to the little adobe hut. If only there was medicine for her. But medicine cost money, and Pedro earned hardly enough for food from the sale of firewood.

Pedro sighed as he closed the door. Today he must buy beans and if there was enough money left, a small piece of meat. How he would like to buy a Christmas present for his mother! He would buy one of the silver necklaces which the silversmith sold. Or he would buy a pair of silver earrings. But, alas, that could never be.

Pedro placed the saddle baskets on each side of the little brown burro and led him out of the shed. The sunshine was bright, but the air was crisp. He walked behind the donkey, switching his long stick gently over the animal's back. Now and then Pedro would stop to pick up a piece of dried mesquite or a piece of dead cactus. These he loaded into baskets. But wood was hard to find on the desert.

He walked farther than he had ever gone before. He climbed a little rise of ground and stood on the sandy knoll looking down into the little valley below. A tiny stream trickled from a small rocky cliff. It ran into a little pool.

Beside the pool, growing close to the water were some tall pretty red flowers. Their leaves were a glossy green. They shone like the wax candles in the church. Pedro ran down the slope to the flowers.

Wednesday (cont.)

"They're beautiful," he cried. "Like-like Christmas. I'll pick Mama a bouquet for a Christmas surprise." He bent and picked a beautiful bright blossom. But almost as soon he pulled the stalk from its root, it withered. Its petals seemed to shiver and fade. The white sap dripped onto his fingers.

"Oh," Pedro cried, "they bleed. They die! But perhaps if I dig the roots too, they will keep for Mama's Christmas." He took a sharp stick and dug carefully about the roots. Soon he had a soft ball of earth with the red flower standing proudly upright in the middle. Pedro put the plant in the corner of one of his wood baskets. Then he kept on gathering firewood. When the baskets were full, he turned the little burro back toward home. It was still early when he stopped at the house of his first customer.

"Buenos dias," Señora Martinez greeted him. "What a lovely flower you have there, Pedro!"

"A beautiful flower," said a man who was standing beside the donkey. He was a stranger and had difficulty speaking the language.

"It is for my mama," Pedro said. "It is for her Christmas."

"Dr. Poinsett is a great lover of flowers," Señora Martinez said. "At his home in the United States he has a greenhouse where he raises many flowers."

"But that one," the tall doctor said, "Is a new one to me. It is very lovely. Would you sell it, boy?"

"It is for Mama," Pedro said. Then quickly, "But if you are a doctor, perhaps you could help me, sir. My mama is very sick and there is no doctor. If you would come, sir, I could show you where these flowers grow. You could have all of them you want."

"You say your mother is ill?" The doctor had forgotten the flower.

"Oh, yes, and white and thin. I try to help her, but she needs medicine."

"I will come," the doctor said. "One moment and I will be with you."

The good doctor got his black bag, and Pedro led the way to the adobe hut. Pedro waited outside while the doctor made his examination. It seemed a long time before he came out, but Pedro was glad to see a smile on his face.

"Good food and the right medicine will cure her. You and I will go into the village and get what she needs. She is very sick now, but she will get better soon."

Wednesday (cont.)

"Oh, Dr. Poinsett," Pedro cried, "You mean she will be well and strong again?" "Yes," said the doctor, "but she will need fruits and vegetables. Beans are not enough.
Come, we will go shopping.

They went to the village, and the good doctor bought fruit, vegetables, meat, and milk.

"You must eat good foods, too, Pedro," said the doctor. "I will bring some each day while I am staying with Señora Martinez. Then I will leave money for you to buy more good food."

"Gracias, gracias," cried Pedro. He prepared the food for dinner and hurried to wash and put away the dishes. Then he put the baskets on the burro and hurried away to the valley. The sun was going down before he finished digging out the roots of a beautiful red flower like the one he had dug for his mother. He took it to the good doctor.

"Here is your Christmas flower," said Pedro.

"It will be the Christmas flower of many people," said the doctor. "Just wait and we shall see."

"It will be my poinsettia flower," said Pedro. "I shall name it for you. You are making my mother well, and we shall have a good Christmas."

"Poinsettia is a good name," said the doctor. "We shall call it that."

So Pedro's red flower is now the Christmas flower, not only to one nation but to many. It is raised all over the country from which it came. Scarcely a cottage in Mexico is without its tall red flowers that almost cover the house at Christmas time.

Pedro's flower is truly a great gift.

Circle Time: Break a Piñata.
Have children sing and dance. Then use a scarf to blindfold one child at a time. Break the piñata using a stick. Note: Be sure children are standing far away from the child who is trying to break the piñata.

Suggestion: Some children may not want to have their eyes covered. You may just want to show the children the piñata and perhaps read the book *Nine Days To Christmas.*

Food Experience: Bufluelos
Make very thin pancakes and serve with a brown sugar sauce. A simple sauce can be made by diluting brown sugar with water.

Theme Activities: Book
Read *The Christmas Piñata* by Jack Kent.

Thursday

Sharing Time: Finger Play

"Five Little Reindeer" (Traditional)

Five little reindeer prancing in the snow,
Waiting for Santa to say, "Let's go!"
The first little reindeer said, "Let's be on our way."
The second little reindeer said, "It will soon be Christmas Day."
The third little reindeer said, "The sleigh is full of toys."
The fourth little reindeer said, "They'll bring happiness and joy."
The fifth little reindeer said, "We'll travel far tonight."
Then out came Santa with his "Ho! Ho! Ho!"
And the sleigh and reindeer were soon out of sight.

(Start with five fingers and take one away with each line.)

Art: Christmas Tree Stick Puppets
Have children cut out Christmas trees from construction paper. Decorate trees and tape craft sticks to the backs of the trees.

Story Time: Book
Read *The Biggest Most Beautiful Christmas Tree* by Amye Rosenberg.

Circle Time: Book
Read *Rudolph The Red-Nosed Reindeer* by Barbara Shook Hazen.

Food Experiences: Rudolph Sandwiches
Make mini sandwiches out of rye bread with any filling you choose. Put a cherry on top for the nose.

Theme Activities: Flannel Activity See patterns on page 181.

"Christmas Tree" (Traditional)

Here stands a lovely Christmas Tree, Christmas Tree, Christmas Tree, Here stands a lovely Christmas Tree, So early in the morning.

Here is a horn for the Christmas Tree, Christmas Tree, Christmas Tree, Here is a horn for the Christmas Tree, So early in the morning.

Here is a drum for the Christmas Tree, Christmas Tree, Christmas Tree, Here is a drum for the Christmas Tree, So early in the morning.

Here is a star for the Christmas Tree, Christmas Tree, Christmas Tree, Here is a star for the Christmas Tree, So early in the morning.

Here are the lights for the Christmas Tree, Christmas Tree, Christmas Tree, Here are the lights for the Christmas Tree, So early in the morning.

Here stands a lovely Christmas Tree, Christmas Tree, Christmas Tree, Here stands a lovely Christmas Tree, So early in the morning.

Friday

Sharing Time: Fingerplay

"Five Little Bells" (Traditional)

Five little bells ringing in a row. *(Hold up five fingers.)*
The first one said, "Ring me slow." *(Point to thumb.)*
The second one said, "Ring me fast." *(Point to next finger.)*
The third one said, "Ring me last." *(Point to next.)*
The fourth one said, "I'm like a chime." *(Point to next.)*
And the fifth one said, "Ring us all. It's Christmas Time!"
(Hold up last finger and then shake hand as if ringing a bell.)

Art: Bells

Make Christmas bells. Cut an egg carton into twelve cups. Cover each cup with foil. Punch a hole in the top of each. Add yarn or ribbon and knot. Small drinking cups, glitter, and glue can also be used.

Story Time: Book

Read *Christmas Time* by Gail Gibbons.

Circle Time: Ringing Bells

Have bells of different sizes on hand. Give children an opportunity to ring them. When a child rings a bell, ask if the sound is high or low.

Food Experiences: Cheese Ball Bells

- 1 8oz. (225 g) package softened cream cheese

- ½ cup (120 mL) softened shredded sharp cheddar cheese

- 1 small onion, finely chopped

- 1 Tablespoon (15 ml) Worcestershire sauce

Add all ingredients in a mixer bowl and mix at slow speed. Then mix on medium speed. Give each child a bit of the mixture and have them form it into small bell shapes. Serve it on crackers.

Theme Activities: Chain of Children

Have children stand around a Christmas tree. Distribute bells. Children form a human chain and ring bells as they dance to Christmas music. Have a few of the children make chains and let the others count the number of children.

Classroom Additions

These materials can be placed in the learning centers in addition to your regular materials:

- Housekeeping: Christmas trees decorated from each country, stockings
- Circle: flannel board and pieces, globe, piñata
- Book: books about how Christmas is celebrated around the world
- Music: songs from each country mentioned, musical bells
- Table Activities: file folder activities listed, lacing cards, puzzles, games
- Block: old and new blocks, flags from different countries, gift boxes
- Art: green play dough, paper plates, glitter, pipe cleaners, cotton balls, yarn, paints
- Puppet: bell puppets, mask puppets, gingerbread people stick puppets
- Science: items listed under Science Activities
- Science Activities: Show children a real poinsettia plant. Caution: Do not allow the children to touch the plant.

Teachers' Aids

File Folder Activities: Choose the skills you wish to emphasize this week. See directions on pages 5-6.

- Decorate the Tree
- Sort the Stockings
- Old and New Matching
- Matching Presents
- Christmas Card Match
- Christmas Tree Puzzle

Bulletin Board Ideas:
- Continue the theme in your classroom by using some of the bulletin board ideas and patterns.
- German Christmas Tree
- Various Christmas Cards
- Reindeer
- Bells

For Parents

Send these tips home for parents to help enrich their child's education.

- Discuss the different countries with your child.
- Visit the library and check out books that tell about Christmas customs in other countries.
- Discuss customs that your families may have.

Bibliography

Children's Books
Climo, Shirley. *The Cobweb Christmas.* Harper, 1982.
dePaola, Tomie, *Friendly Beasts: An Old English Christmas Carol.* G.P. Putnam, 1981
Ets, Marie Hall and Labastida, Aurora. *Nine Days to Christmas.* Viking Press, 1959
Gibbons, Gail. *Christmas Time.* Holiday, 1982
Hazen, Barbara Shook. *Rudolph, The Red-Nosed Reindeer.* Western,
Kent, Jack. *The Christmas Piñata.* Parents Magazine, 1975
Richardson, I.M. *Christmas Carol.* Troll, 1988
Rosenburg, Amye. *The Biggest Most Beautiful Christmas Tree.* Western, 1985

Patterns

Patterns

Weekly Theme: _Snowmen_   Week of: _____

	Monday	Tuesday	Wednesday	Thursday	Friday
Date					
Sharing Time	Fingerplay: Ten Little Snowmen	Fingerplay: I Built a Little Snowman	Glove Puppet: Five Snowmen	Fingerplay: I am a Snowman	Fingerplay: The Snow
Art	Snowflake Child	Shaving Cream Art	Mittens	Snowman Puppet	Snowflakes
Story Time	Book: *The First Snowfall*	Book: *White Snow, Bright Snow*	Book: *The Mitten*	Book: *The Snowy Day*	Book: *Frosty the Snowman*
Circle Time	Build a Snowman	Snow Ball Walk	Snowman Color Activity	Blowing Cotton Balls	Pretend to be Snowflakes
Food Experiences	Snowballs	Fruit Slushes	Oatmeal and Raisins	Taste Hot and Cold Applesauce	Popcorn Ball Snowman
Theme Activities	Flannel Activity: Ten Little Snowmen	Flannel Activity: I Built a Little Snowman	Flannel Activity: Five Little Snowmen	Flannel Activity: I am A Snowman	Ice Fishing

Monday

Materials Needed For The Week:
  fruit juice, applesauce, papier-mâché, balloons, hats, scarves, mittens, cardboard boxes, coffee filters, oatmeal, raisins, popcorn, syrup

Sharing Time: Fingerplay

"Ten Little Snowmen"

Ten little snowmen dressed up fine: *(Hold up ten fingers.)*
This one melted, and then there were nine. *(Bend down one finger.)*
Nine little snowmen standing tall and straight: *(Nine fingers)*
This one melted, and then there were eight. *(Bend down one finger.)*
Eight little snowmen white as clouds in heaven: *(Eight fingers)*
This one melted, and then there were seven. *(Bend down one finger.)*
Seven little snowmen with arms made of sticks: *(Seven fingers)*
This one melted, and then there were six. *(Bend down one finger.)*
Six little snowmen looking so alive: *(Six fingers)*
This one melted, and then there were five. *(Bend down one finger.)*
Five little snowmen with mittens from the store: *(Five fingers)*
This one melted, and then there were four. *(Bend down one finger.)*
Four little snowmen beneath a green pine tree: *(Four fingers)*
This one melted, and then there were three. *(Bend down one finger.)*
Three little snowmen with pipes and mufflers, too: *(Three fingers)*
This one melted, and then there were two. *(Bend down one finger.)*
Two little snowmen standing in the sun: *(Two fingers)*
This one melted, and then there was one. *(Bend down one finger.)*
One little snowman started to run, *(One finger)*
But he melted away, and then there were none. *(Bend down last finger.)*

Art: Snowflake Child
  Use a coffee filter or a circle cut out of construction paper. Let children cut out snowflakes by folding a circle in half, then half again, and half again. Cut out notches on the rounded edge. Open up the snowflake. Add facial features on the snowflake with crayons or markers. Arms and legs can be added by cutting strips of construction paper. They can be glued or stapled on the snowflake. Display on bulletin board.

Story Time: Book
  Read *The First Snowfall* by Anne and Harlow Rockwell.

Monday (cont.)

Circle Time: Build a Snowman.

If weather permits, build a snowman outside. Otherwise build a papier mâché snowman. Papier-mâché can be bought at craft stores. Follow directions on the bag. Or you can make your own papier mâché by tearing old newspapers or white tissue paper into one inch wide (25 mm) strips. Then dip them in a mixture of equal parts of flour and water or dilute glue with water. Blow up two or three balloons and tie the end of each balloon in a knot. Wrap the strips around each balloon. Smooth it by dipping fingers in the mixture. Continue until each balloon is covered. Tie a piece of yarn or string to each of the knotted ends of the balloons and hang them up until they dry. When they are dry, pop the balloons with a needle. If newspaper was used, paint them with white tempera paint or a can of white spray paint. The snowman can be put together using a hot glue gun.

Suggestions: Glue on rocks or pieces of coal for the eyes, mouth, and nose. Children can bring hats and scarfs from home to decorate the snowman. These can be changed as often as necessary so that the snowman has worn everything the children have brought in. Arms and legs can be added by folding accordion strips of colored construction paper. Mittens can be added for the hands. Boots can be added for the feet. A heavy piece of string can be put through the snowman's body so it can be hung from the ceiling.

Food Experiences: Snowballs

Give each child an ice cream ball. Let them roll it in shredded coconut.

Theme Activities: Flannel Activity

"Ten Little Snowmen"

The finger play from the morning sharing time can also be used for a flannel activity. To do this cut out ten snowmen from white felt using the snowman pattern on page 191. As each snowman melts, take one away.

Tuesday

Sharing Time: Fingerplay

"I Built a Little Snowman " (*Author* Unknown)

I built a little snowman. (*Make circle with hands.*)
He had a carrot nose. (*Point to nose.*)
Along came a bunny. (*Hold up first two fingers, slightly bent.*)
And what do you suppose?
That hungry little bunny, (*Make bunny again.*)
Looking for his lunch, (*Hop bunny around.*)
Ate the snowman's nose. (*Pretend bunny is eating nose.*)
Nibble! Nibble! Crunch! (*Pretend to be eating a carrot.*)

Art: Shaving Cream Art
Spray scented shaving cream onto a table and let the children create snow scenes.

Story Time: Book
Read *White Snow, Bright Snow* by Alvin Tressalt.

Circle Time: Snowball Walk
Using tape, rope, or any other means, mark a spot for the children to stand and another place for them to walk. Divide the children in two equal groups. Have each group line up in single file. Give the first child in each group a cotton "snowball" on a spoon. One at a time have the children walk to the marked place and then back to where the other children are standing and give the next children in line the spoon with the cotton ball. Then that child does the same until every child has had a turn. If the cotton ball falls off, that child must start over.

Food Experiences: Fruit Slushes
Crush ice in a blender or in clean dish towel. Put the ice into small cups. Add fruit juice to make slushes.

Theme Activities: Flannel Activity
Use the same finger play from Sharing Time. This time, however, do this as a flannel board activity. See patterns on page 192.

Follow the directions in parentheses.

"I Built a Little Snowman" (*Author* Unknown)

I built a little snowman. (*Place snowman on the flannel board.*)
He had a carrot nose. (*Place on the carrot.*)
Along came a bunny. (*Put bunny on the flannel board.*)
And what do you suppose?
That hungry little bunny, (*Move bunny toward the snowman.*)
Looking for his lunch, (*Move bunny next to the carrot.*)
Ate the snowman's nose. (*Move bunny on top of the carrot.*)
Nibble! Nibble! Crunch! (*Children can make crunching sounds.*)

Wednesday

Sharing Time: Glove Puppet

Before sharing this finger play, make a glove puppet to use with it. See directions on page 7 and patterns on page 192.

"Five Little Snowmen" (Author Unknown)

Five little snowmen, standing in a row, *(Hold up five fingers.)*
Each with a hat *(Point to top of head.)*
And a bright red bow. *(Point to neck.)*
Five little snowmen dressed for a show. *(Smooth clothes with hands.)*
Now they are ready. Where will they go? *(Put hand above eyebrows.)*
Wait till the sun shines. *(Hold arms in a circle over head.)*
Soon they will go.
Down through the field with the melting snow. *(Pretend to melt away.)*

Art: Mittens

On construction paper, trace around the outside of each child's hands. Use a hole punch and punch a hole at the bottom of each mitten. Tie a piece of yarn in each hole to attach the two mittens together. These can be displayed on the bulletin board.

Story Time: Book

Read *The Mitten* by Alvin Tressalt.

Circle Time: Snowman Color Activity

Give children various colored scarves, mittens, or hats. As a group let them dress themselves as snowmen.

Food Experiences: Oatmeal and Raisins

Cook oatmeal and add raisins. Talk about why this would be a good breakfast on a cold day.

Theme Activities: Flannel Activity

"Five Little Snowmen"

The finger play from the morning sharing time can be used as a flannel activity. Use five of the previous snowmen. See patterns on pages 191-192. Cut out five hats, five bows, and one sun. Place the five snowmen with their hats and bows on the flannel board in a row. When it says, "Wait till the sun shines" place the sun on the flannel board. Then as you say, "Soon they will go down through the fields with the melting snow" slide the snowmen off the flannel board.

Thursday

Sharing Time: Finger Play

I Am A Snowman (Author Unknown)

I am a snowman, cold and white. *(Make a circle with each hand, and put one hand on top of other hand.)*

I stand so still all through the night. *(Hold hands still on top of each other.)*

I have a carrot nose way up high, *(Point to nose.)*

And a lump of coal to make each eye. *(Point to eyes.)*

I have a muffler made of red, *(Point to neck.)*

And a stovepipe hat upon my head. *(Point to top of head.)*

Art: Snowman Puppet
Each child can make a snowman by cutting out three white circles. Overlap them and glue together. Draw on facial features with crayons or markers. Add a craft stick to the back of the snowman.

Story Time: Book
Read *The Snowy Day* by Ezra Jack Keats.

Circle Time: Blowing Cotton Balls
Form children into several teams. Give each team a cotton ball. Have teams take turns and blow the cotton ball across a table or on the floor. A variation is to give each child a cotton ball and hold it with the tip of their thumb and first finger. Have them tilt their heads upward and hold the cotton ball above their mouths. As they blow, they should release the cotton ball and it will go up in the air and fall to the ground. The children can try to catch the cotton ball. This resembles the falling snow. Every child should be praised for a good job.

Food Experiences: Taste Hot and Cold Applesauce
Serve children both hot and cold applesauce. Let them compare and decide which one they like better.

Theme Activities: Flannel Activity
"I am a Snowman" (Author Unknown)

The finger play from the morning sharing time can be used as a flannel activity. Use one of the snowmen, carrot, and hat. Also, cut out a red muffler (scarf) and two black coal eyes out of felt. Place flannel pieces on the flannel board as they are mentioned in the story. See patterns on pages 191 and 192.

Friday

Sharing Time: Finger Play

"The Snow"

This is the way the snow comes down, *(Fingers flutter downward.)*
Upon a winter day, *(Wrap arms around body as if it were cold.)*
But soon the golden sun comes out, *(Hold arms in a circle above head.)*
And melts it all away. *(Pretend to melt away.)*

Art: Snowflakes

Snowflakes can be made from coffee filters or circles cut from tissue or construction paper. Let children cut out snowflakes by folding a circle in half, then half again, and half again. Cut out notches on the rounded edge and the folded sides. Then open up the snowflake. These can be displayed on the bulletin board.

Story Time: Book

Read *Frosty The Snowman* as retold by Carol North.

Circle Time: Pretend to be Snowflakes

Have children move around the room pretending to be snowflakes. Let them lazily drift down to the ground.

Food Experiences: Popcorn Ball Snowman

Pop popcorn. Use a syrup recipe and pour over the popcorn and mix until coated. Put butter on children's hands and let each child make a snowman.

Theme Activities: Ice Fishing

Pretend to fish in ice. Use fishing pole. See page 7 for directions on how to make a fishing pole. Cut out different size fish from various colored construction paper. (See fish pattern on page 30.) Attach a paper clip to each fish. Place fish on a large piece of white butcher paper that has been cut into a shape of a pond and put on the floor. As children catch fish, let them tell what color each is.

 Suggestions: The fish can be laminated or covered with clear contact paper first so they will last longer. Dots, shapes, or numerals can be added for shape recognition, counting activities, or numeral recognition.

Classroom Additions

Here are some materials that can be placed in the learning centers in addition to your regular materials.

- Housekeeping: mittens, scarves, hats

- Circle: flannel board with the flannel snowmen, hats, bows, carrots, eyes, and bunny

- Books: books about winter, snow, and snowmen

- Music: records about snowmen

- Table Activities: file folder activities, mitten matching, snowman matching

- Blocks: Sled-This can be made from the bottom or the sides of a cardboard box. To the front of the cardboard attach a piece of rope for the children to hold.

    Skis-Use the sides of a cardboard box. Cut two four-inch-wide (10 cm) strips of the cardboard and make them twelve inches long (30 cm). In the middle of each strip, staple a piece of elastic across the width. The elastic should be long enough so a child's foot can slide in and the skis will stay on. One inch (25mm) wooden dowel rods or old mop and broom handles can be used for the ski poles.

- Art: blue construction paper, white paint, and paint brushes

- Puppets: snowmen puppets (Make the same as the art activity from Thursday, page 187.)

- Science: Complete some of the science activities below throughout the week.

    Pans of snow or crushed ice can be put on a science table for the children to feel, measure, and see how much is melting throughout the day. Paint snow with food coloring. Small clear plastic containers can be placed on the table along with bottles of food coloring. The children can get a scoop of snow or crushed ice and place it in one of the small containers. Let them add drops of food coloring to watch it change colors. An ice sculpture can be made by freezing a bowl of water. Remove the block of ice from the bowl and place it in a dishpan. Put some rock salt on top of the block of ice and watch what happens. More rock salt can be added as desired for creating the ice sculpture.

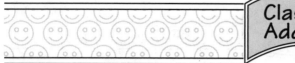

Classroom Additions (cont.)

Teachers Aids

File Folder Activities: Choose the skills you wish to emphasize this week. See directions on pages 5 and 6.

- Snowmen with Matching Hats
- Color Mitten Matching

- Snowman Puzzle: Draw a snowman on a poster board and cut into pieces. Children can then put the puzzle together. Use the pattern on page 192.

- Snowman Building: Cut three different size circles from white construction paper. Children can build a snowman by arranging the circles from the largest to the smallest. A hat, scarf, eyes, nose, and mouth can be cut out for children to place on the snowman.

- Paper Bag Puppets: Stuff a paper bag half full. White bakery bags work well for this. Tie a string around the opening of the bag. Use the patterns on page 192 and let children decorate the puppets.

Bulletin Board Ideas:

- Snow Scene

- Snowmen

- Snowflakes

- Children Wearing Winter Clothing (Cotton balls or cotton batting can be used for the snow.)

For Parents

- Build a snowman with your child.

- Have a gentle snowball fight.

- Take a snow walk.

- Read books to your child about snowmen.

- Make an angel in the snow with your child and compare sizes.

- Discuss why we wear coats, mittens, and boots.

Bibliography

Childrens' Books
Keats, Ezra Jack. ***The Snowy Day.*** Puffin Books, 1962
North, Carol, retold by. ***Frosty The Snowman.*** Western, 1990
Rockwell, Anne and Harlow. ***First Snowfall.*** Macmillan, 1987
Tressalt, Alvin. ***The Mitten.*** Scholastic, 1964
ressalt, Alvin. ***White Snow, Bright Snow.*** Lothrop, Lee and Shepard Books, 1947

Reference Book
Sullivan, Dianna J. ***Paper Bag Art Projects.*** Teacher Created Resources, 1987

Patterns

Patterns

Weekly Theme: _Bears_   Week of: _____

	Monday	Tuesday	Wednesday	Thursday	Friday
Date					
Sharing Time	Fingerplay: Ten in the Bed	Activity: Bear Hunt	Fingerplay: Five Little Bears	Song: The Bear Went Over the Mountain	Activity: Teddy Bear
Art	Brown Play Dough	Moving Bear	Bear Lacing Cards	Easel Paint	Bear Overalls
Story Time	Book: *The Three Bears*	Flannel Story: Why the Bear Has a Short Tail	Book: *Corduroy*	Book: *Brown Bear, Brown Bear, What Do You See?*	Poem: This Little Bear
Circle Time	Flannel Story: The Bear and the Bees	Activity: Bear Walk	Song: Teddy Bear Song	Activity: Sharing Bear Hugs Song Fingerplay: Ten in the Bed	Activity: Bear Tracks
Food Experiences	Honey	Jelly	Maple Sugar Surprise	Berries	Marshmallow Bears
Theme Activities	Book: *The Biggest Bear*	Book: *Blueberries for Sal*	Book: *Bear Shadow*	Book: *Ten Bears in My Bed*	Book: *A Pocket for Corduroy*

Monday

Materials Needed For The Week:

felt, buttons, brass fasteners, yarn, corduroy material, honey, sure-jell, maple sugar, marshmallows, stuffed bears, berries

Sharing Time: Fingerplay

"Ten In The Bed" (Traditional)

There were ten in the bed,
And the little one said,
Roll over, roll over. *(Roll hands.)*
And they all rolled over,

And one fell out. *(Hold up one finger.)*
There were nine in the bed,
And the little one said,
Roll over, roll over.

(Start by holding up ten fingers. Continue until there are none in the bed.)

Art: Play Dough Bears

Let children play with brown play dough and make bears. (Recipe is on page 6.)

Story Time: Book

Read *The Three Bears* by Yuri Salzman.

Circle Time: Flannel Story

Do this as a flannel story using the patterns on page 204.

"The Bear and the Bees"

Once there was a big brown bear who lived inside a cave with his wife. "Please, dear," she said to him one day, "Run down to the brook and catch some fish for dinner. But don't go near the beehive in the old dead tree. Remember what the bees did to you last time!" The big brown bear walked slowly toward the brook. Before he knew it, he was at the old dead tree. As soon as he reached the tree, he pushed his paw into the hive and grabbed a piece of honeycomb. Inside, the busy bees were making wax and honey. But the minute they saw that big paw wrecking their home and stealing their precious honey, they rushed out. Swarming after him in a big cloud, the bees were ready to zoom down on his head. So the poor bear had to act fast. Pulling and kicking and tugging, he tore himself loose at last, leaving a great deal of his fur in the brush. He ran toward the brook, jumped into the water, and hid there with only his nose showing. Suddenly the bees spotted him and swooped down smack on his nose. "Ouch! Ouch!" he cried and ran out of the brook into a grassy field. And he was supposed to catch some fish for dinner! Back he went to the brook and quickly caught a trout. Then he ran toward home, looking over his shoulder fearfully. He was so happy to be home that he gave his wife a great big bear hug and kissed her on both ears. His wife was quite surprised by such a greeting and guessed right away he had done something wrong. And as soon as she saw his nose, she knew what he had done. She asked him why he went near those bees, but he had no excuse. He promised his wife he would never go near that tree again. She gave him the biggest piece of trout and bandaged his nose. But deep down inside he wished the trout would have been some of that nice honey.

Food Experiences: Honey

Drizzle some honey on a cracker and let children taste it.

Theme Activities: Book

Read *The Biggest Bear* by Lynd Kendall Ward.

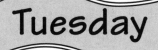

Tuesday

Sharing Time: Activity

"Bear Hunt"

I'm going on a bear hunt. *(Slap thighs.)*
I see a swamp, *(Hold hand as if looking.)*
Can't go under it, *(Take hands down low.)*
Can't go over it, *(Hold hands high.)*
Have to go through it.
Slush, slush, slush, slush, slush. *(Rub hands together.)*
I'm going on a bear hunt.
I see a bridge.
Can't go under it,
Can't go through it,
Have to go over it.
Thump, thump, thump, thump, thump. *(Pound chest.)*
I'm going on a bear hunt.
I see a stream.
Can't go under it,
Can't go over it,
Have to go through it.
Splash, splash, splash, splash, splash. *(Swimming strokes.)*
I'm going on a bear hunt.
I see a tree.
Let's go see.
Up, up, up, up, up. *(Fingers climb up.)*
I see a cave.
Down, down, down, down, down. *(Fingers climb down.)*
Let's go see.
I feel something. *(Feel with hands.)*
I feel something furry.
It feels like a bear.
It looks like a bear.
It is a bear!
Up.
Down.
Splash, splash, splash.
Thump, thump, thump.
Slush, slush, slush.
WOO!

Art: Moving Bear

Cut the bear's body pieces on page 203 out of brown construction paper. Attach with paper fasteners. Attach the head last. Watch the bears as they dance.

Story Time: Flannel Story

"Why The Bear Has a Short Tail" (American Folk Tale)

One cold morning when the fox was coming up the road with some fish, he met a bear. "Good morning, Mr. Fox," said the bear.

"Good morning, Mr. Bear," said the fox. "The morning is brighter because I have met YOU."

"Those are very good fish, Mr. Fox," said the bear. "I have not eaten such fish for many a day. Where do you find them?"

"I have been fishing, Mr. Bear," answered the fox.

"If I could catch such fish as those, I should like to go fishing, but I do not know how to fish."

"It would be very easy for you to learn, Mr. Bear," said the fox. "You are so big and strong that you can do anything."

"Will you teach me, Mr. Fox?" asked the bear.

"I would not tell everybody, but you are such a good friend that I will teach you. Come to this pond, and I will show you how to fish through the ice."

So the fox and the bear went to the frozen pond, and the fox showed the bear how to make a hole in the ice.

"That is easy for you," said the fox, "but many an animal could not have made that hole. Now comes the secret. You must put your tail down into the water and keep it there. That is not easy, and not every animal could do it, for the water is very cold, but you are a learned animal, Mr. Bear, and you know that the secret of catching fish is to keep your tail in the water a long time. Then when you pull it up, you will pull with it as many fish as I have."

The bear put his tail down into the water, and the fox went away. The sun rose high in the heavens, and still the bear sat with his tail through the hole in the ice. Sunset came, but still the bear sat with his tail through the hole in the ice, for he thought, "When an animal is really learned, he will not fear a little cold."

It began to get dark, and the bear said, "Now I will pull the fish out of the water. How good they will be!" He pulled and pulled, but not a fish came out. Worse than that, when he finally broke himself loose, not all of his tail came out, for the end of it was frozen fast to the ice.

He went slowly down the road, growling angrily, "I wish I could find that fox." But the cunning fox was curled up in his warm nest, and whenever he thought of the bear, he laughed.

See bear patterns page 204 and fox pattern in Nutrition section.

Circle Time: Bear Walk

Have children pretend to be bears. Have them walk on all fours and then growl like a bear.

Food Experiences: Jelly

Let children taste several different types of jelly. Spread the jelly on crackers.

Theme Activities: Book

Read *Blueberries for Sal* by Robert McCloskey.

Wednesday

Sharing Time: Fingerplay

"Five Little Bears" (Traditional)

Five little cubby bears, tumbling on the ground, *(Hold up five fingers.)*
The first little bear said, "Let's look around." *(Hold hand to eyes.)*
The second one said, "See the little bunny." *(Point finger.)*
The third one said, I smell honey!" *(Sniff the air.)*
The fourth one said, "It's over in the trees." *(Point finger.)*
The fifth one said, "Look out! Here comes the bees!" *(Run fingers.)*

Art: Bear Lacing Cards

Trace the bear pattern on page 202 onto tag board. Punch holes around the edges. Give each child a length of yarn that has tape on one end. Have them lace yarn through the holes.

Story Time: Book

Read *Corduroy* by Don Freeman.

Circle Time: Song

"Teddy Bear Song" (Traditional)

Teddy bear, teddy bear, turn around.
Teddy bear, teddy bear, touch the ground.
Teddy bear, teddy bear, reach up high.
Teddy bear, teddy bear, touch the sky.
Teddy bear, teddy bear, bend down low.
Teddy bear, teddy bear, touch your toe.
(You may continue adding more verses. See page 199.)

Food Experiences: Maple Sugar Surprise

Boil maple syrup until thick and foamy. Spoon into pans of crushed ice. When syrup turns waxy, twist it up onto a popsicle stick.

Theme Activities: Book

Read *Bear Shadow* by Frank Asch. Play some shadow games. Let one child pretend to be a bear and the other its shadow.

Thursday

Sharing Time: Song

"The Bear Went Over the Mountain" (Traditional)

The bear went over the mountain,
The bear went over the mountain,
The bear went over the mountain,
To see what he could see.
But all that he could see,
But all that he could see,
Was the other side of the mountain,
The other side of the mountain,
The other side of the mountain,
Was all that he could see.

Art: Easel Painting

Provide easels, brown, red, and black paints, and brushes. Encourage children to paint bears.

Story Time: Book

Read *Brown Bear, Brown Bear, What Do You See?* by Bill Martin Jr.

Circle Time: Sharing Bear Hugs

Explain that a bear hug is a hug that is big like a bear. If they wish, let children share bear hugs. Repeat the finger play "Ten in the Bed." See page 194 for the words.

Food Experiences: Berries

Let children taste raspberries, blackberries, or blueberries. Ask them why they think bears might enjoy these tasty treats.

Theme Activities: Book

Read *Ten Bears In My Bed* by Stan Mack.

Friday

Sharing Time: Activity

"Teddy Bear" (Old American Rhyme)

Teddy Bear, Teddy Bear, turn around,
Teddy Bear, Teddy Bear, touch the ground,
Teddy Bear, Teddy Bear, go up stairs,
Teddy Bear, Teddy Bear, say your prayers,
Teddy Bear, Teddy Bear, turn out the light,
Teddy Bear, Teddy Bear, say good night.
Have children perform actions when mentioned.

Art: Bear Overalls

Use the pattern on page 203. Cut it out of tag board. Use the pattern and cut a jumper for the bear out of corduroy. Provide children with buttons, lace, and scrap materials to decorate the jumper.

Story Time: Poem

"This Little Bear"

This little bear has a soft fur suit,
This little bear acts very cute,
This little bear is bold and cross,
This little bear rests his head on moss,
This little bear likes bacon and honey,
But he can't buy them. He has no money.

Circle Time: Bear Tracks

Use the pattern on page 201 and cut several large bear footprints. Place them all around the room. Have the children then take turns walking in the bear tracks.

Food Experiences: Marshmallow Bears

Give children some chocolate icing and both large and small marshmallows. Let them use the chocolate icing to form the marshmallows into bears.

Theme Activities: Book

Read *A Pocket For Corduroy* by Don Freeman. Let children listen with their teddy bears in overalls that they made as an art project.

Classroom Additions

Here are some materials that can be placed in the learning centers in addition to your regular materials.

- Housekeeping: stuffed bears, empty plastic honey bottles
- Circle: flannel board and pieces, weather bear chart
- Books: books about bears, stuffed bears
- Music: lively records
- Table Activities: file folder activities listed, Teddy Bear Bingo game, button bears, puzzles
- Blocks: blocks, stuffed bears
- Art: brown paints, play dough, brass fasteners, brown paper, corduroy material
- Puppets: bear puppets
- Science: pictures of bears, stuffed bears, bear facts, papier mâché cave
- Science Activities: Have available a teddy bear with different types of clothing appropriate for different types of weather. Have children dress the weather bear daily in the appropriate clothing.

Teachers' Aids
- Button Bears
- Teddy Bear Bingo
- Bear Lacing Cards
- Bear Sequence Cards
- Dress the Teddy Bear
- Teddy Bear Name Tags
- File Folder Activities: Choose the skills you wish to emphasize this week. See directions on pages 5 and 6.
- Bears and Honey Pots   • Matching Bears

Bulletin Board Ideas:
- Bears   • Children's Art Work   • Weather Bear   • Weather Chart

For Parents
- Do the Bear Hunt with your child.
- Visit the library and check out books about bears.
- Provide your child with a teddy bear.
- Discuss the weather with your child.
- Give your child a bear hug every day.
- Discuss the different types and colors of bears.
- Discuss why bears hibernate and where they sleep.

Bibliography

Childrens Books
Asch, Frank. ***Bear Shadow.*** Prentice Hall, 1985
Freeman, Don. ***A Pocket For Corduroy.*** Viking, 1978
Freeman, Don. ***Corduroy.*** Viking, 1968
Mack, Stan. ***Ten Bears In My Bed.*** Pantheon, 1974
Martin, Bill Jr. ***Brown Bear, Brown Bear What Do You See?*** Henry Holt, 1983
McCloskey, Robert. ***Blueberries for Sal.*** Viking, 1948
Salzman, Yuri. ***The Three Bears.*** Western, 1987
Ward, Lynd Kendall. ***The Biggest Bear.*** Houghton-Mifflin, 1952

Patterns

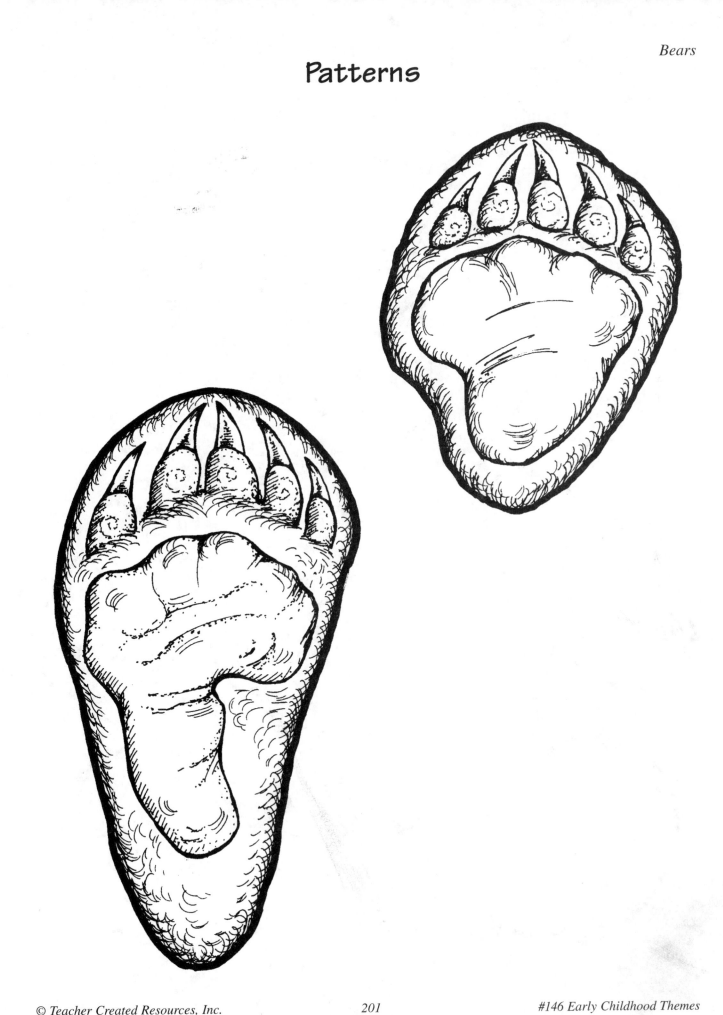

Patterns

Patterns

Patterns

Weekly Theme: *Birthdays*   Week of: _____

	Monday	Tuesday	Wednesday	Thursday	Friday
Date					
Sharing Time	When is Your Birthday?	Birthday Groups	Count the Candles	Pat-a-Cake	*Birthday Bear and the Runaway Skateboard*
Art	Play Dough Cakes	Easel Paint	Birthday Necklace	Birthday Candle Hat	Balloon Party Hat
Story Time	Book: *Happy Birthday Thomas*	Book: *Birthday Presents*	Book: *Georgie and the Runaway Balloon*	Book: *The Birthday Party*	Book: *Happy Birthday Oliver*
Circle Time	Song: Somebody's Birthday	Birthday Chart	Poem: Balloons	Activity: Count the Balloons	Song: Happy Birthday
Food Experiences	Field Trip to the Bakery	Cupcakes	Balloon Cookies	Birthday Cake Toast	Birthday Cake
Theme Activities	Pass the Presents	Book: *Happy Birthday Moon*	Balloon Toss	Activity: Balloon Bounce	Activity: Pin the Tail on the Donkey

Monday

Materials Needed For The Week:
balloons of various colors and sizes; small decorated boxes in an assortment of shapes; birthday cake for Friday; birthday candles; food coloring; cake mix; frosting

Sharing Time: When is Your Birthday?
Talk with children about their birth dates. See who knows the month and day in which they were born. Tell those who do not know.

Art: Play Dough Cakes
Make play dough (see recipe on page 6) and let children make their own birthday cakes. Provide some candles for them to stick in their play dough. Birthday cookie cutters and plastic knives can be used.

Story Time: Book
Read *Happy Birthday Thomas* by Rev W. Awdry.

Circle Time: Song
Play "Somebody's Birthday" from the record *Greg and Steve Holidays and Special Times.*

Food Experiences: Field Trip to the Bakery
Make arrangements ahead of time so that someone will be doing cake decorating. Take the children to a bakery and let them watch the people decorate a cake. Let them taste the frosting.

Theme Activities: Pass the Presents
Wrap up some small boxes of different sizes with colored construction paper. One box for each child would be ideal. Give each child a box; and, as you play music, have the children pass the presents. When the music stops, ask the children what is the color of their present. Repeat as long as the children enjoy the activity.

Tuesday

Sharing Time: Birthday Groups

Put children in groups by the months in which their birthdays land. This will help them relate to other children who have a birthday during the same month.

Art: Easel Painting

Let children paint a birthday cake using pastel colors of tempera paint on white construction paper. Children can help make pastel colors by adding white tempera paint to regular colors of tempera paint.

Story Time: Book

Read *Birthday Presents* by Cynthia Rylant.

Circle Time: Birthday Chart

Make a chart listing the months at the top of poster boards. Write the names of the children who were born during a particular month under that month. This can be hung on the wall to help children recognize the month in which they were born and see which children were born in the same month.

Food Experiences: Cupcakes

Use a package mix and follow directions to make cupcakes for the children. Provide plastic knives and ready made frosting. Let each child decorate a cupcake. Add a candle to each and have the children sing "Happy Birthday" to themselves.

Theme Activities: Book

Read *Happy Birthday Moon* by Frank Asch. Ask children what gift they would give the moon.

Wednesday

Sharing Time: Count The Candles

Make a flannel cake and candles. (See patterns on page 212.) Place the birthday cake on the flannel board. Then place a certain number of candles on the cake. Ask the children how many candles are on the cake. Ask if anyone is that old. Repeat as many times as the activity holds the children's attention.

Art: Birthday Necklace

Trace the numerals of each child's age onto construction paper. Cut out the numeral, punch a hole in the top, and add yarn to go around child's neck. They can decorate them any way they want.

Story Time: Book

Read *Georgie and the Runaway Balloon* by Robert Bright.

Circle Time: Poem

"Balloons"

This is the way we blow our balloon;
Blow, Blow, Blow.
This is the way we break our balloon:
Oh, Oh, Oh!

Food Experiences: Balloon Cookies

Give each child a round sugar cookie. Provide white frosting and some food coloring. Let children dye the frosting different colors. Let children decorate the cookies to look like balloons.

Theme Activities: Balloon Toss

Use different sizes and colors of balloons. Have children toss them to each other.

Thursday

Sharing Time: Rhyme

> **"Pat-A-Cake"** (Old English Rhyme)
> Pat-a-cake, Pat-a-cake, baker's man,
> Bake me a cake as fast as you can;
> Prick it, and pat it, and mark it with a B,
> And put it in the oven for baby and me.

Art: Birthday Candle Hat

Cut out large candles and write each child's age on them. Then cut out a band to fit child's head, attach candle, and decorate.

Story Time: Book

Read *The Birthday Party* by Helen Oxenbury

Circle Time: Count the Balloons

Cut balloon shapes from various colors of felt. Attach yarn to the back of each balloon. Children can count the number of balloons on the flannel board or name the colors of the balloons.

Food Experiences: Birthday Cake Toast

Use a Bread Birthday Cake cutter or a cookie cutter. Press into a slice of bread but not all the way through. Toast. Butter and sprinkle on cinnamon.

Theme Activity: Balloon Bounce

Use the same balloons from Wednesday's Theme Activity. Let the children hit the balloons into the air. Have them keep hitting the balloons without letting them hit the floor.

Friday

Sharing Time: Book

Read *Birthday Bear and the Runaway Skateboard* by Michael J. Pellowski.

Art: Balloon Party Hat

Let children make a party hat from different types of materials. Show them how to fold and staple them together or glue them. Decorate them with crayons. Blow up balloons; tape them at the knotted end and add them to the hats.

Story Time: Book

Read *Happy Birthday Oliver* by Pierre Le-Tan.

Circle Time: Song

Sing the "Happy Birthday" song. Do it several times substituting different names.

Food Experiences: Birthday Cake

Make or buy a birthday cake with all the children's names on it. If all the names won't fit, put them on a piece of tagboard, decorate it, and make it a cake decoration.

Theme Activities: Pin the Tail on the Donkey

Play the classic Pin the Tail on the Donkey game or a variation of it such as Pin the Nose on the Clown. Use tape instead of pins and don't insist that children be blindfolded.

Classroom Additions

Here are some suggestions of materials that can be placed in the learning centers in addition to your regular materials.

- Housekeeping: party hats, balloons, streamers
- Circle: flannel board, flannel birthday cake and candles, felt balloon shapes with yarn
- Books: books about birthdays
- Music: streamers, lively music
- Table Activities: file folder activities, games, puzzles, balloons of different sizes and colors
- Art: collage materials, newspapers, construction paper, tempera paint
- Puppets: happy faces drawn on balloons with a permanent marker, party hats, streamers
- Science: water, food color
- Science Activities: Let children mix small amounts of water and food coloring. Explain that like the water, the frosting used during the week will also change colors. Ask them what happens as more food coloring is added.

Teachers' Aids

File Folder Activities: Choose the skills you wish to emphasize this week. See directions on pages 5 and 6.
- Candle Number Matching
- Balloon Matching, Colors, Shapes, Numbers

Bulletin Board Ideas:
- Birthday Cake and Candles
- Balloons
- Clown
- Calendar with Birthdays marked

For Parents
- Send these tips home for parents to help enrich their child's education.
- Help your child learn his or her birthdate.
- Buy your child a balloon.
- Visit the bakery and look at the different sizes, shapes, and decorations of the cakes.
- Take a walk and hold streamers.
- Visit the library.

Bibliography

Children's Books
Asch, Frank. *Happy Birthday Moon.* Prentice Hall, 1982
Awdry Rev. W. *Happy Birthday Thomas.* Random House Inc., 1990
Bright, Robert. *Georgie and the Runaway Balloon.* Doubleday, 1983
Le-Tan, Pierre. *Happy Birthday Oliver.* Random, 1979
Oxenbury, Helen. *The Birthday Party.* Walker, 1983
Pellowski, Michael J. *Birthday Bear and the Runaway Skateboard.* Willowisp Press, Inc., 1986
Rylant, Cynthia. *Birthday Presents.* Trumpet Club, 1992

Records
Steve Millang and Greg Scelsa. *Greg and Steve Holidays and Special Times.* Youngheart Records, 1989

Patterns

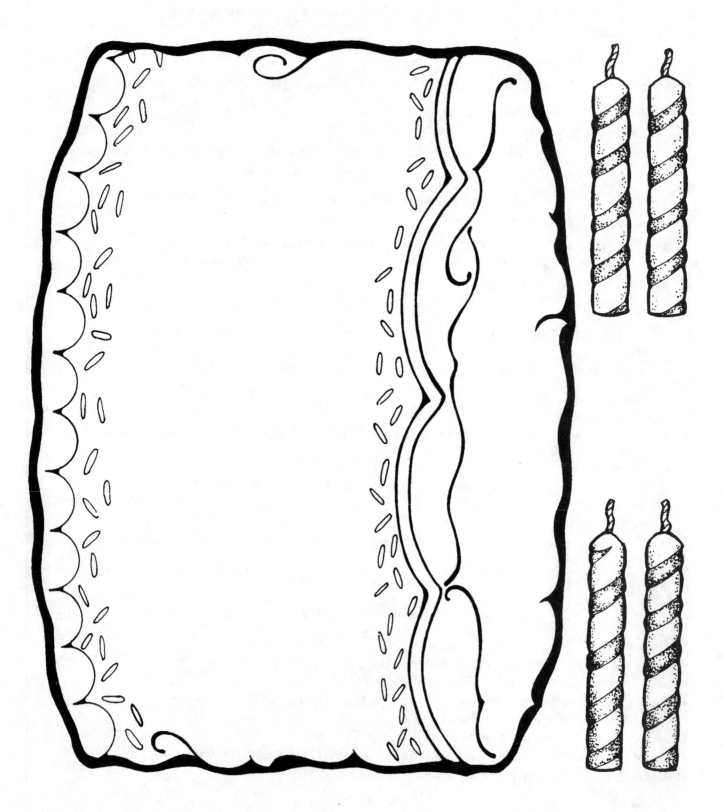

Weekly Theme: _Monsters_   Week of: _____

	Monday	Tuesday	Wednesday	Thursday	Friday
Date					
Sharing Time	Song: Down in the Sea	Song: Monsters in My Room	Song: Misbehaving Monster	Song: Old McMonster	Song: Monstery A B C's
Art	Monster Color Necklace	Monster Bag	Paper Plate Monster Face	Monster Pictures	Foot Monster
Story Time	Book: *How to Deal with Monsters*	Book: *Where the Wild Things Are*	Book: *There's a Nightmare in My Closet*	Book: *Thump, Thump, Thump*	Book: *Monster Bubbles*
Circle Time	Activity/Song: Monster Color Game	Activity/Song: Bag Monster Rag	Activity/Song: Monster Mask	Activity/Song: Boogie Man Boogie	Book: *Little Monsters*
Food Experiences	Monster Muffins	What a Face!	Monster Shakes	Monster Surprise	Monster Cookies
Theme Activities	Book: *Maybe a Monster*	Song: The Monster Song	Song: Footprints	Book: *What's Under My Bed*	Activity: Monster Hugs

Monday

Materials Needed For The Week:

yarn, grocery bags (one per child), paper plates, craft sticks, 1 gallon (3.8 liters) size self-sealing bags (one per child), English muffins, food coloring, pastry brush, old white sheet, cottage cheese, raisins, edibles etc.

Note: All songs in this lesson will be found on the record *Monsters And Monstrous Things.* See bibliography on page 220.

Sharing Time: Song
Sing "Down In The Sea."

Art: Monster Color Necklace
Have children cut out a circle from red, yellow, blue, or green construction paper. Punch a hole and attach the same color yarn that is long enough to go around the child's neck. The color word can be printed on the circle, for children to associate the color with the color name. Use at Circle Time with "Monster Color Game."

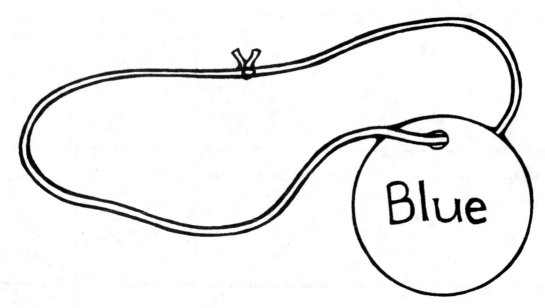

Story Time: Book
Read *How to Deal With Monsters* by Richard Powell.

Circle Time: Activity/Song
Sing and do the "Monster Color Game." Use the monster color necklace children made during art time.

Food Experiences: Monster Muffins
Give each child half an English muffin. Mix up several colors of food coloring with milk. Let children use a pastry or new paint brush to paint monster faces on the English muffins. Toast and eat.

Theme Activities: Book
Read *Maybe A Monster* by Martha Alexander.

Tuesday

Sharing Time: Song
    Sing "Monsters in My Room."

Art: Monster Bag
    Give each child a large brown grocery bag. Cut it into a vest by making a large slit and cutting arm holes. If it has writing on the outside, turn it so children can decorate the clean side. Children can design their monsters with crayons, paint, or glue on tissue paper, yarn scraps, sequins, or anything else that can be glued on. Use at Circle Time with "Bag Monster Rag."

Story Time: Book
    Read *Where the Wild Things Are* by Maurice Sendak. Talk about monsters and share with the class common fears children might have.

Circle Time: Activity/Song
    Sing "Bag Monster Rag" while wearing monster bags.

Food Experiences: What a Face!
    Give each child a scoop of cottage cheese. Provide food coloring for each child to color the cottage cheese. Give them raisins, nuts, and other edibles to make a monster face to eat.

Theme Activities: Acitivty/Song
    Sing *"The Monster Song"* sun to "The Bus Song"

The feet on the monster go
Stomp-stomp-stomp,
stomp-stomp-stomp,
stomp-stomp-stomp.
The feet on the monster go
Stomp-stomp-stomp,
All through the town.
Then hand/mouth/eyes/belly on the monster go/goes...
Clap-clap-clap-growl-growl-growl-growl/blink/blink-blink/wiggle-wiggle-wiggle.

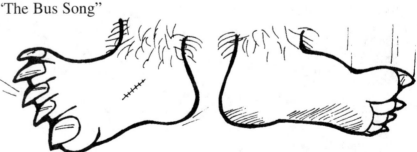

Wednesday

Sharing Time: Song
Sing "Misbehaving Monster."

Art: Paper Plate Monster Face
Children can draw monster faces on plates. Cut out circles for children's eyes. Add ears, yarn, or any other scrapes. Punch a hole on each side of plate and attach yarn to tie around children's heads. Use the masks during circle time.

Story Time: Book
Read *There's a Nightmare in My Closet* by Mercer Mayer.

Circle Time: "Monster Mask"
Before this activity, prepare for each child: a resealable bag containing one paper plate, one square, one rectangle, four triangles, and three circles. These pieces can be covered with clear contact paper and kept for future years, or label the bags and let the children take them home. (Volunteers can help with this.)

Sing "Monster Mask," then have children design their own monster face. Children like to see how many monsters they can create with these pieces. You may wish to do this as a flannel board activity, letting the children create shapes on the flannel board.

Food Experiences: Monster Shakes
Use chocolate ice cream and milk. Put in blender until mixed. Pour in cups.

Theme Activities: Song
Sing the song "Footprints." Talk about the kinds of footprints a monster might make and how children would determine it is a monster's footprints. Put monster footprints (see pattern on page 221) on the floor for children to follow.

Thursday

Sharing Time: Song

Sing **"Old *McMonster.*"** sung to "Old McDonald" (Dona Herweck)

Old McMonster had farm
E-I-E-I-0.
And on that farm he had a snake
E-I-E-I-0.
With a hiss-hiss here,
And a hiss-hiss there,
Here a hiss, there a hiss,
Everywhere a hiss-hiss,
Old McMonster had a farm
E-I-E-I-0.
Old McMonster had a farm
E-I-E-I-0.
And on that farm he had a rat/bat/spider/frog/fly..
E-I-E-I-0,
With a scurry-scurry/flutter-flutter/creep- creep/ribbit-ribbit/bzz- bzz here.

Art: Monster Picture

Children can draw or paint a monster picture. Provide construction paper, crayons, paint.

Story Time: Book

Read *Thump, Thump, Thump* by Anne Rockwell.

Circle Time: Activity/Song

Sing "Boogie Man Boogie." The paper plate monster face or monster bags made earlier in the week can be used with this song.

Food Experiences: Monster Surprise

Let each child put a slice of cheese on bread. Cut green olives in half and put them on the cheese for eyes. Slices of olives can be used for the nose and mouth. Bake and serve.

Theme Activities: Book

Read *What's Under My Bed* by James Stevenson.

Friday

Sharing Time: Song

Sing "Monstery ABC'S."

Art: Foot Monster

Trace each child's foot onto construction paper. Let the children draw a face and attach yarn for hair.

Story Time: Book

Read *Monster Bubbles* by Dennis Nolan.

Circle Time: Book

Read *Little Monsters* by Jan Pienkowski.

Food Experiences: Monster Cookies

Prepare the cookie dough in the recipe given below. You may wish to let the children help with this step. Give children monster cookie cutters or use round cookie cutters. Let them cut out the cookies and decorate with chocolate chips for eyes, raisins for a nose, and licorice for mouth.

Bake at 375° (190°C) for 8 minutes.

- 1½ (225 g) cups margarine
- 2 eggs
- 1½ cups (375 mL) sugar
- 1 tablespoon (15 mL) vanilla
- 4 cups (950 mL) flour
- 2 tablespoons (30 mL) milk
- 3 teaspoons (15 mL) baking powder
- ½ teaspoon (2 mL) salt

Cream together margarine, sugar, eggs, and vanilla until light and fluffy. Stir in milk. Sift together, flour, baking powder, and salt. Stir dry ingredients into creamed mixture until well blended. Chill one hour.

Roll out dough on lightly floured surface. Cut with cutters, decorate, and bake. Makes about 2 dozen cookies.

Theme Activities: Monster Hugs

Children can pretend to be monsters and give the other children different kinds of hugs.

Classroom Additions

Center Ideas

Here are some suggestions of materials that can be placed in the learning centers in addition to your regular materials.

- Circle: flannel monster pieces

- Book: books about monsters

- Music: records about monsters

- Table Activities: monster file folder matching

- Art: construction paper, tempera paint, and sponges for creating a monster

- Puppets: monster stick puppets

- Science: flashlight, monster stick puppets, weather monster

- Science Activities: Weather Monster-Trace the monster pattern on page 222 onto tag board. You may wish to cover the monster with clear contact paper. On a 9" (23 cm) paper plate draw a sun, cloud, sun partly behind a cloud, rain drops that will fit inside the square. Put a brass fastener in the middle of the plate and through the monster so that pictures will show inside the square. If it snows in your area, add snowflakes. The children can turn the plate until the picture matches the weather for the day.

Monster Shadows: Make a monster stick puppet using the same pattern found on the file folder activity. Trace the pattern on construction paper or tag board and cover with clear contact paper. Attach a craft stick to the back with tape. Hold a flashlight behind the stick puppet and shadow will appear on the wall.

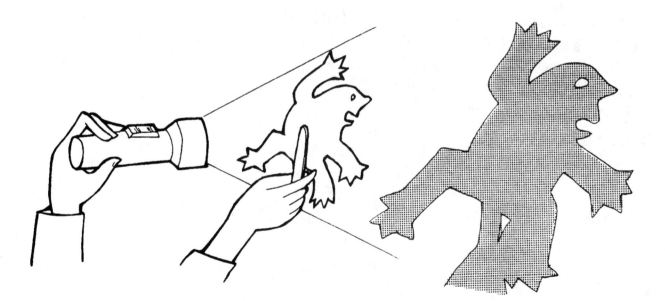

Teacher's Aids

File Folder Activities: Choose the skills you wish to emphasize this week. See directions on pages 5 and 6.

• Monsters Matching   • Monster Footprints

• Use the pattern on page 221. Trace on a sheet with a permanent marker. Color each footprint a different color with crayons. Children can throw a bean bag on a footprint and name the color.

• Shapes can be drawn in the center of each footprint. Numerals and dots can be used. Teachers can instruct a child to throw the bean bag on a certain footprint.

Bulletin Board Ideas:

• Display children's monster masks, drawings and foot monster made in art this week.

• Discuss monsters with your child. Explain that they don't have to be scary.

For Parents:

• Discuss manners.

• Make monster muffins for entire family. Let children help.

• Visit the library and check out books about monsters.

• Use a flashlight and make monster shadows on the wall.

Bibliography

Children's Books

Alexander, Martha. *Maybe a Monster.* Dial, 1979

Mayer, Mercer. *There's a Nightmare in My Closet.* Dial, 1968

Nolan, Dennis. *Monster Bubbles.* Prentice-Hall, 1976

Pienkowski, Jan. *Little Monsters.* Price/Stern/Sloan, 1986

Powell, Richard. *How to Deal With Monsters.* Watermill Press, 1990

Rockwell, Anne. *Thump, Thump, Thump.* Dutton, 1981

Sendak, Maurice. *Where the Wild Things Are.* Harper and Row, 1963

Stevenson, James. *What's Under My Bed?* Greenwillow, 1983

Record

Kathleen Patrick, Camille Core Gift, Libby Core Beardon. *Monsters and Monstrous Things.* Kimbo Education, 1986

Patterns

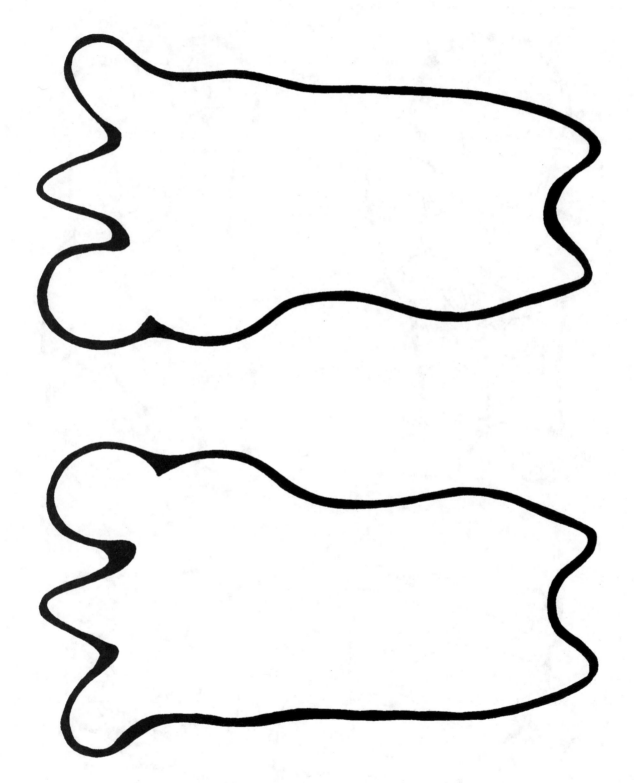

Patterns

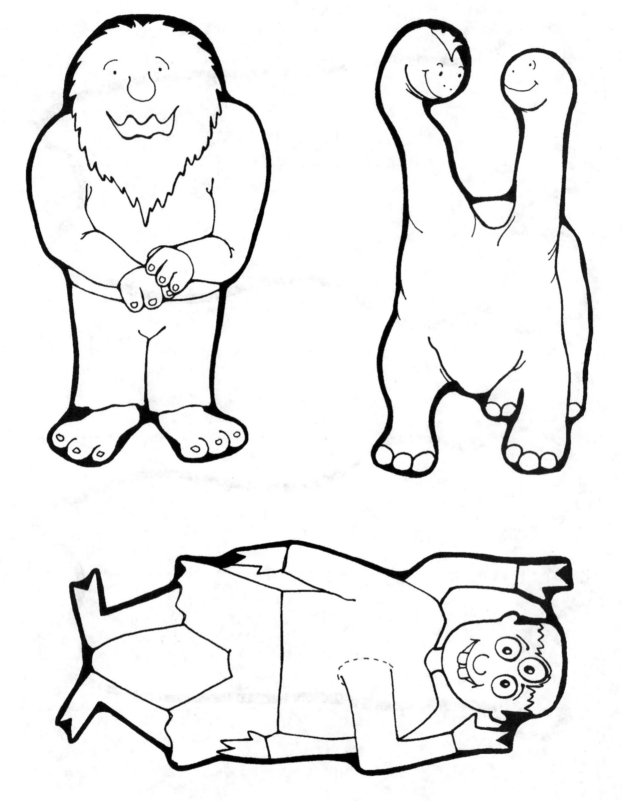

Weekly Theme: *Shadows and Groundhogs* Week of: _____

	Monday	Tuesday	Wednesday	Thursday	Friday
Date					
Sharing Time	Discuss Groundhog Facts	Discuss February Second	Book: *Groundhog's Day at the Doctor's*	Is Today a Shadow Day?	Fingerplay: What is a Shadow?
Art	Groundhog Stick Puppet	Groundhog Mask	Draw Groundhog and His Burrow	Brown Play Dough	Easel Painting
Story Time	Book: *Wake Up Groundhog*	Book: *Will Spring Be Early? Or Will Spring Be Late?*	Book: *Bear Shadow*	Book: *My Shadow and I*	Book: *Shadow*
Circle Time	Activity: Groundhog's Tunnel	Activity: Groundhog's Hole	Activity: Groundhog's Maze	Activity: Shadow Hand Play	Song/ Activity: Shadow Dancing
Food Experiences	Foods with Holes	Early Spring Vegetables	Groundhog Stew	Making Shadows	Shadow Cookies
Theme Activities	Book: *Woodchuck*	Book: *Tongue Twister How Much Wood?*	Activity: Groundhog Suprise	Song: My Shadow	Acitivty: Shadow Play

Monday

Sharing Time: Discuss Groundhog Facts

Talk to children about the groundhog. A groundhog is a furry animal that is bigger than a cat. It is also called a woodchuck. Groundhogs are vegetarians. They dig tunnels under the ground and sleep there all winter. They eat alfalfa and clover.

Art: Groundhog Stick Puppets

Let children cut out a groundhog and color it brown. (See pattern page 230.) Tape to craft stick.

Story Time: Book

Read *Wake Up Groundhog* by Carol Cohan.

Circle Time: Groundhog's Tunnel

Cut a hole in each end of a large cardboard box. Have children crawl in one end and out the other end.

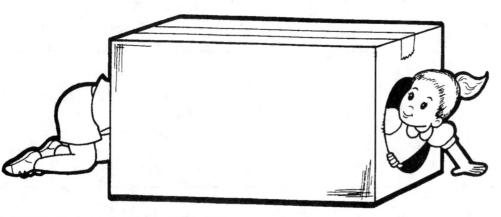

Food Experiences: Foods With Holes

Since ground hogs are known for poking out of holes, let children sample some foods with holes such as donuts, bagels, or Swiss cheese.

Theme Activities: Book

Read *Woodchuck* by Faith McNulty.

Tuesday

Sharing Time: Discuss February Second

Discuss that on February the second, it is believed that the groundhog comes out of his burrow (underground home). If the sun is shining, he sees his shadow and there will be six more weeks of winter weather. If it is cloudy, the groundhog cannot see his shadow, so he will come out and that is a sign of an early spring.

Art: Groundhog Mask

Have children color a paper plate brown and then cut out holes for the children's eyes. Cut a nose and mouth from construction paper and glue on a plate. Punch a hole on each side of the plate and attach yarn and tie around each child's head.

Story Time: Book

Read *Will Spring Be Early? Or Will Spring Be Late?* by Crockett Johnson.

Circle Time: Groundhog's Hole

Several boxes can be taped together. Leave both ends open. Holes can be cut in the top of the boxes large enough for children to poke their heads out of them.

Food Experiences: Early Spring Vegetables

Try some spring time vegetables that might be available in the produce department of a local market or at a farmer's market.

Theme Activities: How Much Wood?

Let children try this classic tongue twister.
How much wood would a woodchuck, chuck
If a woodchuck could chuck wood?
A woodchuck would chuck
All the wood he could chuck
If a woodchuck could chuck wood.

How Much Wood?

Wednesday

Sharing Time: Book

Read *Groundhog's Day at the Doctor's* by Judy Delton.

Art: Groundhog in a Burrow

Children can draw a picture of a groundhog and his burrow. Provide various art materials.

Story Time: Book

Read *Bear Shadow* by Frank Asch.

Circle Time: Groundhog Maze

Set up a maze in the classroom by using tables and chairs. Children can pretend they are groundhogs crawling through their tunnels.

Food Experiences: Groundhog Stew

- 4 lbs. (1.8 kg) beef for stew, cut in 1½" (3.75 cm) cubes

- 1 lb. (450 g) carrots, sliced

- 2½ lbs. (1.125 kg) potatoes, quartered

- ½ lb. (225 g) celery, chunks

- 1 onion, diced

In large pan, cook the beef in water until it is almost done. Add vegetables and cook until tender. Two envelopes of brown gravy mix can be added for extra flavor.

Suggestion: This could be on the menu for the meal.

Theme Activities: Groundhog Surprise

Use a cardboard box big enough that a child can sit in it. Have child get in the box and close the top flaps. Have the rest of the children recite the following poem:

Groundhog, Groundhog

Groundhog, groundhog, (Child's name can be used.)
What do you think?
Will the sun be shining,
Or cloudy today?

Use the light switches in the classroom. If the lights are on, the groundhog (child) will see his/her shadow and go back inside. If the lights are off, the groundhog (child) won't see his/her shadow and will come outside. Change it around so that the child inside wonders whether the lights will be on or off.

Thursday

Sharing Time: Is Today a Shadow Day?

Check the weather outside today and ask the children if today would be a good day to see your shadow.

Art: Brown Play Dough.

Let children play with brown play dough and make groundhogs. See the recipe on page 6.

Story Time: Book

Read *My Shadow and I* by Patty Wolcott.

Circle Time: Shadow Hand Play

Use an overhead projector or film projector. Experiment on how to hold your hands to make different kinds of animals. Then hold your hands in front of the light projector and project the shapes onto the wall or a screen. See if children can guess what the shapes are supposed to be. The library may also have some books on how to do this.

Food Experiences: Making Shadows

Using chocolate chips and butterscotch or peanut butter chips let children create shadows. Using the light colored chips have them make a small shape, and next to it use the darker chips to create its shadow. The shadow may be larger than the original shape.

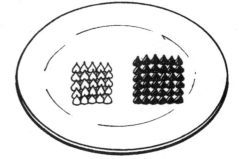

Theme Activities: Song

Sing "My Shadow" from the record *Kids In Motion*.

Friday

Sharing Time: Finger Play

"What Is A Shadow"

If I walk, my shadow walks. *(Use first two fingers, in walking motion.)*

If I run, my shadow runs. *(Same fingers in running motion.)*

And when I stand still, as you can see *(Same fingers, standing still.)*

My shadow stands beside me. *(Use first two fingers on other hand and stand beside the first two fingers.)*

When I hop, my shadow hops. *(First two fingers, hopping.)*

When I jump, my shadow jumps. *(Same fingers, jump.)*

And when I sit still, as you can see, *(Same fingers, bend at knuckles to sit.)*

My shadow sits beside of me. *(Use as before both set of fingers sitting beside each other.)*

Art: Easel Painting

Easel paint with white tempera paint on black paper to create a shadow like effect.

Story Time: Book

Read *Shadow* by Gomi.

Circle Time: Song/Activity

Sing "Shadow Dancing" from the record *Kids In Motion*.

Food Experiences: Shadow Cookies

Give children two different types of cookie dough. (Refrigerated sugar and chocolate chips cookie dough would work well.) Let them make two balls and push them into each other. Then have them flatten the cookies and bake them to create a shadow cookie.

Theme Activities: Shadow Play

Make sure children do this in a place where they can see each other's shadows. Have them try to step on each other's shadows.

Classroom Additions

Here are some suggestions of materials that can be placed in the learning centers in addition to your regular materials.

- Circle: flannel board, flannel pieces with shadows
- Books: books about groundhogs
- Table Activities: file folder activities listed
- Puppets: groundhog stick puppets, groundhog masks (Make the same as the art activities.)
- Science: flashlight, film strip projector, groundhog puppets
- Science Activities

   Provide a pan of dirt (use a sand and water table if available) for children to dig groundhog tunnels.

   Under adult supervision let children put their hands in front of a film projector to make shadows on the wall.

Teachers' Aids
- File Folder Activities: Choose the skills you wish to emphasize this week. See directions on pages 5 and 6.
- Flashlight Matching   • Groundhog and Groundhog Hole Number Matching

Bulletin Board Ideas:
- Groundhogs and Their Holes   • Sun
- Groundhog Shadows   • Cloud

For Parents
- Play shadow tag with your child.
- Talk about groundhogs with your child.
- With your child investigate to find out if the groundhog saw his shadow on February 2nd.
- Look for brown items around the house and yard.
- Let your child dig in the dirt.
- Discuss the differences between burrows where groundhogs live and houses where people live.

Bibliography

Children's Books
Asch, Frank. *Bear Shadow.* Prentice Hall, 1985
Cohan, Carol. *Wake Up Groundhog.* Crown, 1975
Delton, Judy. *Groundhog's Day at the Doctor.* Parents', 1981
Gomi. *Shadow.* Heian, 1981
Johnson, Crockett. *Will Spring Be Early? Or Will Spring Be Late?* Harper and Row, 1959
McNulty, Faith. *Woodchuck.* Harper, 1974
Wolcott, Patty. *My Shadow and I.* Addison-Wesley, 1975

Record
Steve Millang and Greg Scelsa. *Kids In Motion.* Youngheart Records, 1987

Patterns

Patterns

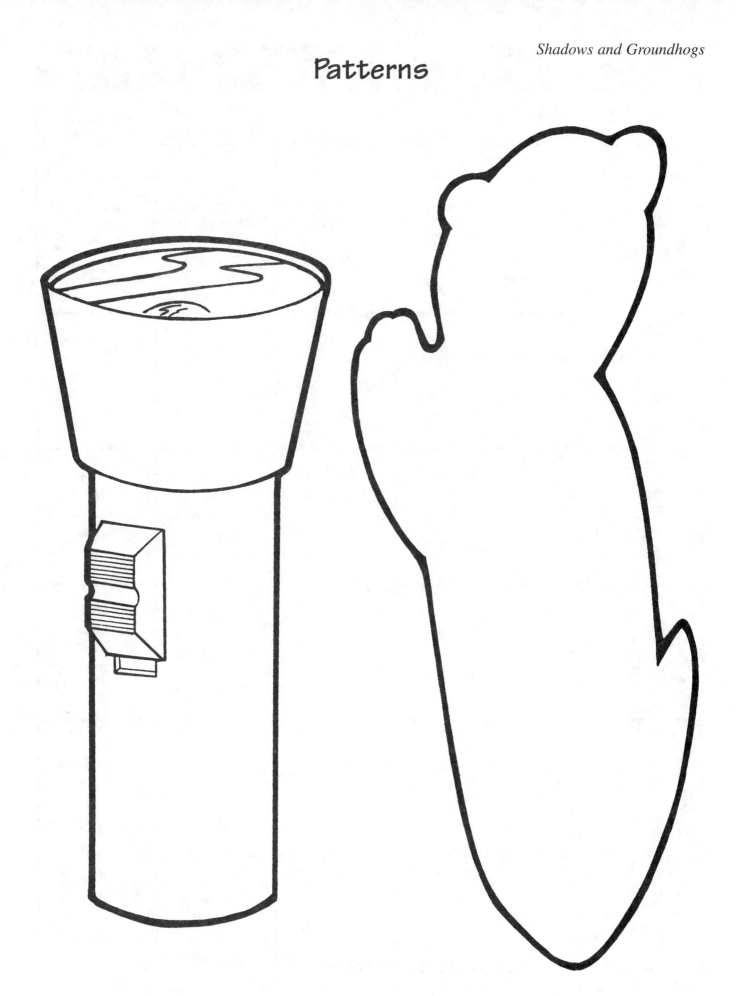

Weekly Theme: _Valentines_   Week of: _____

	Monday	Tuesday	Wednesday	Thursday	Friday
Date					
Sharing Time	Discuss: People You Love	Fingerplay: Five Little Valentines	Poem: To My Valentine	Fingerplay: Valentine's Good Morning	Song: Love Somebody, Yes I Do
Art	Valentine Necklace	Valentine Holder	Smelly Valentines	Valentine Fans	Valentine Puzzle
Story Time	Book: _The Valentine Bears_	Book: _Teeny Witch and the Perfect Valentine_	Book: _Valentine Cat_	Book: _Love is a Special Way of Feeling_	Book: _One Zillion Valentines_
Circle Time	Positional Activity: Hearts and Circles	Discuss Feelings	Activity: Exercise for Your Heart	Flannel Activity: Five Little Valentines	Activity: Pass Out Valentines
Food Experiences	Tomato Juice	Valentine Punch	Cherry Gelatin	Valentine Cookies	Cranberry Juice
Theme Activities	Activity: Fish for Hearts	Poem: Valentine for You	Book: _Be My Valentine_	Poem: How Much Do You Love Me?	Activity: Teacher Pass Out Valentines and Give Valentine Hugs

Monday

Materials Needed For The Week:
heart shaped paper lace doilies, perfume, cotton balls, plastic yarn needles, yarn, tomato juice, paper plates, fruit punch, ginger ale, cherry gelatin, heart-shaped cookie cutter, white frosting, red candies or sugar

Sharing Time: Discuss People You Love
Let children tell you who they love. Don't forget to tell the children who you, the teacher, love.

Art: Valentine Necklace
Use the clay dough recipe below and let children create their own necklaces.

Clay Dough
- 3 cups (700 mL) flour
- 1 cup (250 mL) salt
- 1 cup (250 mL) water
- ½ cup (125 mL) vegetable oil
- red food coloring (optional)

Mix flour and salt together in a large bowl. Add water, oil, and food coloring slowly. Knead the dough thoroughly. Make into balls. Give each child a ball. They can flatten it and use heart cookie cutters to cut out a heart. Punch hole in the top with a pencil or straw. Child's name can be etched on the heart with a pencil. Then they can be baked at 225°F (110°C) for 2 hours. Be sure to turn them several times while baking. This prevents them from curling. They should also be put in a warm place to dry. Turn them over each day. When dry, attach yarn and they are ready to wear.

Story Time: Book
Read *The Valentine Bears* by Eve Bunting.

Circle Time: Positional Activity
Play Hearts and Circles. Give each child a heart. When a child's name is called, he/she is instructed to put his/her heart on the circle, below the circle, or above the circle.

Food Experiences: Tomato Juice
Pour chilled canned tomato juice in cups. Help children identify the color red.

Theme Activities: Fish For Hearts
Use a previously made fishing pole. (See instructions on page 7.) Cut out three sizes of hearts, one each from red, pink, and purple paper. Instruct a child to fish for a certain size and color.

Valentines

Sharing Time: Finger Play

   "Five Little Valentines"

   One little valentine said, "I love you." *(Hold up 1 finger.)*
   Tommy made another; then there were two. *(Hold up 2 fingers.)*
   Two little valentines, one for me;
   Mary made another; then there were three. *(Holdup 3 fingers.)*
   Three little valentines said,
   "We need one more."
   Johnny made another; then there were four. *(Hold up 4 fingers.)*
   Four little valentines, one more to arrive;
   Susan made another; then there were five. *(Hold up 5 fingers.)*
   Five little valentines, all ready to say, *(Keep up 5 fingers.)*
   "Be my valentine on this happy day."

Art: Valentine Holder

   Use two paper plates; cut one in half. Staple the half piece onto the bottom of the whole paper plate.
   Children can decorate them with hearts cut from construction paper or they can draw and color
   hearts on them. Punch a hole in the top of the whole paper plate and attach a piece of yarn for a
   hanger.

Story Time: Book

   Read *Teeny Witch and the Perfect Valentine* by Liz Matthews.

Circle Time: Discuss Feelings

   Discuss different feelings. Let children tell you how they feel when they are happy, sad, mad, etc.

Food Experiences: Valentine Punch

   Mix together fruit punch and ginger ale. Serve for an afternoon refreshment.

Theme Activities: Poem

   "Valentine for You"
   A valentine for you,
   A valentine for you,
   A valentine, a valentine,
   A valentine for you.

Wednesday

Sharing Time: Poem

"*To My Valentine*"
If apples were pears,
And peaches were plums,
And the rose had a different name;
If tigers were bears,
And fingers were thumbs
I'd love you just the same!

Art: Smelly Valentines
Have children sew two paper lace hearts together with yarn and plastic yarn needles. Leave a small opening to stuff with cotton balls that have been sprayed with perfume. Finish sewing and tie the ends together into a bow. Punch a hole at the top and attach yarn so it can be hung up. "Happy Valentine's Day" can be written on it with a fine tip permanent marker.

Story Time: Book
Read *Valentine Cat* by Clyde Robert Bulla.

Circle Time: Exercise for Your Heart
Do some exercises that are good for the heart. Touching toes, Running in place, and sit ups can be done. Tell children that exercising is good for your heart.

Food Experiences: Cherry Gelatin
Follow the directions on package for cherry gelatin. As children eat it, point out that it is the color red.

Theme Activities: Book
Read *Be My Valentine* by Charles M. Schulz

Thursday

Sharing Time: Finger Play

"Valentine's Good Morning" (Traditional)

Good morning to you, Valentine, *(Point to a child.)*
Curl your locks as I do mine; *(Point to your hair.)*
Two before, and three behind. *(Hold 2 fingers up in front of shoulders for 2. Hold 3 fingers behind shoulder for 3.)*
Good morning to you, Valentine. *(Point to a child.)*

Art: Valentine Fans

Have children cut out a heart from colored tagboard. Have them decorate it. Attach a craft stick to each to create a valentine fan.

Story Time: Book

Read *Love is a Special Way of Feeling* by Joan Walsh Anglund. Let children share how they feel when they know someone loves them.

Circle Time: Flannel Activity

Make five flannel hearts using the patterns on page 239. Use the "Five Little Valentines" finger play from Tuesday's Sharing Time. Put a valentine on the board when the story increases in number.

Food Experiences: Valentine Cookies

Give children heart shaped cookies or prepare dough and let them use heart shaped cookie cutters or cut around using a pattern. Decorate the cookies using red candies or red sugar and white frosting.

Theme Activities: Poem

"How Much Do You Love Me?" (Traditional)

How much do you love me?
A bushel and a peck and a hug around the neck,
That's how much I love you!

Let children pantomime a kiss and a hug as they say the poem.

Friday

Sharing Time: Song

> ***"Love Somebody, Yes I Do"*** (Folk Song)
>
> Love somebody, yes I do,
> Love somebody, yes I do,
> Love somebody, yes I do,
> Love somebody, but I won't tell who.
> *(Continue with these additional verses)*
> Love my Daddy, yes, I do...
> Love my Mommy, yes, I do...
> Love my Grandma, yes, I do ...
> Love my Grandpa, yes, I do ...

Art: Valentine Puzzle

Cut a large heart or other valentine shape out of tagboard. Use one of the patterns on pages 239-240. Red or pink tagboard will add a special touch. Make one for each child and store in plastic bags with children's names on them. Cut up the valentine into several large pieces, so children can put it together again. These can be stored in plastic bags with children's names on them.

Story Time: Book

Read *One Zillion Valentines* by Model.

Circle Time: Pass Out Valentines

Let children pass out valentine cards. Teach them this song to the tune of "Skip To My Lou" to sing as they pass out cards.

Pass, pass, pass out cards,
Pass, pass, pass out cards,
Pass, pass, pass out cards
Celebrating Valentine's.

Food Experiences: Cranberry Juice

Chill and serve some cranberry juice. Let the children tell you what color it is.

Theme Activities: Teacher Gives Valentine Cards

Teacher can pass out valentine cards and say the poem from Tuesday. If you wish give a special valentine hug to each child.

Classroom Additions

Here are some suggestions of materials that can be placed in the learning centers in addition to your regular materials.

- Housekeeping: child's medical kit, large heart shapes cut from red construction paper and covered with clear contact paper to be used as place mats
- Circle: flannel board, assortment of felt hearts
- Books: books about valentines and the heart
- Table Activities: file folder activities listed
- Puppets: valentine stick puppets (See patterns on page 239. Draw on facial features and attach craft stick.)
- Science: pictures of the human heart
- Science Activities

    Have children feel each other's heart before and after running.

    Have a nurse visit the classroom to discuss the heart and take blood pressures.

Teachers' Aids

File Folder Activities: Choose the skills you wish to emphasize this week. See directions on pages 5 and 6.

- Heart Wallpaper Matching   • Heart Shape Matching
- Heart Puzzles

Bulletin Board Ideas:

- Hearts   • Arrows   •   Cupid

For Parents

- Discuss the meaning of Valentine's Day with your child.
- Talk about who you love.
- Help your child make valentines.
- Discuss your heart and the benefits of exercise.
- Exercise with your child.
- Take your child to the library.
- Bake a valentine cake with your child.

Bibliography

Children's Books

Anglund, Joan Walsh. *Love is a Special Way of Feeling.* Harcourt, Brace and World Inc, 1969

Bulla, Clyde Robert. *Valentine Cat.* Thomas Y. Crowell, 1959

Bunting, Eve. *The Valentine Bears.* Clarion Books, 1983

Matthews, Liz. *Teeny Witch and the Perfect Valentine.* Troll, 1991

S. *One Zillion Valentines.* The Trumpet Club, 1981

M. Charles. *Be My Valentine.* Random House, 1976

Patterns

Patterns

Weekly Theme: _Time_   Week of: _____

	Monday	Tuesday	Wednesday	Thursday	Friday
Date					
Sharing Time	Poem: Starlight Star Bright	Hours in a Day	Poem: A Diller a Dollar	Song: Good Morning to You	Poem: Hickory Dickory Dock
Art	Easel Paint	Play Dough	Digital Clock	Moon Puppet	Paper Plate Clock
Story Time	Flannel Story: A Starry Night	Book: *The Year at Maple Hill Farm*	Book: *The Grouchy Ladybug*	Book: *Goodnight Moon*	Book: *Clocks and How They Go*
Circle Time	Activity: Fly Around Space	Clocks	Telling Time	Fingerplay: Goodnight	Poem: The Big Clock
Food Experiences	Orbit Ring	Timing It	Three Minute Eggs	Star Toast and Orange Moon Slices	Clock Pancakes with Syrup Hands
Theme Activities	The Moon	A Year	How Long Does It Take?	Poem: One Misty Moisty Morning	Poem: The Clocks

Monday

Materials Needed For The Week:

brass fasteners, clock-digital and sweep-second hand, calendar, kitchen timer, pancake mix, syrup, star cookie cutter, pineapple rings, cherries

Sharing Time: Poem

"Starlight, Star Bright" (Traditional)

Starlight, star bright,
First star I see tonight,
Wish I may, wish I might
Have the wish I wish tonight.

After you say the poem, talk about the night time. Let children tell you how long they think nighttime is. Place a star on flannel board and let the children make a wish.

Art: Easel Painting

Let children create their own picture of night time. Provide dark blue construction paper and yellow tempera paint.

Story Time: Flannel Story

(See patterns on page 250.)

"A Starry Night" (Anonymous)

One summer evening Harry and his little brother Paul sat down on the grass to rest. It began to grow dark. One by one the stars came out. At last it was quite dark. The sky was dotted with bright stars.

Paul watched the stars quietly for some time; then he said, "Where are the stars in the daytime?"

"They are shining just as they are now," said Harry.

"Are they always shining, day and night?" asked Paul.

"Yes, they are like the sun; they shine all the time"

"Then why can't we see them during the day?"

"Because the sun gives much more light than the stars," said Harry. "You know that if you turn the porch light on in the daytime you can hardly see it. When we first sat down here, we could not see even one star. But then it grew dark enough to see the brightest stars. As it grew darker still, we saw other stars. If something should happen at noon to make it quite dark, then we could see the stars."

Monday (cont.)

"How strange that seemsi" said Paul. "I did not know before that the stars were up in the sky in the daytime."

"Did you know that you can tell which way is north by looking at the stars?" said Harry.

"How is that done?" asked Paul.

"All you have to do is find the North Star," said Harry.

"Look where I am pointing. Do you see seven stars in a group?"

"They seem to make the shape of a dipper. Four of these stars make a square. That is the bowl of the Dipper. The other three bend away and make the handle. Two stars at the front of the bowl are called the Pointers. They point toward the North Star."

"The Dipper moves about, but these two stars always point to the North Star. People long ago thought that these two stars made the shape of a bear, so they called this group the Big Bear."

"There is a little Bear too. It looks like a little dipper to us. The North Star is at the end of its handle."

"Why should I know where the North Star is?" asked Paul.

"Because if you're lost in the woods at night, that is the only star that can tell you the direction. Then if you know where north is, you can find your way home again."

"It is fun to lie and study the stars," said Paul.

"Yes," said Harry. "And some people study about the sun and stars and outer space all their lives. These people are called astronomers. It is very exciting to study about the sun and stars and outer space because there is so much to learn."

Circle Time: A Time In Space

Have children pretend they are flying around space in a spaceship. How long does it take them to get from planet to planet? To the moon?

Food Experiences: Orbit Ring

Using a pineapple ring and a cherry, let each child put the cherry in the pineapple slice and make an orbit ring.

Theme Activities: The Moon

How long does it take for the moon to change from a new moon to a full moon and back again? The answer is 29 1/2 days. Let children begin to understand how long a time this is. Use a blank calendar (see page 249) and a moon face. Each day let a different child mark the calendar with a moon face. At the end of 30 days count how long it took.

Tuesday

Sharing Time: Hours In A Day

Ask how many hours are in a day. Explain that 24 hours make a day, and that 7 days make a week, etc. Use both clocks and calendars to explain.

Art: Play Dough

Provide play dough, a number of cookie cutters, and plastic knives, and let the children be creative and try to make clocks. See recipe for play dough on page 6.

Story Time: Book

Read *The Year at Maple Hill Farm* by Alice and Martin Provenson. Talk about how the time passes and how the seasons show this happening.

Circle Time: Clocks

Bring in different types of clocks. Listen for the sounds they make. Let children imitate the sounds.

Food Experiences: Timing It

Find a simple recipe to follow that requires monitoring the time. This could include the time needed to cool, to set, to bake, or to freeze. Use a kitchen timer to keep track of the time.

Theme Activities: A Year

How long is a year? Show children a calendar and explain that each page is equal to a month. Talk about the seasons of the year, Summer, Fall, Winter, and Spring. Ask them which season they are in now. What is the weather like? What happens during each season? Does anyone know when their birthday is? As you look at the calendar, have the children with birthdays in the month you are showing stand and tell the others which day is their birthday. A blank calendar is found on page 249.

month

Wednesday

Sharing Time: Poem

> *"A Diller, a Dollar"*
> A diller, a dollar
> A ten o'clock scholar,
> What makes you come so soon?
> You used to come at 9 o'clock,
> But now you come at noon.

Talk about being on time to school and how important it is to be on time. Ask children if they know what time school begins. Show them on a clock both the starting and ending times.

Art: Digital Clock

Use the patterns provided on pages 252-253. Reproduce them onto index paper. Cut the slits in the clock. Color the clocks and let the children thread the numbers through to show the time.

Story Time: Book

Read *The Grouchy Ladybug* by Eric Carle.

Circle Time: Telling Time

Use the digital clocks that the children have made in art. On a flannel board or chalkboard, show them the times the grouchy lady bug wanted to eat, and let them move their clocks to those times.

Food Experiences: Three Minute Eggs

Let children boil an egg for three minutes and enjoy eating it. Be sure and use a timer.

Theme Activities: How Long Does it Take?

Ask the children how long they think it takes to do certain tasks such as buttoning a jacket, picking up their crayons, and getting in line. Then time them and share the results.

Thursday

Sharing Time: Song

"Good Morning To You" (Traditional)
Good morning to you, good morning to you,
Good morning everybody, good morning to you.

Discuss night and day with the children.

Art: Moon Puppet
Make a moon puppet. Cut a moon out of construction paper and attach a craft stick. Let children choose if they want a full, half, or quarter moon. See patterns on page 251.

Story Time: Book
Read *Goodnight Moon* by Margaret Wise Brown.

Circle Time: Finger Play

"Good Night"
Two little hands go clap, clap, clap. *(Clap hands.)*
Two little arms lie in my lap. *(Lay arms in lap.)*
Two little feet go bump, bump, bump. *(Bump feet.)*
Two little legs give one big jump. *(Jump one time.)*
Two little eyes are shut up tight. *(Shut eyes.)*
One little voice whispers soft, "Good night." *(Whisper good night.)*

Food Experiences: Star Toast and Orange Moon slices
Toast the bread and cut with a star cookie cutter and toast. Serve with orange slices.

Theme Activities: Poem

"One Misty Moisty Morning" (Mother Goose)
One misty moisty morning,
When cloudy was the weather,
I chanced to meet an old man,
Clothed all in leather.
He began to compliment
And I began to grin.
How do you do? And how do you do?
And how do you do again?

Friday

Sharing Time: Finger Play

"Hickory Dickory Dock" (Nursery Rhyme)

Hickory dickory dock.
The mouse ran up the clock. *(Use first 2 fingers, run upwards.)*
The clock struck one. *(Hold up 1 finger.)*
The mouse ran down. *(Use first 2 fingers, run back down.)*
Hickory dickory dock.

Discuss time with the children.

Art: Paper Plate Clock

Use 9 inch (23 cm) paper plates to make clocks.
Use tagboard to make hands. Attach with brass
fasteners.

Story Time: Book

Read *Clocks and How They Go* by Gail Gibbons.

Circle Time: Poem

"The Big Clock"

Slowly ticks the big clock;
Tick-tock, tick-tock!
But the cuckoo clock ticks double-quick;
Tick-a-tock-a, tick-a-tock-a,
Tick-a-tock-a, tick!

Food Experiences: Clock Pancakes With Syrup Hands

Use a box of pancake mix. Follow the directions on
box. Pour on syrup in the 9 o'clock position.

Theme Activities: Poem

"The Clocks" (Mother Goose)

There's a neat little clock,—
In the schoolroom it stands,—
And it points to the time
With its two little hands.
And may we, like the clock,
Keep a face so clean and bright,
With hands ever ready
a face so clean and bright,
With hands ever ready
To do what is right.

Classroom Additions

Here are some suggestions of materials that can be placed in the learning centers in addition to your regular materials.

- Housekeeping: clock, watches, telling time clock, rain coats, umbrellas
- Circle: calendar
- Books: books about space, time, weather
- Table Activities: file folder activities listed
- Blocks: toy spaceships, mobile of the solar system
- Science: globe, clock, watches
- Science Activities: Using a milk carton make a house by cutting out windows. Use a flashlight to shine through it. Ask the children what time of day it is when the light is shining through the milk carton house.

Teachers' Aids
- File Folder Activities: Choose the skills you wish to emphasize this week. See directions on pages 5 and 6.
- Sun and Moon   • Clock Faces

Bulletin Board Ideas:

- Moon   • Sun   • Stars   • Spaceship   • Clocks (both types)

For Parents
- Discuss time with your child.
- Discuss what we do in the daytime/night time.
- Go star gazing at night.
- Check out books at the library on these topics.
- Have your child look at the moon every night this week.
- Talk about the shape of the moon each night.
- Talk about how the moon changes shape.
- Make a moon chart with your child.

Bibliography

Children's Books
Brown, Margaret Wise. *Goodnight Moon.* Harper and Row, 1974
Carle, Eric. *The Grouchy Ladybug.* Harper and Row, 1986
Gibbons, Gail. *Clocks And How They Go.* Crowell, 19799
Provenson, Alice and Martin. *A Year At Maple Hill Farm.* Aladdin, 1988

Patterns

month

Patterns

Patterns

Patterns

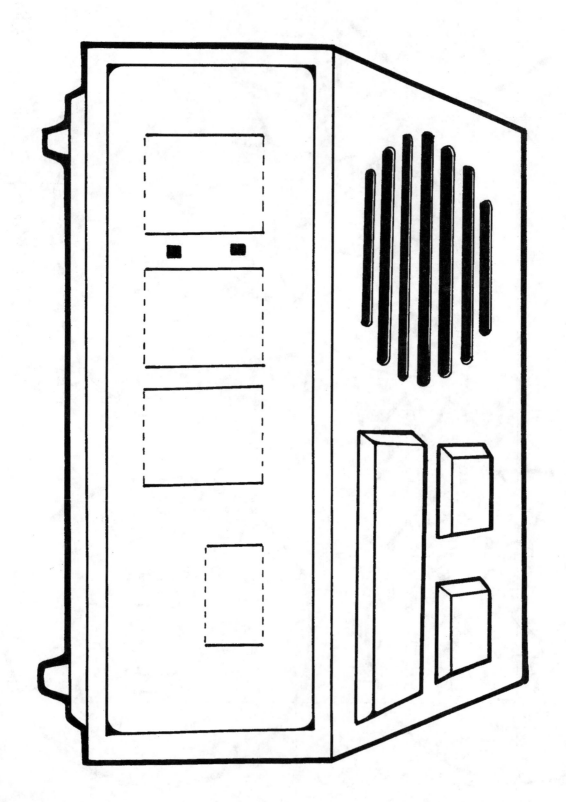

Patterns

1	0	0	7		6
2	1	1	8	AM	7
3	2	2	9	PM	8
4	3	3	10	AM	9
5	4	4	11	PM	
6	5	5	12	0	

Weekly Theme: _Dinosaurs_   Week of: _____

	Monday	Tuesday	Wednesday	Thursday	Friday
Date					
Sharing Time	Discuss Dinosaurs Introduce Word: Extinct	Introduce Word: Paleontologist	Discuss Dinosaur Facts	Song/ Activity: The Dinosaur Bop	Spatial Concepts: Up And Down
Art	Dinosaur Eggs	Dinosaur Rubbing	Dinosaur Finger Painting	Paper Bag Dinosaur	Play Dough Dinosaurs
Story Time	Book: _The Day of the Dinosaur_	Book: _Danny and the Dinosaur_	Book: _If the Dinosaurs Came Back_	Book: _King of the Dinosaurs Tyrannosaurus Rex_	Song: Dinosaurs
Circle Time	Activity: Dinosaur Bone Hunt	Song: Tyrannosaurus Rex	Activity: Pre-Historic Parade	Activity: Dinosaur May I?	Song: Dinosaur Hunt
Food Experiences	Dinosaur Toast	Dinosaur Bones	Deviled Dinosaur Eggs	Dinosaur Dip	Celery and Smoked Sausage
Theme Activities	Song/ Activity: Dinosaur, Dinosaur	Activity: Dinosaur Fishing	Activity: Dinosaur Bean Bag Toss	Song: Triceratops	Dinosaur Hunt

Monday

Materials Needed For The Week:
chicken or turkey bones that have been boiled and dried, plaster of Paris, various sizes and kinds of dinosaurs (plastic, stuffed, inflated, stickers, cookie cutters), canned biscuits (one per child), eggs, pistachio pudding, fresh celery, smoked sausage, and bread for food experiences

Sharing Time: Discuss Dinosaurs; New Word: Extinct
Introduce the word "extinct." Ask children if they know what it means. Explain that it is something that no longer exists. Using a stuffed or inflatable dinosaur, work on the spatial concepts of "front" and "back." Have a child stand or sit in front of the dinosaur, then in back of the dinosaur.

Art: Dinosaur Eggs
Let children cut out dinosaur egg shapes and decorate them to put on the bulletin board display.

As a group project, let all children help create a papier-mâché dinosaur egg. Use the same recipe that was used in the Snowmen Theme week (page 184). Wrap the paper all around the balloon until it's completely covered. When dry it can be cut as though it has been cracked open. A dinosaur can be placed inside. This could become a guessing game. You can put a dinosaur inside and the children can guess which dinosaur is inside.

Story Time: Book
Read *The Day of the Dinosaur* by Stan and Jan Berenstain.

Circle Time: Dinosaur Bone Hunt
Cut out dinosaur bones from cardboard and hide bones around the room. See pattern on page 261. Let children pretend they are paleontologists.

Food Experiences: Dinosaur Toast
Toast wheat bread. Use dinosaur cookie cutters to cut bread into dinosaur shapes.

Theme Activities: Song
Sing the song "Dinosaur, Dinosaur" from the record *Dynamic Dinosaurs.*

Tuesday

Sharing Time: New Word: Paleontologist

Introduce the word "paleontologist," which refers to a person who hunts and digs up fossils. Ask the children when they acted as a paleontologist (on Monday during circle time).

With the same dinosaur you used during Monday's sharing time, work on the spatial concepts of "on" and "off." Have a child put his/her hands on the dinosaur and then off.

Art: Dinosaur Rubbing

Using one pattern of a dinosaur on pages 262-263, make a template out of a plastic coffee can lid and cut out the shape. Put the dinosaur under a piece of paper. Peel the paper off of old crayons. Lay the crayons flat and rub over the pattern.

Story Time: Book

Read *Danny and the Dinosaur* by Sid Hoff.

Circle Time: Song

Sing "Tyrannosaurus Rex" from the record *Dynamic Dinosaurs.*

Food Experiences: Dinosaur Bones

Make soft pretzel dough and let each child shape a bone. Bake, then eat. Or use canned biscuits which can also be rolled into dinosaur-shaped bones. Allow one biscuit per child.

Theme Activities: Dinosaur Fishing

Cut out colored eggs from construction paper. You can attach small dinosaur stickers. Attach small paper clips. Use dowel rods that have an attached string with a magnet on the end for fishing pole. (See directions on page 7.)

256

Wednesday

Sharing Time: Dinosaur Facts/Above And Below

Talk about dinosaur facts, such as size, diet, and distinctive features. Using the same stuffed or inflatable dinosaur from Monday and work on the spatial concepts. A child can put hands above the dinosaur and then below.

Art: Dinosaur Finger Painting

Cut dinosaur shapes out of finger paint paper, and put a spoonful of green and a spoonful of brown on each shape. Let children finger paint with the mixture and then hang the dinosaurs from the ceiling.

Story Time: Book

Read *If the Dinosaurs Came Back* by Bernard Most.

Circle Time: Pre-Historic Parade: Play different types of instrumental music and let the children pretend to be different types of dinosaurs stomping around the room. As the "dinosaurs" rest, work on the concept of "big." Measure the length of different "dinosaurs" using a piece of rope or yarn.

Food Experiences: Deviled Dinosaur Eggs

Make them the same as you would regular deviled eggs. Explain to the children that dinosaurs laid eggs.

Theme Activities: Dinosaur Bean Bag Toss/Balancing Skills

Using some of the patterns on pages 262-263 to decorate boxes with different dinosaurs. Have the children toss bean bags into them. You may wish to assign points to different dinosaurs and make the toss more challenging. Use a balance beam or a strip of masking tape on the floor. Have children pretend they are walking on a dinosaur's back.

Thursday

Sharing Time: Song/Left And Right

Sing "The Dinosaur Bop" from the record *Dynamic Dinosaurs*.

Using the same stuffed or inflatable dinosaur from Monday work on the spatial concepts of "left" and "right." Have a child stand to the left of the dinosaur and then to the right.

Art: Paper Bag Dinosaur

Trace simple outlines of a dinosaur on brown paper bags, one per child, and have children cut them out. (See patterns on pages 262-263.) Children can decorate their dinosaurs as they wish. Staple around the edges leaving an opening. Have children stuff newspaper into the dinosaur and staple the opening.

Story Time: Book

Read *King of the Dinosaurs Tyrannosaurus Rex* by Michael Berenstain.

Circle Time: Dinosaur May I?

Play this game like "Mother May I?' The teacher is the dinosaur; and, as children ask if they may take steps, the dinosaur allows them to. Let them take dinosaur-type steps such as a Tyrannosaurus Hop or Triceratop's Skip.

Food Experiences: Dinosaur Dip

Mix instant pistachio pudding mix according to the directions on the package. Cut fruit into bite size pieces. Dip fruit and marshmallows into pudding and use as a dip.

Theme Activities: Song

Sing "Triceratops" from the record *Dynamic Dinosaurs*.

Friday

Sharing Time: Up And Down

Using the same stuffed or inflatable dinosaur from Monday, work on the spatial concepts of "up" and "down." A child can hold the dinosaur up in the air and then lay it down on the floor.

Art: Play Dough Dinosaurs

Using the play dough recipe on page 6 let children make dinosaurs out of play dough. Add food coloring to the play dough if you wish to give it different colors for each dinosaur.

Story Time: Song

Listen to the song "Dinosaurs" from the record *Monsters and Monstrous Things.*

Circle Time: Song

Sing "Dinosaur Hunt" from the record *Dynamic Dinosaurs.*

Food Experiences: Celery And Smoked Sausage

Let children taste both celery and smoked sausage. Discuss meat and plant eaters and that some dinosaurs ate meat and others didn't. Ask children what type of eaters they would be considered.

Theme Activities: Dinosaur Hunt

Have children go on a dinosaur hunt in the classroom. Using the patterns on pages 262-263, prepare several different dinosaurs. Let children hunt with a partner or in small groups to try to find one of each type of dinosaur you have hidden for them.

Classroom Additions

Here are some suggestions of materials that can be placed in the learning centers in addition to your regular materials:

• Housekeeping: stuffed dinosaurs
• Circle: flannel dinosaurs
• Book: books on dinosaurs
• Music: records about dinosaurs
• Table Activities: dinosaur puzzles (These can be purchased at local school supply stores.)
• Block Area: inflated dinosaur, plastic dinosaurs
• Art: sponges, brown and green tempera paint, construction paper, dinosaur stencils.
• Puppet Area: dinosaur puppets, plastic dinosaurs
• Science: fossils, skeleton of a dinosaur (This can be purchased at local school supply store.)
• Science Activities
  Display a lizard.
  Make a dinosaur using clay and turkey or chicken bones. Bones need to be boiled clean and air dried.
  Dinosaur Fossils: Mix up plaster of Paris. Let children use plastic dinosaurs to make an imprint in the plaster. Let dry.
  Dinosaur Hunt: Bury small plastic dinosaurs in the sand table. Let children go on a dinosaur hunt.

Teachers Aids

• Dinosaur Puzzles: Using the patterns on pages 262-263 draw dinosaurs on construction paper and cut out. Cut dinosaurs in half and use dots on one side and numerals on the other. The children can match the numerals to the dots.
  Bulletin Board Ideas:
• Create a pre-historic scene with dinosaurs, ferns, grass, and children's dinosaur eggs they made in art.

For Parents

• Take your child to the library and check out books on dinosaurs.
• Do dinosaur activities at home this week.
• Pretend you are going on a dinosaur hunt.
• Talk about dinosaurs, their names and what they eat.
• Volunteer in the classroom this week.

Bibliography

Children's Books

Berenstain, Stan and Jan. *The Day of the Dinosaur.* Random House, 1987

Berenstain, Michael. *King of the Dinosaurs, Tyrannosaurus Rex.* Western, 1989

Hoff, Sid. *Danny and the Dinosaur.* Harper and Row, 1958

Most, Bernard. *If the Dinosaurs Came Back.* Harcourt Brace Jovanovich, 1978

Records

Shera, Janice K. *Dynamic Dinosaurs.* Oklahoma City, Melody House, 1985.

Kathleen Patrick, *Camille Core Gift,* Libby Core Bearden. *Monsters and Monstrous Things.* Upbeat Basics, 1983.

Patterns

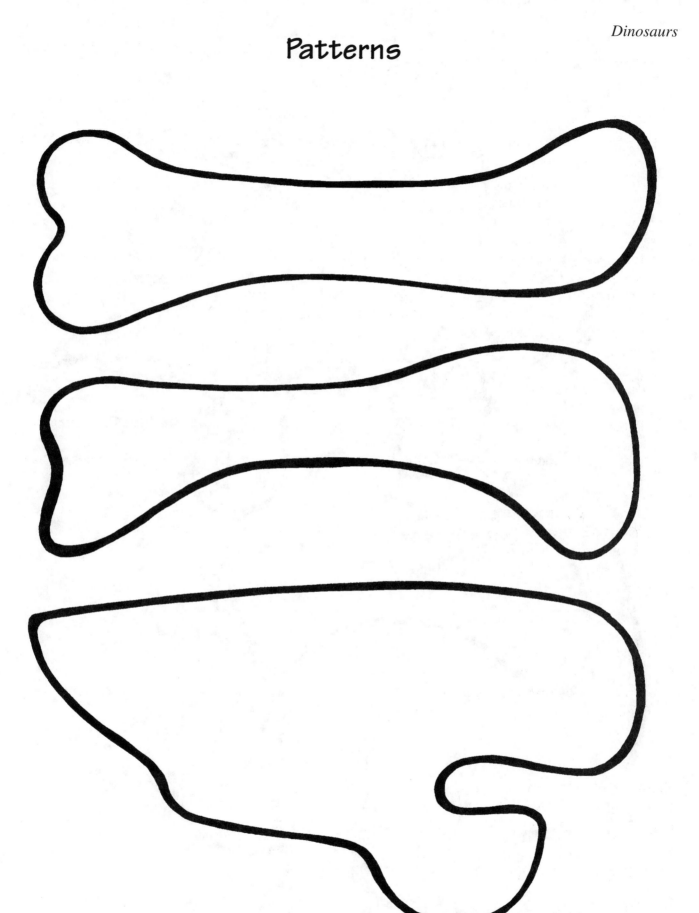

Patterns

Patterns

Weekly Theme: _Pigs_ Week of: _____

	Monday	**Tuesday**	**Wednesday**	**Thursday**	**Friday**
Date					
Sharing Time	Rhyme: To Market, To Market,	Fingerplay: This Little Pig	Fingerplay: Five Little Pigs	Song: Old Woman and the Pig	Fingerplay: Two Mother Pigs
Art	Easel Painting	Pink Play Dough	Paper Plate Pig	Circle Pig	Paper Plate Wolf
Story Time	Book: *The Three Little Pigs*	Book: *Humphrey, the Dancing Pig*	Flannel Story: Old Woman and Her Pig	Flannel Story: Old Woman and Her Pig	Book: *Pig Pig Grows Up*
Circle Time	Flannel Activity: Two Mother Pigs	Rhyme: Sing If a Pig Wore a Wig	Book: *Tales of Oliver Pig*	Fingerplay: Five Little Pigs	Face Mask Story: Three Little Pigs
Food Experiences	Ham Sandwiches	Bacon	Pig in a Blanket	Pork Chops	Apple Pigs
Theme Activities	Poem: Barber, Barber	Finger Puppet: This Little Pig	Finger Puppet: Five Little Pigs	Rhyme: Tom, Tom the Piper's Son	Fingerplay: This Little Pig

Monday

Materials For The Week:

paper plates, corn starch, canned biscuits, hot dogs, bacon, pig butcher chart, ham, bread, mayonnaise or mustard, apples, raisins, toothpicks

Sharing Time: Rhyme Time

"To Market, To Market" (Mother Goose)

To market, to market, to buy a fat pig,
Home again, home again, jiggety jig.
To market, to market, to buy a fat hog,
Home again, home again, jiggety jog.
To market, to market, to buy a plum bun,
Home again, home again, market is done.

Art: Easel Painting

Easel paint with pink tempera paint. Let children paint pigs if they wish.

Story Time: Book

Read *The Three Little Pigs*. Use any classic version of the story. Teacher Created Resources 551 Big Book is an appropriate one to use with preschool children.

Circle Time: Flannel Activity

(See patterns on page 273. You will need two mother pigs and eight babies.)

"Two Mother Pigs"

Two mother pigs lived in a pen,
Each had four babies, and that made ten.
These four babies were black as night,
These four babies were black and white.
But all eight babies loved to play
And they rolled and rolled in the mud all day.
At night, with their mother, they curled up in a heap,
And squealed and squealed till they went to sleep.

(Add flannel pieces as you read.)

Food Experiences: Ham Sandwiches

Give children bread, ham, and some mayonnaise or mustard. Let them make their own sandwiches.

Theme Activities: Poem

'Barber, Barber' (Mother Goose)

Barber, barber
Shave a pig.
How many hairs to make a wig?
Four and twenty; that's enough.
Give the barber a pinch of snuff.

Tuesday

Sharing Time: Finger Play

"This Little Pig" (Nursery Rhyme)
This little pig went to the market.
This little pig stayed home.
This little pig had roast beef.
This little pig had none.
And this little pig went
Wee, wee, wee, wee, all the way home.
(Hold up a finger for each pig, starting with the thumb.)

Art: Pink Play Dough
Make pink play dough. See directions on page 6. Let children use the play dough to make pink pigs.

Story Time: Book
Read *Humphrey the Dancing Pig* by Arthur Getz.

Circle Time: Rhyme

"If a Pig Wore a Wig" (Nursery Rhyme)
If a pig wore a wig,
What could we say?
Treat him as a gentleman,
And say "Good day."
If his tail chanced to fall,
What could we do?
Send him to the talloress
To get one new.

Food Experiences: Bacon
Cook and eat some bacon. Discuss what part of the pig bacon comes from.

Theme Activities: Finger Puppet

"This Little Pig" (Nursery Rhyme)
Make finger puppets and use with the finger play from sharing time. See patterns on page 274.

Wednesday

Sharing Time: Finger Play

"Five Little Pigs"

The first little pig danced a merry, merry jig.
The second little pig ate candy.
The third little pig wore a blue and yellow wig.
The fourth little pig was dandy.
The fifth little pig never grew very big,
So they called him Tiny Little Andy.
(Hold up a finger for each pig, starting with the thumb.)

Art: Paper Plate Pig

Have children cut out two ears and glue onto the top of a paper plate. They can draw on eyes and nose and color if desired.

Story Time: Flannel Story

See patterns on pages 275-278.

"Old Woman And Her Pig" (Mother Goose Tale)

An old woman was sweeping her house, and she found a sixpence. "What shall I do with this sixpence?" she said.
I know. I will go to market and buy a little pig."
So she went to the market and she bought a little pig. On the way home, they came to a stile.
But the pig would not go over the stile.
She went a little farther, and she met a dog.
So she said to the dog,

"Dog, dog, bite pig!
Pig won't go over the stile,
And I shan't get home tonight."
But the dog would not.
She went a little farther,
And she met a stick.
So she said to the stick,
"Stick, stick, beat dog!
Dog won't bite pig,
Pig won't go over stile,
And I shan't get home tonight."
But the stick would not.

She went a little farther,
And she met a fire.
So she said to the fire,
"Fire, fire, burn stick!
Stick won't beat dog,
Dog won't bite pig,
Pig won't go over stile,

And I shan't get home tonight."
But the fire would not.
She went a little farther,
And she met some water.
So she said to the water,
"Water, water, quench fire!
Fire won't burn stick,
Stick won't beat dog,
Dog won't bite pig,
Pig won't go over stile,
And I shan't get home tonight."
But the water would not.
She went a little farther,
And she met an ox.

Wednesday (cont.)

So she said to the ox,
"Ox, ox, drink water!
Water won't quench fire,
Fire won't, burn stick,
Stick won't beat dog,
Dog won't bite pig,
Pig won't go over stile,
And I shan't get home tonight."
But the ox would not.
She went a little farther,
And she met a butcher.

So she said to the butcher,
"Butcher, butcher, kill ox!
Ox won't drink water,
Water won't quench fire,
Fire won't burn stick,
Stick won't beat dog,
Dog won't bite pig,
Pig won't go over stile,
And I shan't get home tonight."
But the butcher would not.
She went a little farther,
And she met a rope.

So she said to the rope,
"Rope, rope, hang butcher!
Butcher won't kill ox,
Ox won't drink water,
Water won't quench fire,
Fire won't burn stick,
Stick won't beat dog,
Dog won't bite pig,
Pig won't go over stile,
And I shan't get home tonight."
But the rope would not.
She went a little farther,
And she met a rat.

So she said to the rat,
"Rat, rat, gnaw rope!
Rope won't hang butcher,
Butcher won't kill ox,
Ox won't drink water,
Water won't quench fire,
Fire won't burn stick,
Stick won't beat dog,
Dog won't bite pig,
Pig won't go over stile,
And I shan't get home tonight."
But the rat would not.
She went a little farther,
And she met a cat.

So she said to the cat,
"Cat, cat, kill rat!
Rat won't gnaw rope,
Rope won't hang butcher,
Butcher won't kill ox,
Ox won't drink water,
Water won't quench fire,
Fire won't burn stick,
Stick won't beat dog,
Dog won't bite pig,
Pig won't go over stile,
And I shan't get home tonight."

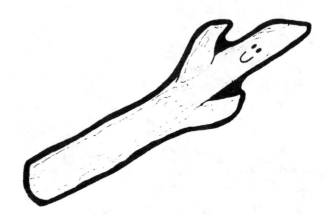

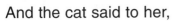

Wednesday (cont.)

And the cat said to her,
"If you will go over to the cow in the next field and fetch me a saucer of milk, I will kill the rat."
So the old woman went over to the cow in the next field.
And the cow said to her,
"If you will go over to the haystack and fetch me a handful of hay, I will give you milk."
So the old woman went over to the haystack to fetch a handful of hay for the cow. After the cow had eaten the hay, she gave the old woman the milk.
The old woman went back to the cat with the milk in a saucer. As soon as the cat had lapped up the milk
The cat began to kill the rat
The rat began to gnaw the rope
The rope began to hang the butcher
The butcher began to kill the ox
The ox began to drink the water
The water began to quench the fire
The fire began to burn the stick
The stick began to beat the dog
The dog began to bite the pig
The pig jumped over the stile
And the old woman got home that night!

Circle Time: Book
Read *Tales of Oliver Pig* by Jean Van Leeuwen.

Food Experiences: Pig in a Blanket
Wrap a pig in a blanket. Use canned biscuits. Let each child flatten a biscuit and wrap around a hot dog. Bake and enjoy.

Theme Activities: Finger Puppets
***"Five Little* Pigs"** (Author unknown)
Use the same finger puppets from Tuesday's "This Little Pig" Finger Play and the "Five Little Pigs" finger play from today's sharing time. Let children take turns saying the rhyme with the finger puppets.

Thursday

Sharing Time: Song

"Old Woman and the Pig" (Folk Song)

There was an old woman and she had a little pig, oink, oink, oink.
There was an old woman and she had a little pig.
He didn't cost much 'cause he wasn't very big, oink, oink, oink.

Art: Circle Pig

Have children cut out different size circles to make a pig face. Let them color on ears and a face.

Story Time: Flannel Story

Retell the story "Old Woman and Her Pig."

Circle Time: Finger Play

Five Little Pigs (Nursery Rhyme)

Let us go to the woods, said this little pig; *(Hold up thumb.)*
What to do there? says that little pig; *(Hold up first finger.)*
To look for my mother, says this little pig; *(Hold up tall finger.)*
What to do with her? says that little pig; *(Hold up ring finger.)*
Give her a kiss, says this little pig. *(Hold up little finger.)*

Food Experiences: Pork Chops

Discuss what part of the pig pork chops come from. If possible, fix pork chops for the children to sample.

Theme Activities: Rhyme

"Tom, Tom the Piper's Son" (Nursery Rhyme)
Tom, Tom the piper's son,
Stole a pig and away he run;
The pig was eat,
And Tom was beat,
And Tom went howling down the street.

Friday

Sharing Time: Finger Play

"Two Mother Pigs"

Two mother pigs lived in a pen, *(Hold up thumb on each hand.)*
Each had four babies, and that made ten. *(Hold up ten fingers.)*
These four babies were black as night, *(Hold up four fingers on one hand.)*
These four babies were black and white. *(Hold up four fingers on other hand.)*
But all eight babies loved to play *(Hold up eight fingers.)*
And they rolled and rolled in the mud all day. *(Roll hands.)*
At night, with their mother, they curled up in a heap, *(Make fists with each hand.)*
And squealed and squealed till they went to sleep.

Art: Paper Plate Wolf

Have children cut out two ears out of brown paper. Then cut a nose and mouth out of pink paper and glue on a paper plate. Draw on eyes. The plate can be colored if desired.

Story Time: Book

Read *Pig, Pig Grows Up* by David McPhail.

Circle Time: Face Mask Story

"The Three Little Pigs"

Have children act out the story. Face masks can be made the same as in art activities except cut out the eyes. Punch a hole on each side of plate and add yarn to tie around children's heads.

Food Experiences: Apple Pigs

Using raisins and toothpicks let children create a face for a pig by attaching them to an apple with toothpicks.

Theme Activities: Finger Play

"This Little Pig" (Nursery Rhyme)

Use this finger play from Tuesday's sharing time again but omit the last word in each line and let the children fill in the blanks.

Classroom Additions

Here are some suggestions of materials that can be placed in the learning centers in addition to your regular materials.

- Housekeeping: stuffed toy pigs
- Books: books about pigs
- Table Activities: file folder activities listed
- Blocks: plastic pigs
- Puppet: pig snouts - masks made like art activities
- Science: pig butcher chart, pictures of different type pigs, plastic pigs, dirt and water in a sand and water table, brown gooey mixture (See recipe on page 7.)

Teachers' Aids

File Folder Activities: Choose the skills you wish to emphasize this week. See directions on pages 5 and 6.

- Matching Number Pigs   • Matching Color Pigs
- Pig and Matching Mud Puddle (Dots to numerals)

Bulletin Board Ideas:
- Pigs
- Pig Pen

For Parents

- March 1st is National Pig Day.
- Visit the library and check out pig books
- Dress your child in pink this week.
- Discuss the color pink with your child.
- Look for pink items around the house.
- Make cupcakes with pink icing.
- Prepare some type of pork for dinner one night.
- If you know anyone who has a pig, take your child to see it.
- Go to your local petting zoo.

Bibliography

Children's Books

Getz, Arthur. *Humphrey the Dancing Pig.* Dial, 1980

Lobel. *A Treeful of Pigs.* Greenwillow, 1979

McPhail, David. *Pig, Pig Grows Up.* Dutton, 1980

The Three Little Pigs. Teacher Created Resources, 1992

Van Leeuwen, Jean. *Tales of Oliver Pig.* Dial, 1979

Patterns

Patterns

274

Patterns

Patterns

Patterns

Patterns

Weekly Theme: _Nutrition_   Week of: _____

	Monday	Tuesday	Wednesday	Thursday	Friday
Date					
Sharing Time	Discuss Dairy Foods	Discuss Fruits and Vegetables	Discuss Meats and Protein Foods	Discuss Breads and Cereals	Discuss Peanuts
Art	Collage of Dairy Foods	Collage of Fruits and Vegetables	Make a Pizza	Collage of Bread and Cereals	Thank You Card
Story Time	Book: *Dinner Time*	Book: *Bugs Bunny Carrot Machine*	Book: *Green Eggs and Ham*	Flannel Activity: Pancake Man	Book: *Peanut Butter and Jelly*
Circle Time	Book: *Milk and Cookies*	Poem: I Eat My Peas with Honey	Book: *Horton Hatches the Egg*	Book: *Bread and Jam for Frances*	Activity: Peanuts Growing
Food Experiences	Crunchy Mix	Vegi and Fruit Tray	Child's Pizza	Pancakes and Blueberries	Peanut Butter
Theme Activities	Book: *Who's Got the Apple?*	Flannel Story: The Big Turnip	Book: *Curious George and the Pizza*	Fingerplay: One Potato, Two Potato	Song/Fingerplay: Peanut Sitting on a Railroad Track

Monday

Materials Needed For The Week:
old magazines with pictures of food in them, food models, nutritional poster, small paper plates, silver spray paint, canned biscuits, pizza sauce, pepperoni, cereals, nuts, pretzels, carrots, celery, apples, oranges, grapes, pancake/waffle mix, can of blueberries

Sharing Time: Discuss Dairy Foods
Discuss why bodies need good nutritious foods. Show children food models or containers of dairy products such as cheese, milk, and yogurt.

Art: Collage Of Dairy Foods
Give children magazines, scissors, construction paper, and glue. Have them cut out pictures of dairy foods from magazines or use the patterns at the end of the Nutrition section.

Placemats: Purchase a package of paper placemats. Prepare in advance stencils of a plate (make a circle or buy paper plates), fork, knife, spoon, cup, and napkin. See patterns on page 289. Let children trace these items onto the paper placernat in the correct positions. Children then may color their placernat if they want.

Story Time: Book
Read *Dinner Time* by Jan Pienkowski.

Circle Time: Book
Read *Milk and Cookies* by Frank Asch.

Food Experiences: Crunchy Mix
Mix up different types of cereals, nuts, and pretzels. Serve with milk for a snack.

Theme Activities: Book
Read *It Looks Like Spilt Milk* by Charles G. Show. Take a class survey to see who likes milk.

Tuesday

Sharing Time: Discuss Fruits And Vegetables

Show children food models or real fruits and vegetables. Let children know they should be eating 3-5 of these each day.

Art: Collage of Fruits and Vegetables

Have children cut out pictures of fruits and vegetables from a magazine or use the patterns at the end of the Nutrition section. Glue on construction paper.

Story Time: Book

Read *Bugs Bunny Carrot Machine* by Clark Carlisle.

Circle Time: Poem

"I Eat My Peas With Honey"
I eat my peas with honey;
I've done it all my life.
It makes the peas taste funny,
But it keeps them on the knife.

Food Experiences: Vegi & Fruit Tray

Include some of the following vegetables and fruit on a tray for children to choose from: carrots, apples, celery, oranges, cabbage, grapes.

Theme Activities: Flannel Story

"The Big Turnip" (Traditional)
See patterns on page 290. Children also like acting this story out.

A farmer once planted a turnip seed. And it grew, and it grew, and it grew. The farmer saw it was time to pull the turnip out of the ground. So he took hold of it and began to pull.

He pulled and he pulled and he pulled and he pulled, but the turnip wouldn't come up. He pulled and he pulled, but the turnip wouldn't come up.

Tuesday (cont.)

So the farmer called to his wife who was getting dinner.

"Fee, fi, fo, fum. I pulled the turnip, but it wouldn't come up."

And the wife came running, and she took hold of the farmer, and they pulled and pulled and they pulled and they pulled. But the turnip wouldn't come up,

So the wife called to the daughter who was feeding the chickens nearby.

"Fee, fi, fo, fum. We pulled the turnip, but it wouldn't come up."

And the daughter came running. The daughter took hold of the wife. The wife took hold of the farmer. The farmer took hold of the turnip. And they pulled and they pulled and they pulled and they pulled. But the turnip wouldn't come up.

So the daughter called to the dog who was chewing a bone.

"Fee, fi, fo fum. We pulled the turnip, but it wouldn't come up."

And the dog came running. The dog took hold of the daughter. The daughter took hold of the wife. The wife took hold of the farmer. And the farmer took hold of the turnip. And they pulled and they pulled and they pulled and they pulled. But the turnip wouldn't come up.

So the dog called to the cat who was chasing her tail.

"Fee, fi, fo, fum. We pulled the turnip, but it wouldn't come up."

And the cat came running. The cat took hold of the dog. The dog took hold of the daughter. The daughter took hold of the wife. The wife took hold of the farmer. The farmer took hold of the turnip. And they pulled and they pulled and they pulled and they pulled. But the turnip wouldn't come up.

So the cat called the mouse who was nibbling spinach nearby.

"Fee, fi, fo, fum. We pulled the turnip, but it wouldn't come up."

And the mouse came running.

"That little mouse can't help," said the dog. "He's too little." "Phooey," squeaked the mouse. "I could pull that turnip up myself, but since you have all been pulling I'll let you help, too."

So the mouse took hold of the cat. The cat took hold of the dog. The dog took hold of the daughter. The daughter took hold of the wife. The wife took hold of the farmer. The farmer took hold of the turnip. And they pulled and they pulled and they pulled and they pulled. And UP came the turnip. And the mouse squeaked, "I told you so!"

Wednesday

Sharing Time: Discuss Meats and Protein Foods

Show children food models of meats and protein foods. Ask them what happens to the way foods look after they're cooked.

Art: Make A Pizza

Use the patterns on page 291 and cut out cheese strips from yellow construction paper, mushrooms from tan construction paper, pepperoni from brown construction paper, onions from white construction paper, and green peppers from green construction paper. Trace large circles on off white construction paper for crust and trace medium circles on red construction paper for tomato sauce. Have children cut out circles and glue on their favorite toppings. Small paper plates can be spray painted with silver paint for the pizza pan.

Story Time: Book

Read *Green Eggs and Ham* by Dr. Seuss.

Circle Time: Book

Read *Horton Hatches the Egg* by Dr. Seuss.

Food Experiences: Child's Pizza

Use canned biscuits and have different toppings so children can roll out and make their own pizzas. Bake in a toaster oven.

Theme Activities: Book

Read *Curious George and the Pizza* by H. Rey. Ask children what they like or dislike about pizza. Ask them what toppings are their favorites and what they dislike.

Thursday

Sharing Time: Discuss Breads And Cereals

Show children food models or actual breads and cereals.

Art: Collage of Breads and Cereals

Children can find and cut out pictures of breads and cereals from magazines or use the patterns at the end of the Nutrition section. Glue onto construction paper.

Story Time: Flannel Story

See patterns on page 292.

"Pancake Man" (Traditional)

There was a little old woman and a little old man. One day the old woman had a pancake in a little old pan. She went to the door and said, "Come, little old man, and look in this pan." The little old man looked in the little old pan and said, I see just what I want for my dinner. I am going to eat that pancake." The pancake jumped away from the little old man. He jumped out of the pan to the floor. He rolled over the floor to the door. Then out the door he went in a hurry! "Stop, Pancake!" said the old man. "Come back to this little old pan!" The pancake did not stop. He rolled out of the gate and called back, "Run, run, as fast as you can. You cannot catch me. I am the Pancake Man." The old woman and the old man ran after the pancake, but they could not catch him.

Thursday (cont.)

Pancake rolled on and on. Soon he met a big black dog.

"Stop, Pancake!" said the dog. Pancake did not stop. He rolled on and sang, I ran away from a little old woman and a little old man and I can run away from you too. I am the Pancake Man!"

Pancake rolled on and on. Soon he met a big brown bear.

"Stop, Pancake!" said the bear. Pancake rolled on and he sang, I ran away from a little old woman and a little old man. I ran away from a big black dog, and I can run away from you too. I am the Pancake Man!"

On rolled the pancake. Next he met a fox. "Good day, Pancake," said the fox. "Did I hear you sing as you rolled down the hill? Come here and sing for me."

The Pancake Man sang, I ran away from a little old woman and a little old man. I ran away from a big black dog and a big brown bear. I can run away from you too. I am the Pancake Man!"

"My, my!" said the fox. I do not want to run after you. Stay here and sing for me again."

The pancake sat next to the fox and sang, I ran away from a little old woman and a little old man. I ran away from a big black dog and a big brown bear. I can run away from you, too. I am the Pancake Man!"

"You will never run away again," said the fox. "You are just what I want for my dinner. I am going to eat you up!" And that is just what he did!

Circle Time: Book
Read *Bread and Jam for Frances* by R. Hoban.

Food Experiences: Pancakes and Blueberries
Use a prepared pancake mix. Let children help pour pancakes. Provide proper guidance around the griddle. Top pancakes with blueberries.

Theme Activities: Finger Play
"One Potato, Two Potato" (Traditional)
One potato, two potato, three potato, four,
Five potato, six potato, seven potato, more.
(Hold up one finger at a time as you count. Clap on more.)

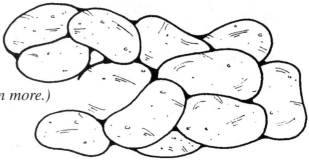

Friday

Sharing Time: Discuss Peanuts

Discuss peanuts in their different forms. Review the food groups you discussed during the week.

Art: Thank You Card

Make a classroom thank you for the school cook or for whoever cooks at home to show them how much they are appreciated for the good nutritious foods they prepare.

Story Time: Book

Read *Peanut Butter and Jelly* by Nadine Bernard Westcott.

Circle Time: Peanuts Growing

Let children pretend to be peanuts in a shell. Have them choose a partner; then one child can pretend to crack the peanut and take it out of its shell.

Food Experiences: Peanut Butter

Make peanut butter with the children. Follow the directions below.

Ingredients

• 1 cup (225 g) roasted shelled peanuts

• 1 teaspoon (5 mL) oil

Directions:

1. Place ingredients in blender and close top.

2. Blend several minutes.

3. Use rubber spatula to scrape mixture from blender.

4. Blend until it is easy to spread.

Serve on crackers with a drink.

Theme Activities: Song/Finger Play

"Peanut Sitting On A Railroad Track"
A peanut sat on a railroad track
His heart was all aflutter *(Pat hand over heart.)*
Around the bend came number ten, *(Hold up ten fingers.)*
Choo-Choo Peanut Butter. *(Pretend you are pulling whistle.)*
Smack! *(Clap hands together.)*

Classroom Additions

Here are some suggestions of materials that can be placed in the learning centers in addition to your regular materials.

- Housekeeping: various plastic play food, pictures of food cut from magazines and laminated

- Circle: Make a pizza - use the same directions as for the Wednesday art, except make pieces from felt. Cover a paper plate with foil or spray with silver spray paint for the pizza pan.

- Books: books on foods

- Table Activities: file folder activities listed; foods cut from magazines and laminated, paper plates for children to arrange their own breakfast, lunch, or supper meal

- Puppets: aprons, chef hats, small pizza boxes (make the pizza as in the art activity to put in the boxes). Children can pretend to be a pizza delivery person.

- Science: grow a vegetable or fruit plant, nutrition posters

- Science Activity: Make bread. Frozen bread dough loaves can be purchased. Take the dough from the freezer and put it in a greased pan. Grease the top of the loaf and cover with wax paper. Put in a warm place. Children can observe it several times throughout the day as it rises. Bake the bread according to the directions on the package.

Teachers' Aids

File Folder Activities: Choose the skills you wish to emphasize this week. See directions on pages 5 and 6.

- Pickle   • Cupcake   • Any of the foods

Bulletin Board Ideas:

- Each food group displayed on paper plates

- Food posters purchased at local school supply stores

Classroom Additions (cont.)

For Parents

- Let your child help you prepare nutritious meals and snacks.

- Take children grocery shopping.

- Keep fresh fruits and vegetables around for children to eat for a snack.

- Encourage exercise with your child.

- Talk with children about the food groups.

Bibliography

Children's Books

Asch, Frank. *Milk and Cookies.* Parents Magazine Press, 1982

Carlisle, Clark. *Bugs Bunny Carrot Machine.* Western, 1978

Hoban, R. *Bread and Jam for Frances.* Scholastic, 1964

Loof, Jan. *Who's Got the Apple?* Random House, 1975

Pienkowski, Jan. *Dinner Time.* Gallery Five LTD., 1981

Rey, H. *Curious George and the Pizza.* Houghton Mifflin, 1985

Seuss, Dr. *Green Eggs and Ham.* Beginners Books, 1960

Seuss, Dr. *Horton Hatches the Egg.* Random House, 1940

Shaw, Charles G. *It Looked Like Spilt Milk.* Harper, 1947

Westcott, Nadine Bernard. (Illustrated by) *Peanut Butter and Jelly.* The Trumpet Club, 1987

Free Teaching Materials

Teaching materials are available by writing and requesting materials.

Peanut Lessons and Materials
National Peanut Council
1000 16th St. N.W. Suite 700
Washington, D.C. 20036

Growers Peanut Food Promotions
109 S. Main Street
P.O. Box 11709
Rocky Mount, N.C. 27801

Nutrition Posters, Food Models
National Dairy Council
6300 North River Road
Rosemont, Ill. 60018

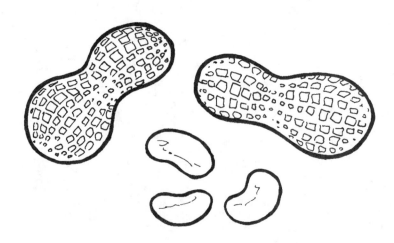

Patterns

Patterns

Patterns

Patterns

Patterns

Patterns

Patterns

Weekly Theme: _St. Patrick's Day_ Week of: _____

	Monday	Tuesday	Wednesday	Thursday	Friday
Date					
Sharing Time	Discuss the Visit from the Leprechauns	Read Note From Leprechauns	Read Note From Leprechauns	Read Note From Leprechauns	Read Note From Leprechauns
Art	Easel Painting	Elf Ears	Shamrock Paper Doily Leprechauns	Green Heart Art	Shamrock Hat
Story Time	Book: _Green Eggs and Ham_	Flannel Story: Myrtle, the Turtle, Meets a Leprechaun	Book: _St. Patricks Day in the Morning_	Flannel Story: Looie, the Leprechaun	Flannel Story: The Three Wishes
Circle Time	Dance: Irish Jig	Activity: Leprechaun Leap	Song: Irish Folk Song	Irish Counting-Out Game	Activity: Leprechaun, May I?
Food Experiences	Green Scrambled Eggs	Green Milk Shakes	Green Mashed Potatoes	Fresh Mushrooms	Pistachio Salad
Theme Activities	Activity: Note to Leprechauns	Activity: Note to Leprechauns	Activity: Note to Leprechauns	Activity: Note to Leprechauns	Treat from Leprechauns

Monday

Materials Needed For The Week:
poster-sized paper, shamrock-shaped doilies, green tempera paint, world map, shamrock shaped cookies, potatoes or mashed potatoes mix, green food coloring, vanilla ice cream, milk, mushrooms, pot of flowers, pistachio pudding mix, carton of whipped topping, can of crushed pineapple

Sharing Time: Visit from the Leprechauns
Before the children arrive, mess up the room and add tiny green footprints around the room with green paint. Make sure there is green paint in cups on the easel. Some can be spilled on the floor with green footprints leaving the area. The bigger the mess, the more excited the children are. When the children arrive, tell them that the leprechauns came to visit. They must have had a good time and forgot to clean up the mess they made. Suggest to the children that in case the leprechauns come back tonight, we need to leave them a note and tell them we like our room clean. This afternoon we will write the note. Have the children help clean up the room.

Art: Easel Paint
Have children paint trees with shamrock leaves.

Story Time: Book
Read *Green Eggs and Ham* by Dr. Seuss.

Circle Time: Dance
Do an Irish jig from the record *Folk Dance Fun.*

Food Experiences: Green Scrambled Eggs
Serve green scrambled eggs. When scrambling the eggs, put in some green food coloring.

Theme Activities: Note to Leprechauns
Write a note to the leprechauns. Let the children help tell you what to say or use the letter below. Write it on a piece of poster-sized paper so the children can help you and see it at the same time.

Hi, Little Leprechauns!

We are glad you came to visit us. We did not like the mess you left for us to clean up. All the boys and girls here try very hard to keep our room clean so we can find the toys we want. Please help us keep it clean and neat!

Let children sign their names.

Tuesday

Sharing Time: Read Note From Leprechauns

Before the children arrive today, mess up the room again, but not as much as yesterday. Don't forget the footprints. Have a note posted from the leprechauns that reads:

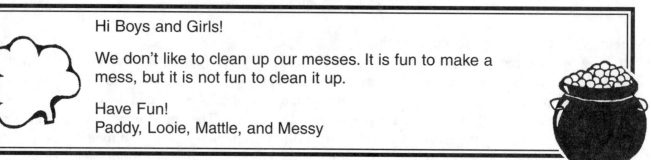

Hi Boys and Girls!

We don't like to clean up our messes. It is fun to make a mess, but it is not fun to clean it up.

Have Fun!
Paddy, Looie, Mattle, and Messy

Suggest to the children that we must write them another note this afternoon and tell them that clean up time can be fun.

Art: Elf Ears

Cut out two large elf ears. Attach to band to fit child's head. See the pattern on page 306.

Story Time: Flannel Story

Use flannel story patterns on pages 307-308.

"Myrtle, the Turtle, Meets a Leprechaun"

Myrtle the Turtle was creeping along the road, minding her own business and enjoying the smooth, soft feel of spring.

Suddenly she saw a quick movement among a group of yellow daisies on the roadside.

"Who's that?" she asked, in a slow way. "Who's there?"

"Nobody here but us daisies," said a small voice.

Myrtle smiled her slow smile. "Come on out," she said. "I won't hurt you, I promise."

A very small green man, with a pointed hat, a bunch of whiskers on his chin, and a crooked walking cane in his hand, pushed his way through the daisies.

"Why, hi there, Mr. Leprechaun," said Myrtle.

"Sure and you know who I am now?" asked the little green man.

"Of course," said Myrtle, "Everyone knows a leprechaun when she sees one! But what are you doing so far from home?"

"I decided me to be takin'a little trip and here I am," said the leprechaun. "Now suppose you'll be wantin' me pot o' gold."

"No, thank you," said Myrtle, "I most surely would not."

"Well," said the leprechaun, sighing with relief. He sat down on the grass, looking like a blade of grass himself. "Now then, I'll just be givin' you your wish, then."

"I don't wish for anything, thank you," said Myrtle.

"Sure now," said the leprechaun, "there must be something special that you're wanting."

"Well,yes," said Myrtle slowly. "I would like some pink ribbons for Ruthie Rabbit's birthday present. Fancy ones-or better yet, one big lovely one!"

"Whoosh," said the leprechaun. "You've got to be a wishin' for your ownself now—according to proper form."

"Then I haven't any wishes," said Myrtle.

"You have to have," said the leprechaun. "It's one of the rules of the Brotherhood of Leprechauns. If ya' don't take the gold, you get yourself a wish. It's a rule now, I'm tellin' ya!"

Myrtle thought hard. The little green man twiddled his thumbs impatiently. Then he said, "Maybe you'd like to swim. Why don't you wish you could swim like a fish?"

"I can swim," said Myrtle.

"Well, sure now, and you're makin' it difficult. I can't be leavin' here till you've wished yourself a wish. Now then, wouldn't ya fancy yourself in a fine fur coat like Ruthie Rabbit's say?"

"I would not," said Myrtle, smiling her slow smile. "I've grown accustomed to my shell."

The leprechaun tugged at his little beard. Then he snapped his fingers. "I know," he shouted. "Wouldn't it be grand to be the only turtle in the world with wings? And think how fast you could get around with wings."

Myrtle thought. After a long while she said, "Silver wings?" The leprechaun nodded. "All right, I'll take them," said Myrtle.

"You have to use the regular wording," said the leprechaun.

Myrtle closed her little eyes and said, "I wish I had a pair of silver wings." Before her words were finished, there on her shell back was a pair of lovely silver wings.

"Go on," said the leprechaun. "Try your wings."

Myrtle spread her wings, and first thing she knew, there she was, flying high above the daisies and over the leprechaun. Up and up she flew, faster and faster. She looked down. The ground was far away. Myrtle felt a little dizzy. She closed her eyes. Then she heard a familiar voice.

"Why, Myrtle, think of seeing you up here!" And there was Robin Redbreast flying beside her.

"Yes," said Myrtle. "Just think of it."

"I'm here for the summer," said the Robin. "And I must say I'm surprised to see you. I never saw a turtle fly. I must say I'm surprised."

"I think I'm surprised myself," said Myrtle. "And I do wish these wings wouldn't fly so fast. "

"Try moving them more slowly," said the Robin.

Myrtle tried. "I'm still going faster than I really want to," she said.

Tuesday (cont.)

"I don't think you're so happy flying," said Robin.

"I know I'm not-how do I land?"

Robin showed her how to use the wings for landing. Then he flew on. Myrtle came down with a dull thud. She looked all around. She was back where she had started.

There was a little movement among the daisies. "Mr. Leprechaun," said Myrtle, "come out at once, please."

The little green man slowly pushed his way through the daisies.

"Have a nice flight?" he asked.

"No," said Myrtle, "I didn't."

"Oh, dear now," said the leprechaun. "You're supposed to be happy when your wish is granted. Whatever shall I be doing now?"

"Look," said Myrtle. "You gave me a wish, so you obeyed the rules. If you give me another wish, you'll be obeying the rules twice."

"Sure and you're right," said the little green man. "Close your eyes and be making it then!"

Myrtle closed her eyes. "I wish I didn't have a pair of silver wings," she said, and suddenly she didn't! "I hope you're not offended," she said.

"It's all right," said the leprechaun. "Now I'm off to make my report to the Brotherhood. And good luck to ye, Myrtle. 'Tis not many I meet who are to be satisfied with things as they be."

Myrtle glanced at her back just to be sure the wings were gone. When she turned around again the leprechaun had disappeared.

But there on the road where he had been standing was something pink and shiny. Myrtle crept up to it. There was a fancy pink ribbon with a lovely card reading, "Happy Birthday to Ruthie, from Myrtle, the Turtle."

Myrtle smiled happily. "Well now," she said to herself, "Wasn't that a kind thing for him to do? He was certainly a nice fellow, wasn't he?"

Circle Time: Leprechaun Leap

Have children pretend to be leprechauns. Practice leaping and hiding behind various objects and pretending they are bushes.

Food Experiences: Green Milk Shakes

Add green food coloring to vanilla ice cream and milk.

Theme Activities: Note To Leprechauns

Write the note you talked about at the beginning of the day.

Hi Paddy, Looie, Mattie and Messy!

We told you that we like our room clean. When we came to school today you had left us another mess. Cleaning up the room can be fun. Try singing or playing music.

Have children sign their names again.

Wednesday

Sharing Time: Read Note From Leprechauns

Before the children arrive today, make a little mess. A note from the leprechauns could read:

Hi Boys and Girls!

You have so many nice things to play with, and your room is so nice and clean. Do you always keep your room clean?

Have Fun!
Paddy, Looie, Mattle, and Messy

Tell the children that this afternoon we will write another note to the leprechauns.

Art: Shamrock Paper Doily Leprechauns

Have children draw a leprechaun face on a shamrock doily. Then have them cut out green arms and legs to attach to the doily.

Story Time: Book

Read *St. Patrick's Day in the Morning* by Eve Bunting.

Circle Time: Song

Sing this old Irish folk song.

When Irish hearts are happy
Sure the world is bright and gay,
And when Irish eyes are shining
Sure they'll steal the hearts away.

Food Experiences: Green Mashed Potatoes

Use an instant mashed potato mix or make mashed potatoes of your own. Add green food coloring to mashed potatoes.

Theme Activities: Note To Leprechauns

This note may be left for the Leprechauns.

Hi Paddy, Looie, Mattie, and Messy!

Yes, we always keep our room clean, so we can find our toys and walk around the room safely. We would like to know more about you. Where do you live and what kind of house do you live in? Thank you for not leaving us a big mess to clean up.

Love,
Children's names

Thursday

Sharing Time: Read Note From Leprechauns

Before the children arrive today, you can keep the room clean or have just a few things out of place. Have a piece of green material caught in a window or a door and footprints leading to the place. Have children write their note in the afternoon.

The note from the leprechauns could read:

Hi Boys and Girls!

We live in a tree and our beds are made of green shamrock leaves. We eat berries and drink the morning dew. Our home is found in Ireland.

Your Friends,

Paddy, Looie, Mattie, & Messy

Art: Green Heart Art

Make stencils of hearts. (See patterns on page 306.) Have children cut out hearts and glue onto construction paper to make a shamrock.

Story Time: Flannel Story

Use patterns on page 308.

"Looie, The Leprechaun"

Once upon a time in the Land of Make-Believe, there lived a tiny leprechaun named Looie. He wore a tiny green hat with a bell on the tip, a tiny green, fringed coat with bells on the fringes, tiny green trousers and tiny green shoes with pointed toes and bells on the tips. When Looie flitted about, you could hear a merry tinkle of leprechaun bells.

Now Looie was a very special leprechaun because he had an unusual hobby. He collected bright, white, shiny teeth. Looie found these teeth under little children's pillows at night. In his little green house under a large maple leaf in Make-Believe Land, Looie had a row of shelves, and on these shelves he kept his large collection of bright, shiny, white teeth. Every night, Looie flitted from pillow to pillow looking for teeth. When he found a tooth he always left something for the owner of the tooth. Usually Looie exchanged the tooth for a shiny dime. Looie, the Leprechaun, really liked the children who brushed their teeth after every meal, because theirs were the shiniest and prettiest. He didn't like the dull teeth which hadn't been brushed very often.

Thursday (cont.)

One night Looie peeked under a little girl's pillow. Under the pillow he found a note instead of a tooth. It said, "Dear Good Fairy ... My tooth came out in school and I wanted to bring it home to put under my pillow, but I lost it. The janitor swept the schoolroom and my tooth is gone. Please leave a dime for me anyhow. Love, Cheryl."

"Ha!" said Looie. "Why should I leave a dime when I'm not getting a tooth for my collection?" He turned with a tinkle of leprechaun bells to go look under someone else's pillow. As he turned, he noticed Cheryl sleeping peacefully. She was smiling in her sleep. Looie could see the space where the tooth had been.

"Oh, leprechaun bells," said Looie. "She couldn't help it if she lost her tooth. I would have liked it for my collection because her teeth are so white and bright. Maybe I'll get the next one." He took the note and slipped a shiny dime under her pillow. Then Looie flitted out the window to the next house, looking for some more teeth.

When Cheryl woke up the next morning, she reached under her pillow and found the dime. She was very happy and as she pushed her tongue in the spot where her tooth had been, she felt the next tooth wiggle, wiggle, wiggle. Soon this tooth will fall out and Looie will find it and add it to his collection.

Circle Time: Irish Counting-Out Game

Recite this fun rhyme with the children.

Riggedy, higgedy, wiggedy, rig,
Paddy dances an Irish jig,
While feeding potatoes to his pig,
Riggedy, higgedy, wiggedy, rig,
Out goes Y-O-U.

Food Experiences: Fresh Mushrooms

Bring in some fresh mushrooms. Wash them very well and slice them. Let the children taste them. You may want to provide some kind of dressing for them.

Theme Activities: Note to Leprechauns

First show the children where Ireland is on a map in relationship to where they live; then write this letter.

Note To The Leprechauns:

Hi Paddy, Looie, Mattie, and Messy!

Our teacher showed us where Ireland was on the map. You all live very far away. Our room looked better today when we came to school. One of you tore a piece of your clothes last night, we are leaving it here for you. We love you!
Children's names

Friday

Sharing Time: Read Note From Leprechauns

Today the room will be very clean with a pot of flowers for the teacher and a special treat for each child. Shamrock cookies are a good treat. Don't forget the note from the leprechauns.

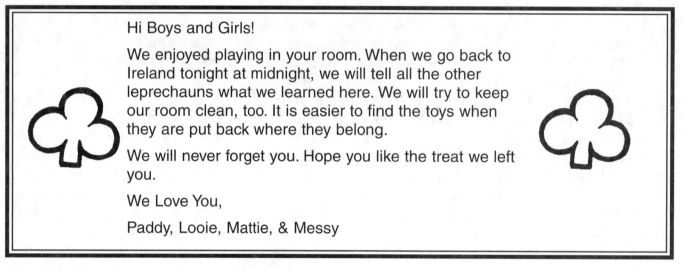

Hi Boys and Girls!

We enjoyed playing in your room. When we go back to Ireland tonight at midnight, we will tell all the other leprechauns what we learned here. We will try to keep our room clean, too. It is easier to find the toys when they are put back where they belong.

We will never forget you. Hope you like the treat we left you.

We Love You,

Paddy, Looie, Mattie, & Messy

Art: Shamrock Hat

Have children cut out shamrock shapes (see pattern page 306) and glue on a head band.

Story Time: Flannel Story

Do *The Three Wishes* as a flannel story. (Patterns and story located in Self Concept week, pages 113-114. You may wish to substitute a leprechaun for the fairy. Use the patterns on pages 309.)

Circle Time: Leprechaun May I

Play "Leprechaun, May I?" This is played like Mother May I?

Food Experiences: Pistachio Salad

To make pistachio salad, fix two packages of pistachio pudding according to directions on box. Add a container of whipped topping and a can of drained, crushed pineapple. Green cherries can be cut in half and put on top if desired.

Theme Activities: Treat From Leprechauns

Pass out the treats left by the leprechauns. This can be anything you want. Shamrock cookies with green icing are a good choice.

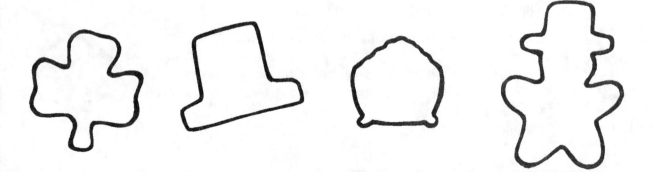

Classroom Additions

Center Ideas

Here are some suggestions of materials that can be placed in the learning centers in addition to your regular materials.

- Housekeeping: shamrock-shaped placemats (cut out of green bulletin board paper or construction paper and covered with clear contact paper)
- Circle: flannel shamrock shapes
- Books: books about leprechauns
- Music: Irish Jig from the record *Folk Dance Fun*
- Table Activities: file folder activities listed
- Art: green food coloring, bowls, and water
- Blocks: metal coins, green footprints from construction paper
- Puppets: green clothing, shamrock hats
- Science Activities

  Have four-leaf clovers on hand, if possible.
  Provide water, green food coloring, and bowls. Let children see how many shades of green they can make.

Teachers Aids

- File Folder Activities: Choose the skills you wish to emphasize this week. See directions on pages 5 - 6.
- Matching Shamrocks
- Shamrock Counting
- Shamrock Puzzle

Bulletin Board Ideas:
- Tree with Shamrocks Leaves
- Leprechauns and Green Tiny Footprints
- Pot of Gold at the End of a Rainbow

For Parents

- Discuss the color green.
- Serve green foods to your child.
- Encourage child to clean up around the house.
- Discuss why we need to keep our rooms clean.
- Talk about imagination and make believe.
- Let your child wear green on St. Patrick's Day.

Bibliography

Children's Books

Bunting, Eve. *St. Patrick's Day in the Morning.* Clarion, 1980

Seuss, Dr. (1960). *Green Eggs and Ham.* Random House, Inc. 1960

Record

Stewart, Georgianna. *Folk Dance Fun.* Long Branch, N.J.: Kimbo Education, 1984.

Patterns

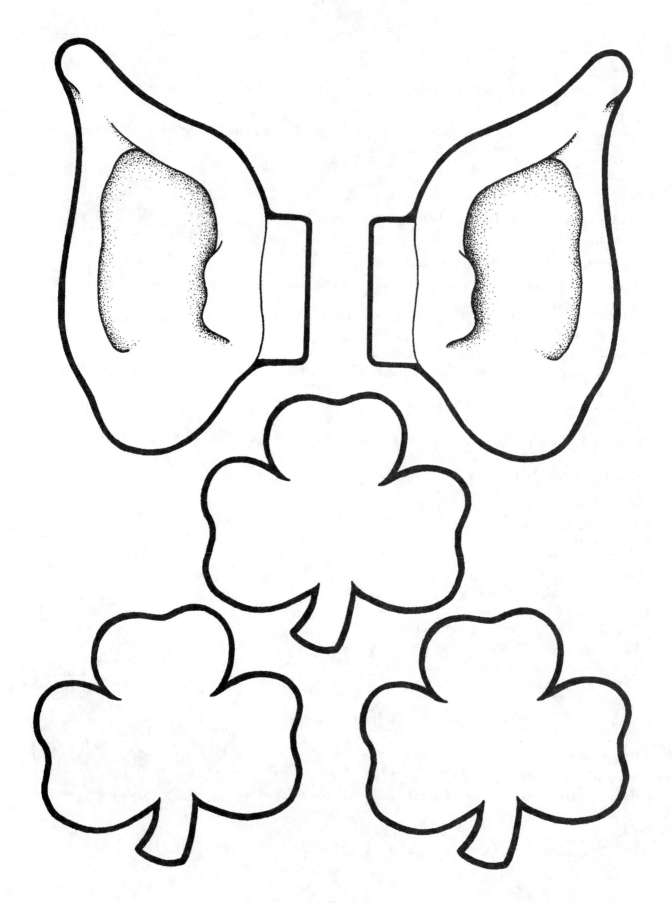

Patterns

Patterns

Patterns

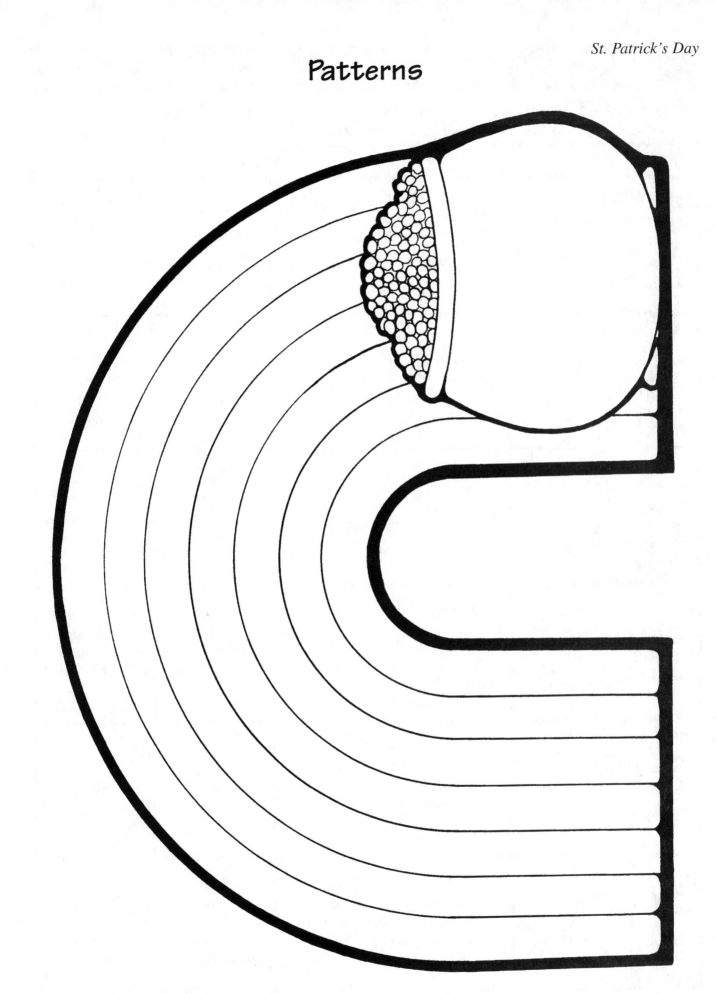

Weekly Theme: _Easter_ Week of: _____

	Monday	**Tuesday**	**Wednesday**	**Thursday**	**Friday**
Date					
Sharing Time	Finger Play: Little Bunny Foo-Foo	Finger Play: Five Little Easter Rabbits	Flannel Activity: Five Little Easter Rabbits	Action Story: _The Tale of Peter Rabbit_	Flannel Story: Why Rabbits Have Long Ears
Art	Easter Baskets	Egg Headband	Bunny Ears	Painting Fun	Dye Easter Eggs
Story Time	Flannel Story: The Child Who Found Spring	Book: _Easter Parade_	Book: _Bunnies In School_	Book: _Johnny's Egg_	Book: _Little Bunny Follows His Nose_
Circle Time	Hop Like A Bunny	Activity: Bunny May I	Song/Activity: Bunny Hop	Song/Activity: Hop Like A Bunny	Activity: Easter Egg Hunt
Food Experiences	Eat Lettuce	Egg Salad Sandwich	Carrots	Hard Boiled Egg	Peanut Butter Egg
Theme Activities	Book: _Rupert: the Tired Rabbit_	Book: _Easter Bunny's Lost Egg_	Book: _Happy Easter Little Critter_	Book: _The Tale of Peter Rabbit_	Book: _Teeny Tiny and the Tricky Easter Bunny_

Monday

Materials Needed For The Week:

Easter baskets, plastic eggs, Easter grass, egg carton, eggs, mayonnaise, bread, bunny cookie cutter, different types of lettuce, pint milk cartons or gallon plastic milk jugs, food coloring, cotton swabs, carrots

Sharing Time: Finger Play

"Little Bunny Foo Foo" (Traditional)

Little Bunny Foo Foo, *(Hold up first 2 fingers, slightly bent.)*
Hopping through the forest, *(Make your bunny hop.)*
Scooping up the field mice *(Scoop up mice.)*
And bopping them on the head! *(Hit 1 hand against the other fist.)*
Down came the good fairy and said, *(Hold fingers up in the air and move downward.)*
"Little Bunny Foo Foo, *(Hold first 2 fingers, slightly bent.)*
I don't like your attitude- *(Point finger at bunny.)*
Scooping up the field mice *(Scoop up mice.)*
And bopping them on the head. *(Hit 1 hand against fist.)*
I'll give you three chances *(Holdup 3 fingers.)*
And if you don't behave, *(Point finger at bunny.)*
I'll turn you into a GOON!" *(Put thumbs in ears and flutter fingers.)*
(Repeat until three chances are gone. Continue with same movements.)
And on the fourth day
Little Bunny Foo Foo....
Down came the good fairy for the last time and said,
"Little Bunny Foo Foo
I gave you three chances
And you still didn't behave.
Now I'll turn you into a GOON!"
(This finger play can be done over and over again because children love it.)

Art: Easter Basket

Make Easter baskets out of empty and cleaned pint milk carton or plastic gallon milk jugs. Use cotton balls to decorate. Attach ears out of pink construction paper. Facial features can be cut from construction paper.

Story Time: Flannel Story

Since Easter is always in the spring, share this story. See patterns on page 319.

"The Child Who Found Spring"

Once upon a time when the winter was over in the city, there was a child who thought he would like to go out into the street and find out for himself if spring had truly come. It was a long, crowded street-full of mighty trucks, and day and night these trucks carrying milk and fruit and vegetables rumbled over the road. It was a long and narrow street, crowded with many workers, and from morning 'til night these people jostled each other as they hurried to their work and home again. It was a loud noisy street, with car horns and grinding, squeaking wheels, and voices-sounds that were never stilled.

Monday (cont.)

But this was the child's street and he loved it. It had given him a bunch of lilacs in the summer, a bag of roasted chestnuts in the fall, and an orange and a toy in winter. So he decided to go down the long stairs from his home in a tall building to walk along it.

His mother was cleaning the glass in their window when the child started. All winter the coal dust and the soot from the factory chimneys had darkened the window, but now it was bright and clear and the golden sunshine was reflected on the floor. His mother smiled as she worked and kissed the child saying, "Don't be gone long and be careful on the busy street."

"I'll come back soon after I have asked the street cleaner at the corner if this nice weather will last." And the child gave his mother a hug and skipped down the flight of dim stairs and ran out into the long, narrow, and noisy street.

"Hoo hoo, Street Cleaner," shouted the child to his friend with the broom and little white cart. "What kind of weather will we be having?"

Street Cleaner stood at the crossing of the street that he had swept clean, and motioned to the child to come close. He put one hand under the child's chin and tilted his head up, and pointed toward a roof. The child saw a beautiful fluttering butterfly drying its new wings in the city sunshine. The yellow butterfly had burst its winter chrysalis and was trying out its frail wings. "A sign," said the street cleaner. "Tis spring."

"A butterfly in our streets! Perhaps tomorrow will be Butterfly Day," laughed the child, and this was such a happy thought that he had decided to go on down the street to ask his friend, the apples-and-oranges lady, about the weather. He ran along singing, even though his voice was small against all the city noises. He jumped and hopped, and took a kind of rabbit road in and out of the crowds and the trucks and the cars. And presently the child reached the place at the corner where the traffic policeman worked. All the cars and buses were stopped. The traffic policeman had his gloved hand raised and the child looked to see why all the traffic had been stopped. There in front of the first trucks and cars was a yellow pool of grain that had fallen from a seed wagon. Around it, chirping and cooing were many kinds of birds. The policeman led the child toward the birds.

Monday (cont.)

"A sign," he said. "Spring has come. See all the birds." And as the birds flew away they sang as if they were trying to say, "Thank you."

"Perhaps tomorrow will be Bird Day," laughed the child, and he went on toward the apple-and-oranges lady. But she had changed. Sure enough, she was wearing the same patched coat and the same faded hat but she had flowers instead of fruit-red tulips and yellow daffodils, pink hyacinth and white daisies.

"Here you are," said the child. "And what will the weather be?" he asked.

The lady smiled and acted as if she knew a secret. She reached into her cart and pulled out a little flower pot with a bright red geranium.

"Here," she said. "Give this to your mother, and ye know what kind of day 'twill be."

"Oh, thank you. It will be Flower Day," laughed the child, and he started toward home. Home through the long, crowded, narrow, noisy street the child hastened, remembering what he had seen. A yellow butterfly, birds singing, beautiful flowers, kindness in people's hearts. It was more than spring. All the city had given him a new feeling in his heart.

His mother had finished cleaning the window and it shone with brightness. It was almost as bright as his mother's smile as he handed her the plant.

"Tomorrow will be Easter Day," he cried. And he knew, from all he had seen and felt, what Easter really means.

Circle Time: Hop Like a Bunny

Let children pretend to hop like a bunny. First hop on two feet, then hop on one.

Food Experiences: Lettuce

Let children taste a few different types of lettuce such as iceberg or red leaf. Ask which they think a rabbit would prefer to eat.

Theme Activities: Book

Read *Rupert: The Tired Rabbit* by R. Schaffner.

Tuesday

Sharing Time: Finger Play

"Five Little Easter Rabbits" (Traditional)

Five little Easter rabbits sitting by the door, *(Hold up five fingers.)*
One hopped away, and then there were four. *(Move one finger hopping away.)*
Hop, hop, hop, hop, see how they run! *(Continue hopping.)*
Hop, hop, hop, hop, They think it's great fun! *(Continue hopping.)*
Four little Easter rabbits under a tree, *(Hold up four fingers)*
One hopped away and then there were three. *(One finger hopping)*
Hop, hop, hop, hop, see how they run! *(Hopping)*
Hop, hop, hop, hop, They think it's great fun! *(Hopping)*
Three little Easter rabbits, looking at you, *(Three fingers)*
One hopped away, and then there were two. *(one finger hopping)*
Hop, hop, hop, hop, see how they run! *(Hopping)*
Hop, hop, hop, hop, They think it's great fun! *(Hopping)*
Two little Easter rabbits resting in the sun, *(Two fingers)*
One hopped away, and then there was one. *(One finger)*
Hop, hop, hop, hop, see how they run! *(Hopping)*
Hop, hop, hop, hop, They think it's great fun! *(Hopping)*
One little Easter rabbit left all alone, *(One finger)*
He hopped away and then there were none! *(One hopped, No fingers)*
Hop, hop, hop, hop, see how they run!
Hop, hop, hop, hop, They think it's great fun!
(This can be done with all 10 fingers)

Art: Egg Headband
Have children cut out a medium-sized egg and decorate it. Attach it to a headband that fits the child's head. Several eggs can be glued around the head band. To reinforce the concept of ten, up to ten eggs can be cut out.

Story Time: Book
Read *Easter Parade* by Eileen Curran.

Circle Time: Activity
Play "Bunny, May I?" This is played like "Mother, May I?" however, encourage bunny-like movement, such as hopping and jumping.

Food Experiences: Egg Salad Sandwich
Make egg salad with the children. Let the them mash the eggs using a fork and add a little mayonnaise. Spread on bread that has been cut with bunny cookie cutters.

Theme Activities: Book
Read *Easter Bunny's Lost Egg* by Sharon Gordon.

Wednesday

Sharing Time: Flannel Activity

See patterns on page 321.

"Five Little Easter Rabbits" (Traditional)

Use the finger play from Tuesday and take one rabbit off the flannel board as each rabbit hops away.

Art: Bunny Ears

Out of pink construction paper trace large bunny ears. See pattern on page 322. Children will cut them out. Attach to a band to fit child's head.

Story Time: Book

Read *Bunnies in School* by K. Paget

Circle Time: Song/Activity

Sing "Bunny Hop" from the record *The Hokey Pokey and Other Favorites.* The directions for the Bunny Hop follow.

1. The first person stands with his or her back facing another person's front. Repeat this pattern for remaining students. Everyone keeps their feet together and holds onto the shoulders of the person in front, except the leader of the one, who keeps his or her hands outstretched.

2. Everyone kicks right foot out to the side and brings it back. Repeat.

3. Everyone kicks left foot out to side and brings it back. Repeat.

4. Everyone hops forward with feet together.

5. Everyone hops backward with feet together

6. Everyone hops forward three times.

Food Experiences: Carrots

Peel and cut carrots into sticks. Serve as an afternoon snack.

Theme Activities: Book

Read *Happy Easter Little Critter* by Mercer Mayer.

Thursday

Sharing Time: Book
Read *The Tale of Peter Rabbit* by Beatrix Potter.

Art: Painting Fun
In small bowls, mix various colors with food coloring and water. Let children use cotton swabs to paint bunnies and eggs.

Story Time: Book
Read *Johnny's Egg* by E. Long.

Circle Time: Song/Activity
Sing and do "Hop Like A Bunny" from the record *It's Fun to Clap.*

Food Experiences: Hard Boiled Eggs
With the children, hard boil eggs. Save these to color and use later for the Easter egg hunt.

Theme Activities: Action Story
Do *The Tale of Peter Rabbit* as an action story. The children should listen to the story and copy the movements and sounds.

Once upon a time, Peter Rabbit went walking in the woods. *(snap fingers)*
He came to the garden of Mr. McGregor. *(stop snapping)*
Peter went under the fence. *(motion fingers of one hand going under the other)*
He found good vegetables to eat. *(sound of chomping)*
Then Mr. McGregor found Peter! *(look surprised, hand to mouth)*
Mr. Mc Gregor ran after Peter. *(pat hand quickly on the knees)*
Peter was afraid. His jacket buttons got stuck in a gooseberry net. *(child pulls on his/her buttons or shirt front)*
He got away and jumped into a water can. *(children say "kertyschooo")*
Mr. McGregor was still chasing him *(pat knees rapidly)*
Peter was lost and afraid. He saw a cat. *(children say "meow")*
Peter ran and hid in a wheelbarrow. *(hide one fist under the other)*
Very quietly Peter looked around. *(extend two fingers like bunny ears from the fist)*
He saw Mr. McGregor and the gate! *(cross hands and touch shoulders)*
Peter ran very fast (pat knees) and got under the gate just in time. (motion finger of one hand going under the other)
He ran all the way home without looking back. *(moves arms back and forth)*
His mother scolded him and put him to bed with a dose of camomile tea. *(children fold their hands in their laps)*

Friday

Sharing Time: Flannel Story
See patterns on page 323.

"Why Rabbits Have Long Ears"

This Chuj (Choog) Indian folk tale comes from the jungles of Guatemala.

Long, long ago, in the forest of Quezaltenango, an argument arose among the animals who lived there as to who should be their King. The animals couldn't decide between the rabbit and the lion.

The lion was very brave and very strong. He let his past deeds speak for him and he talked very little about being king. The rabbit, although weak and small, made great speeches and promises about all the great things that would happen to the other animals if he was elected their king. He had no intention of keeping these promises, but the other animals had no way of knowing this.

Finally, the animals decided to go to the God of All The Beasts and ask his advice in this difficult matter. The rabbit repeated all his promises to the God of All The Beasts. When the lion's turn to speak came, he said simply, "Great One, I feel my past deeds speak louder than words. You see me and you know me. I have no more to say."

After a long pause, the Great One gave his answer. He said that the rabbit should be given a chance to prove himself. To prove that he was wise and resourceful, the rabbit was to bring back the skins of an alligator, a tiger, and three monkeys. Then the Great God would give his answer.

The rabbit tricked his animal friends into trusting him, then he killed them and took their skins. Very proud of himself, he brought his catch before the Great One. "I have done these wonderful deeds," rabbit said. "No one could be more clever than I."

The Great One roared with anger at the rabbit. "All deeds are not wonderful," he said. 'You are not fit to be king. Had you been truly wise you would have known that what I asked could not have been done without betraying your friends," With that he seized the rabbit by the ears and his ears stretched into long slender points.

From that day forward, rabbits have had long, pointed ears. And the lion, not the rabbit, is the King of Beasts.

Art: Dye Easter Eggs
Following the package directions on dye or the directions on food coloring, dye eggs.

Story Time: Book
Read *Little Bunny Follows His Nose* by K. Howard.

Circle Time: Egg Hunt
Have an Easter egg hunt. Hide eggs where children can find them. Make sure to hide enough or set a limit on how many each should find so that all children can find some.

Food Experience: Peanut Butter Eggs
Give children some peanut butter eggs to try. Let them name the colors.

Theme Activities: Book
Read *Teeny Tiny and the Tricky Easter Bunny* by Matthews.

Classroom Additions

Center Ideas

Here are some suggestions of materials that can be placed in the learning centers in addition to your regular materials:

- Housekeeping: Easter basket with plastic eggs, Easter bonnets, dressy clothes, and shoes
- Circle Time: flannel basket, assorted sizes and colors of eggs, rabbit
- Books: books about rabbits and Easter
- Easter Table Activities: file folder activities listed
- Blocks: Easter basket and plastic eggs
- Puppets: rabbit stick puppets
- Science: egg sound cups

Science Activities:

   Incubator with chicken eggs to hatch

Teachers' Aids

File Folder Activities: Choose the skills you wish to emphasize this week. See directions on pages 5 and 6.

- Color Bunnies
- Easter Egg Wallpaper Matching

Bulletin Board Ideas:

- Easter Rabbits
- Easter Eggs
- Easter Baskets
- Artificial Grass

For Parents

- Discuss with your child why we have Easter.
- Make dying eggs a family affair.
- Visit the library.
- Take an Easter stroll with your child.
- Have an Easter egg hunt.
- Discuss the colors of eggs with your child.

Bibliography

Children's Books

Curran, Eileen. *Easter Parade.* Troll, 1985

Gordon, Sharon. *Easter Bunny's Lost Egg.* Troll, 1980

Howard, K. *Little Bunny Follows His Nose.* Golden Press and Inc,. Western, 1971

Long, E. *Johnny's Egg.* Addison-Wesley, 1980

Matthews. *Teeny Tiny and the Tricky Easter Bunny.* Troll, 1991

Mercer, Mayer. *Happy Easter Little Critter.* Western, 1988

Paget, K. *Bunnies In School.* Scholastic, 1974

Potter, Beatrix. *Tale of Peter Rabbit.* Frederick Warne & Co., 1902

Schaffner, R. *Rupert: the Tired Rabbit.* Dandelion Books, 1978

Records

William Janiak. *It's Fun to Clap.* Kimbo, 1982.

The Hokey Pokey and Other Favorites. Melody House Publishing Co.

Patterns

Patterns

Patterns

Patterns

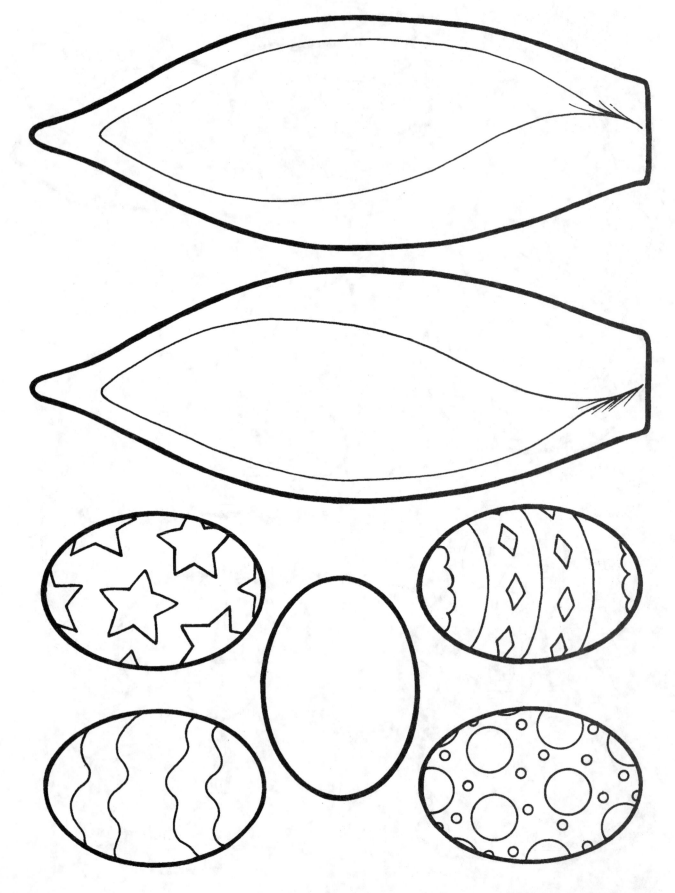

Patterns

Weekly Theme: _Spring_ Week of: _____

	Monday	**Tuesday**	**Wednesday**	**Thursday**	**Friday**
Date					
Sharing Time	Finger Play: Itsy Bitsy Spider	Poem: The Flower	Poem: Rain on the Green Grass	Activity: Planting Pantomine	Rhyme: May Song
Art	Flower Pots	Easel Painting	Fingerpaint	Sunflowers	Seed Collages
Story Time	Flannel Story: The Dog and the Bumblebee	Book: _Will Spring Be Early? Or Will Spring Be Late?_	Book: _Round Robin_	Book: _The Carrot Seed_	Book: _First Comes Spring_
Circle Time	Activity: Spring Walk	Activity: Flower Arranging	Field Trip: Visit a Green House	Poem: Thunger	Activity: Bird Walk
Food Experiences	Flowery Snack	Leafy Foods	Fruit	Sunflower Seeds	Spring Vegetables
Theme Activities	Finger Play: My Garden	Rhyme: Buttercups and Daisies	Book: _Titch_	Poem: Dig a Little Hole	Poem: Mistress Mary, Quite Contrary

Monday

Materials Needed For The Week:

foam cups, potting soil, flower seeds, sunflower seeds, 8 oz. package cream cheese, 1/4 lb. American cheese, round crackers, spinach, lettuce, artificial flowers, cherries, apricots, and a variety of vegetable seeds.

Sharing Time: Finger Play

"Itsy, Bitsy Spider" (Nursery Rhyme)

The itsy, bitsy spider went up the water spout, *(Use first two fingers and walk up other arm.)*
Down came the rain and washed the spider out. *(Flutter fingers down.)*
Out came the sun and dried up all the rain *(Make circle above head with arms.)*
And the itsy, bitsy spider went up the spout again. *(Use first two fingers and walk up other arm.)*

Art: Flower Pots

Use foam cups and let children draw pictures on them. Crayons or colored pencils will work well for this.

Story Time: Flannel Story

Do "The Dog and the Bumblebee" flannel story. The story and patterns are located in Pet Week on pages 29 and 30.

Circle Time: Spring Walk

Take a spring walk with the children. Point out the sights of spring and discuss them.

Food Experiences: A Flowery Snack

Soften a large package (8 oz.) cream cheese and ¾ pound of shredded American cheese. Mix together. Let each child arrange five round shaped crackers on a paper plate. Then they can make a round cheese ball and put it in the center of the crackers. Cover with clear plastic wrap and chill. Have with lunch or as an afternoon snack.

Theme Activities: Finger Play

"My Garden" (Traditional)

This is my garden. I'll rake it with care. *(Pretend to rake.)*
And then some flower seeds I'll plant there. *(Pretend to plant seeds.)*
The sun will shine, *(Put arms over head in a circle.)*
And the rain will fall, *(Put hands in air and bring down as rain.)*
And my garden will blossom and grow straight and tall. *(Make fist then open up slowly as the flower blooms.)*

Tuesday

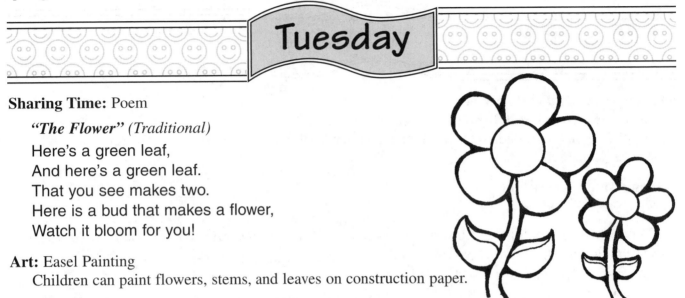

Sharing Time: Poem

"The Flower" (Traditional)
Here's a green leaf,
And here's a green leaf.
That you see makes two.
Here is a bud that makes a flower,
Watch it bloom for you!

Art: Easel Painting
Children can paint flowers, stems, and leaves on construction paper.

Story Time: Book
Read *Will Spring Be Early? Or Will Spring Be Late? by* Crockett Johnson.

Circle Time: Flower Arranging
Give children all types of artificial flowers. Provide plastic vases. Let children work alone or in groups to make a flower arrangement.

Food Experiences: Leafy Foods
Let children see leafy foods such as spinach or several different types of lettuce. Ask them why they're called leafy. Compare the leaves on each. Let them taste the different leaves. Ask them if they all taste the same or different.

Theme Activities: Rhyme
Teach this springtime nursery rhyme.

"Buttercups and Daisies"

Buttercups and daisies,

Oh, the pretty flowers;

Coming 'ere the springtime,

To tell of sunny hours.

While the trees are leafless,

While the fields are bare,

Buttercups and daisies

Spring up here and there.

Wednesday

Sharing Time: Poem

"Rain on the Green Grass"

Rain on the green grass,
And rain on the tree,
And rain on the housetop,
But not upon me!

Art: Fingerpaint Flowers

Give children various colors of fingerpaint in small cups. Let them use their fingers to make flowers, stems, and leaves.

Story Time: Book

Read *Round Robin* by Jack Kent.

Circle Time: Field Trip

Visit a greenhouse or you could tour a nursery or gardens. Let children exerience all the flowers that are in bloom. Let them try to name some of the flowers.

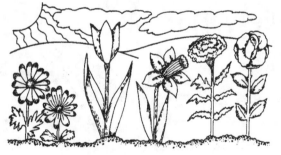

Food Experiences: Fruit

Choose some springtime fruits such as cherries or apricots. Cut them up so that the children can see the pits. Explain that they are really seeds and that the fruit was a flower in bloom at one time.

Theme Activities: Book

Read *Titch* by Pat Hutchins.

Thursday

Sharing Time: Planting Pantomime

Do a planting pantomime. Have children pretend to a dig hole, plant seeds, cover up, and water the seeds.

Art: Sunflowers

Cut out a large yellow circle. Glue on large yellow petals. Attach a stem. See the pattern on page 331.

Story Time: Book

Read *The Carrot Seed* by Ruth Kraus.

Circle Time: Poem

"Thunder" (Traditional)

I hear thunder, I hear thunder.
Hark, don't you? Hark, don't you?
Pitter patter raindrops, pitter patter raindrops,
I'm wet through.
So are you.

Food Experiences: Sunflower Seeds

Let children eat sunflower seeds. If you give them the ones with shells, explain how to crack them. Or show them what the seeds look like with shells and serve a small portion of already prepared seeds. If possible, get a real sunflower to share with the children.

Theme Activities: Poem

"Dig a Little Hole" (Traditional)

Dig a little hole.
Plant a little seed.
Pour a little water.
And pull a little weed.

Friday

Sharing Time: Rhyme

"May Song" (Old English Country Rhyme)
Spring is coming, spring is coming,
Birdies, build your nest;
Weave together straw and feather,
Doing each your best.
Spring is coming, spring is coming,
Flowers are coming, too;
Pansies, lilies, daffodillies
Now are coming through.
Spring is coming, spring is coming,
All around is fair;
Shimmer and quiver on the river,
Joy is everywhere.

Art: Seed Collage
Collect all types of seeds. Have children glue them onto construction paper to create a collage.

Story Time: Book
Read *First Comes Spring* by Anne Rockwell.

Circle Time: Bird Walk
Take the children on a bird walk. Discuss the different colors of the birds you see. Tell the children the names of the birds.

Food Experiences: Spring Vegetables
Show children some vegetable seeds or pictures of some seeds. Serve some of the vegetables grown from the seeds. Let children guess which vegetables grow from which seed.

Theme Activities: Poem

"Mistress Mary, Quite Contrary" (Traditional)
Mistress Mary, quite contrary,
How does your garden grow?
With silver bells and cockleshells
And pretty maids all in a row.

(Let children tell you what they think silver bells and cockleshells might be. Could they really plant a garden like Mistress Mary?)

Classroom Additions

Center Ideas

Here are some suggestions of materials that can be placed in the learning centers in addition to your regular materials.

- Housekeeping: plastic pot and flowers
- Circle: flannel pots and flowers
- Books: books about spring
- Blocks: plastic rakes, hoes, shovels
- Science: plastic pot and flowers, potting soil, critter cage, posters of plant growth
- Science Activities: Try some of these science activities through the week.
  - Plant flower seeds in individual cups.
  - Plant a potato in water by placing a few toothpicks around the center, and placing the potato in a jar of water, letting the toothpicks rest on the rim of the jar.

Teachers Aids

File Folder Activities: Choose the skills you wish to emphasize this week. See directions on pages 5 and 6.

- Flower Pot and Flower Matching

Bulletin Board Ideas:

- Tissue Paper Flowers • Sun • Rain • Birds • Butterflies
- Sunflowers the children made • Rainbow

For Parents

- Plant a flower or vegetable garden with child's help.
- Talk about the change of seasons and weather.
- Talk about plant growth.
- Visit the library.
- Let child water his/her plant daily.
- Discuss the size, shape, and color of the flower or vegetable planted.

Bibliography

Children's Books

Hutchins, Pat. *Titch.* Macmillan, 1971

Johnson, Crockett. *Will Spring Be Early? Or Will Spring Be Late?* Harper & Row, 1961

Kent, Jack. *Round Robin.* Simon & Schuster., 1989

Krauss, Ruth. *The Carrot Seed.* Harper & Row, 1986

Rockwell, Anne. *First Comes Spring.* Harper Collins, 1985

Patterns

Patterns

Weekly Theme: _Farm_			Week of: _____	
Monday	**Tuesday**	**Wednesday**	**Thursday**	**Friday**

	Monday	Tuesday	Wednesday	Thursday	Friday
Date					
Sharing Time	Finger Play: Five Little Farmers	Activity: Galloping Horses	Finger Play: This Little Cow	Poem: Chick Ways	Activity: Discuss Farm Animals and Sounds They Make
Art	Farm Animal Puppets	Corn Cob Painting	Farm Scene	Farm Animal Tracks	Crop Collage
Story Time	Book: _On the Farm_	Book: _The Carrot Seed_	Book: _Little Chick's Breakfast_	Flannel Story: Five Hungry Chicks	Flannel Story: The Big Turnip
Circle Time	Poem: Higgledy, Piggledy	Activity/Song: farmer in the Dell	Finger Play: The Farmer	Book: _Farm Babies_	Field Trip: To a Farm
Food Experiences	Butter	Carrot Salad	Chocolate Milk	Bread	Vegetable Tray
Theme Activities	Song: Salad Salad	Book: _Chick Hatches_	Book: _The Milk Makers_	Book: _The Little Red Hen_	Song/ Activity: Flick a Fly

Monday

Materials Needed For The Week:

old magazines (check with local library for discarded magazines), corn cobs for painting pictures, various raw vegetables and raisins for food experiences, whipping cream, baby food jars, crackers, carrots, mayonnaise, chocolate sauce, milk

Sharing Time: Finger Play

"Five Little Farmers" (Traditional)

Five little farmers woke up in the sun, *(Hold up five fingers.)*
For it was early morning and chores must be done.
The first little farmer went to milk the cow. *(Hold up thumb.)*
The second little farmer thought he'd better plow. *(Hold up first finger.)*
The third little farmer fed the hungry hens. *(Hold up next finger.)*
The fourth little farmer mended broken pens. *(Hold up next finger.)*
The fifth little farmer took his vegetables to town. *(Hold up last finger.)*
Baskets filled with cabbages, and sweet potatoes brown.
When the work was finished and the western sky was red,
Five little farmers tumbled into bed! *(Hold up 5 fingers.)*
Discuss what farmers do.

Art: Farm Animal Puppets

Cut large pictures of different farm animals from magazines or use the patterns on pages 341-342. Cover with clear contact paper. Attach craft sticks.

Story Time: Book

Read *On the Farm* by Richard Scarry.

Circle Time: Poem

"Higgledy, Piggledy" (Mother Goose)

Higgledy, piggledy, my black hen,
She lays eggs for gentlemen;
Sometimes nine
Sometimes ten,
Higgledy, Piggledy, my black hen.

Food Experiences: Butter

Pour some heavy whipping cream into a baby food jar. Let the children take turns shaking the jar until it becomes butter. Pour off the whey and spread it onto crackers.

Theme Activities: Song

"Old MacDonald"

Old MacDonald had a farm. E-I-E-I-0.
And on his farm he had a cow. E-I-E-I-0.
With a moo-moo here and a moo-moo there.
Here a moo, there a moo, everywhere a moo-moo.
Old MacDonald had a farm. E-I-E-I-0.
Continue the song including a pig, horse, chicken, duck, etc.

Stick puppets can be made. See patterns on pages 341-342.

Tuesday

Sharing Time: Galloping Horses

Have children pretend to be horses galloping all around the room.

Art: Corn Cob Painting

Dried corn cobs are good to use for painting pictures. Let children use them as brushes.

Story Time: Book

Read *The Carrot Seed* by Ruth Krauss.

Circle Time: Activity

"Farmer In The Dell" (Traditional)

The Farmer in the dell, The farmer in the dell,
Hi-ho and merry-o, The farmer in the dell.
The farmer takes a wife. The farmer takes a wife.
Hi-ho and merry-o, The farmer takes a wife.
The wife takes the child... The child takes the nurse...
The nurse takes the dog... The dog takes the cat ...
The cat takes the rat... The rat takes the cheese ...
The cheese stands alone. The cheese stands alone.
Hi-ho and merry-o, The cheese stands alone.

Food Experiences: Carrot Salad

Peel and grate carrots. The children can add some raisins and mix with some mayonnaise. Let them try it.

Theme Activities: Book

Read *Chick Hatches* by Joanna Cole.

Wednesday

Sharing Time: Finger Play
"This Little Cow"

This little cow eats grass,
This little cow eats hay,
This little cow drinks water,
This little cow runs away.
This little cow does nothing,
But just lies down all day.

Discuss how cows give us milk.

Art: Farm Scene
Have children draw or paint a farm scene. Let them use patterns (see pages 341-342) to trace around animals they might wish to include. Then paint or color their pictures.

Story Time: Book
Read *Little Chick's Breakfast* by Mary Deball Kwitz.

Circle Time: Finger Play

"The Farmer"

First the farmer sows his seeds, *(Pretend to sow seeds.)*
Then he stands and takes his ease,
He stamps his foot *(Stamp foot.)*
And claps his hands, *(Clap hands.)*
And turns around to view his lands. *(Put hand over eyebrows and look to left and right.)*

Food Experiences: Chocolate Milk
Mix some chocolate into milk (if no food allergies) but don't let the children see you doing this. Ask children to describe the flavor and ask if a cow gives chocolate milk.

Theme Activities: Book
Read *The Milk Makers* by Gail Gibbons.

Thursday

Sharing Time: Poem

"*Chick Ways*"

Come chick, chick, chick,
Come chick, chick, chick,
Here's food for you to eat,
Here's food for you to eat,
SHOO!

Discuss chickens.

Art: Farm Animal Tracks

Have children dip feet of plastic farm animals into paint and press on paper. Let them share their pictures and let others guess which animal tracks they have painted.

Story Time: Flannel Activity

"*Five Hungry Chicks*" (Mother Goose)

Said the first little chicken,
With a queer little squirm,
"I wish I could find
A fat little worm."

Said the second little chicken,
With an odd little shrug,
"I wish I could find
A fat little bug."

Said the third little chicken'
With a sharp little squeal,
"I wish I could find
Some nice yellow meal."

See page 343 for patterns

Said the fourth little chicken,
With a sigh of grief,
"I wish I could find
A little green leaf."

Said the fifth little chicken,
With a faint little moan,
"I wish I could find
A wee gravel stone."

"Now, see here," said the mother,
From the green garden patch,
"If you want any breakfast,
Just come here and scratch!"

Food Experiences: Bread

Make cornbread with the children. Use a simple recipe or use a prepared mix. Serve with butter.

Circle Time: Book

Read *Farm Babies by* Russell Freedman.

Theme Activities: Book

Read *The Little Red Hen* by Paul Galdone.

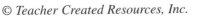

Friday

Sharing Time: Discuss Farm Animals

Discuss farm animals and the sounds they make. Practice the sounds. Then play a game with the sounds. As you or one of the children call out the sound everyone repeats that sound.

Art: Crop Collage

Have children cut out pictures of vegetables and paste on construction paper. Cut these pictures from magazines or patterns on page 340. Use them to create a crop collage. Explain that most vegetables grow together in large rows.

Story Time: Flannel Story

Share *The Big Turnip.* See Nutrition Week, pages 281-290 for the story and patterns.

Circle Time: Field Trip to a Farm

Take a field trip to a farm. Let children see the livestock and the crops being grown, If this isn't possible show pictures of farms, including livestock, crops being grown, and farm machinery used.

Food Experiences: Vegetable Tray

Clean and cut various raw vegetables for a snack. Before preparing any vegetables show them to the children. Make sure that they see things like carrots with the tops and peels, celery leaves, cucumbers with skins, and a whole head of cauliflower.

Theme Activities: Song/Activity

Sing *"Flick A Fly"* from the record *Walter the Waltzing Worm.*

Classroom Additions

Center Ideas

Here are some suggestions of materials that can be placed in the learning centers in addition to your regular materials.

- Housekeeping: straw hats, bib overalls, red handkerchiefs, plaid shirts, plastic vegetables
- Circle: flannel chicken and baby chicks
- Books: books about farms
- Table Activities: file folder activities listed
- Blocks: plastic farm animals, Lincoln Logs®, cardboard box painted like a barn, metal farm equipment
- Science: pan of dirt, small hoe, rake, plastic vegetables that grow under the ground (Children can plant them in the dirt.)
- Science Activities: Try some of the activities with the children

  Plant Bean Seeds
  Cotton (raw if possible)

Teacher's Aids

File Folder Activities: Choose the skills you wish to emphasize this week. See directions on pages 5-6.
- Egg Number Matching

Bulletin Board Ideas:
- Farm Animals
- Farmer   • Farm Scene   • Display Seeds In Plastic Bags

For Parents

- Visit a farm or petting zoo with your child.
- Visit the library and check out books on farms.
- Continue growth chart on plants from last week.
- Make farm animal sounds with your child.
- Sing "Old MacDonald Had a Farm."
- Take your child on a bird walk.
- Let your child help you plant a garden.

Bibliography

Children's Books
Cole, Joanna. *Chick Hatches.* Morrow, 1976
Freedman, Russell. *Farm Babies.* Holiday, 1981
Galdone, Paul. (1973). *The Little Red Hen.* Clarion Books, 1979
Gibbons, Gail. *The Milk Makers.* Macmillan, 1985
Krauss, Ruth. *The Carrot Seed.* Harper & Row, 1986

Records
Hap Palmer. *Walter the Waltzing Worm.* Educational Activities, Inc., 1982.

Patterns

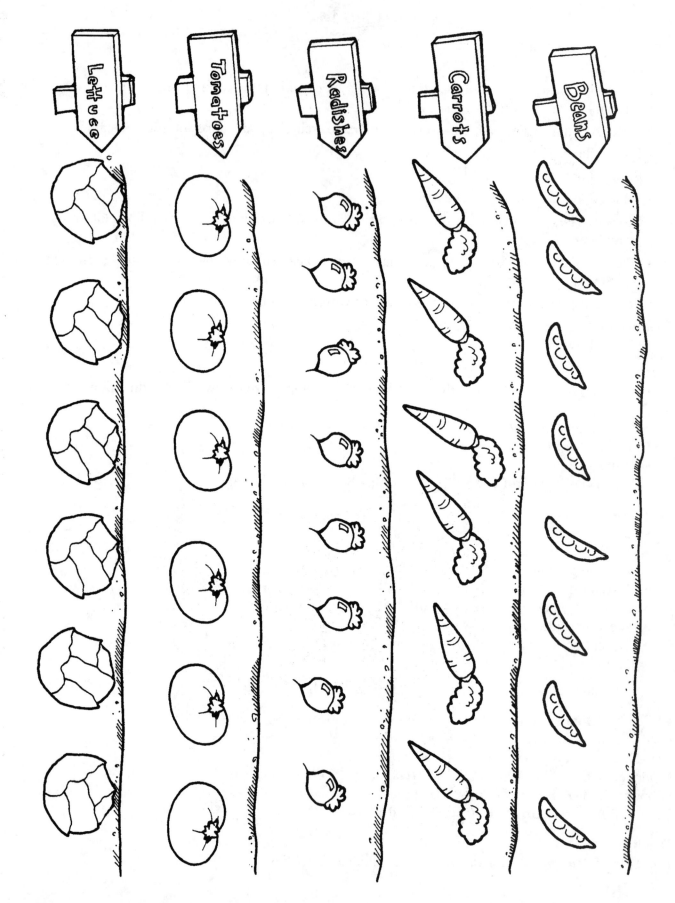

Patterns

Patterns

Patterns

Weekly Theme: *Frogs*   Week of: _____

	Monday	Tuesday	Wednesday	Thursday	Friday
Date					
Sharing Time	Finger Play: Five Little Speckled Frogs	Finger Play: Mr. Green Froggies	Poem: Little Frogs	Finger Play: Mr. Bullfrog	Finger Play: Frogs
Art	Lily Pads	Stuffed Frogs	Easel Painting	Frog Music Maker	Green Play Dough
Story Time	Book: *The Caterpillar and the Pollywog*	Stick Puppets: Five Little Speckled Frogs	Flannel Activity: Mr. Green Froggie	Book: *Jump Frog Jump*	Book: *The Wide Mouthed Frog*
Circle Time	Activity: Leap Froggie	Activity: Jumping Up	Song: Flick a Fly	Activity: Frog Fishing	Activity: Feed the Frogs
Food Experiences	Frog on a Lily Pad	Green Gelatin	Lily Pad Cookies	Biscuit Frogs	Frogs on a Log
Theme Activities	Song: A Frog Went Walking	Finger Play: Five Little Froggies	Activity: Let's Act! Five Little Speckled Frogs	Flannel Activity: Frogs	Activity: Let's Act! Mr. Green Frog

Monday

Materials Needed For The Week:

lime gelatin, celery, cream cheese, raisins, tuna, lettuce leaves, cherry halves, balance beam, craft sticks, frog eggs, canned biscuits, food coloring, round cookies, white frosting, toilet paper tubes, rubber bands, mayonnaise, bread or crackers

Sharing Time: Finger Play

"Five Little Speckled Frogs" (Traditional)

Five little speckled frogs sitting on a speckled log. *(Hold up five fingers.)*
Eating some most delicious bugs, yum, yum. *(Rub belly.)*
One jumped into the pool, where it was nice and cool, *(One finger, jumping in pool-arm rounded.)*
Then there were four speckled frogs, glump, glump. *(All say glump, glump.)*
(Continue until there are no frogs left.)

Put frogs eggs in the science center. Discuss the frog eggs. Explain to the children what they will look like as they develop.

Art: Lily Pads

Give children a large piece of green construction paper. Let them cut out their own lily pads.

Story Time: Book

Read *The Caterpillar and the Pollywog* by Jack Kent.

Circle Time: Leap Froggie

Lay lily pads around the room. Children can leap from lily pad to lily pad.

Food Experiences: Frog on a Lily Pad

Make tuna fish salad and chill. At lunch give each child a lettuce leaf on a small paper plate. Use an ice cream scoop to put the tuna fish salad on the lettuce leaf. Use red cherry halves for eyes. Serve with bread or crackers. Other suggestions include egg salad sprinkled with parsley flakes or cream cheese tinted green.

Theme Activities: Song

"A Frog Went Walking" (Traditional)

A frog went walking on a summer day, a-hum, a-hum.
A frog went walking on a summer day; he met Miss Mousie on the way, a-hum, a-hum.
He said, "Miss Mousie, will you marry me?" A- hum, a-hum.
He said, "Miss Mousie, will you marry me?
We'll live together in an apple tree,"
A-hum, a-hum.
And what do you think they had for supper? A-hum, a-hum.
And what do you think they had for supper?
A fried mosquito and bread and butter,
A-hum, a-hum.

Sharing Time: Finger Play

"Mr. Green Froggie"

Mr. Green Froggie was fast asleep *(put cheek on hand)*
On a lily pad where the pool was deep.

He heard some wings go buzzing by *(flap arms)*

He opened his eyes and there was a fly. *(open eyes wide)*

Snap went the froggie! *(snap fingers)*

Away the fly flew! *(flap arms)*

And Mr. Green Froggie went hopping off, too. *(hop)*

Let children observe the frog eggs. Ask them questions about what they see.

Art: Stuffed Frogs
Cut out two frog shapes from green construction paper using the patterns on page 351. Children can draw on features. Staple around frog leaving an open space. Children can then stuff tissue paper inside the frog and staple the opening closed.

Story Time: Stick Puppets
Use the frog patterns on page 353 and attach a craft stick. Repeat the finger play, "Five Little Speckled Frogs" on page 345.

Circle Time: Jumping Up
Let children pretend to be frogs and see how many ways they can jump.

Food Experiences: Green Gelatin Squares
Make according to directions on box. Pour into oblong pan. When chilled cut into squares.

Theme Activities: Finger Play

"Five Little Froggies" (Traditional)

Five little froggies sitting on a well, *(Hold up five fingers.)*

One peeked in and down he fell. *(Hold up one finger.)*

Froggies jumped high. *(With hand, jump up.)*

Froggies jumped low. *(With hand, jump low.)*

Froggies jumped everywhere, to and fro! *(With both hands, jump forward and sideways.)*

(Continue until none are left. This can be done from ten down.)

Wednesday

Sharing Time: Poem

"Little Frogs"

Hop, hop, hop, I'm a little frog.
See us hopping all together,
In the bright and sunny weather.
For we love the sun, hopping every one.

Again check to see if the frog eggs have changed. Let the children descibe what they see.

Art: Easel Painting
Use green paint and have children create green frogs on lily pads.

Story Time: Flannel Activity
Do "Mr. Green Froggie" on pages 351 and 352 as a flannel activity.

Circle Time: Song
Sing the song "Flick a Fly" from the record *Walter The Waltzing Worm*.

Food Experiences: Lily Pad Cookie
Give each child a round cookie and some white frosting. Let them decorate the cookie to look like a lily pad.

Theme Activities: Let's Act
Let the children act out "Five Little Speckled Frogs." In groups of five, have children sit on a balance beam or a strip of tape on the floor. The rest of the class recites the poem. As they do, groups of five can take turns acting this out. One 'frog' jumps into the pool until the end of the poem.

Thursday

Sharing Time: Finger Play

"Mr. Bullfrog"

Here's Mr. Bullfrog sitting on a rock; *(Hold up one finger.)*
Along comes a little boy; *(With other hand, use first two fingers as a boy.)*
Mr. Bullfrog jumps! Kerflop! *(One finger, jump.)*

Check the eggs for any tadpoles that have broken out of the eggs. Let all the children see. What has happened to the eggs?

Art: Frog Music Maker

Use a toilet paper tube and have children draw pictures of a frog on it. On each end of the tube, make two small cuts directly across from one another. Stretch a rubber band from one end of the tube to the other, placing it in the cuts. Pluck the band at one end to make sounds.

Story Time: Book

Read *Jump Frog Jump* by Robert Kalan.

Circle Time: Frog Fishing

Go frog fishing. Cut a large lilly pad to lay frogs on.

Use the fishing pole and construction paper frogs. Put numbers, shapes, or colors on frogs. Ask children to catch the one you name. See instructions for fishing poles on page 7. Make five frogs from the patterns on page 353.

Food Experiences: Biscuit Frogs

Give each child one canned biscuit. Let them shape it into a frog and paint it with green food coloring before it is baked.

Theme Activities: Flannel Activity

"Frogs"

Five little frogs sat on the shore,
One went for a swim and then there were four.
Four little frogs looked out to sea,
One went swimming and then there were three.
Three little frogs said, "What can we do!"
One jumped in the water and then there were two.
Two little frogs sat in the sun,
This one swam off and then there was one.
One little frog said, "This is no fun."
So he dived in the water and then there were none.
Use patterns on page 353.

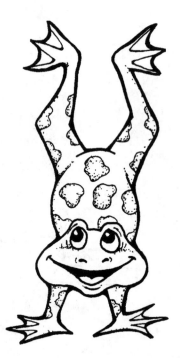

Friday

Sharing Time: Finger Play

Do "Frogs" from Thursday's Theme Activities as a finger play. Start with five fingers, then take one away as the frogs go for a swim.

Observe frog eggs.

Art: Play Dough Frogs

Use green play dough to make frogs. See recipe on page 6.

Story Time: Book

Read *The Wide Mouthed Frog* by Rex Schneider.

Circle Time: Feed the Frogs

Play Feed the Frogs. Draw a large frog on a poster board. Cut out the mouth of the frog. Children can throw bean bags through the frog's mouth.

Food Experiences: Frog on a Log

Clean celery and cut in short pieces for log. Add cream cheese that has been tinted with green food coloring. Children can add raisins for eyes.

Theme Activities: Let's Act

Let children act out "Mr. Green Froggie" from Tuesday's Sharing Time. Give children a lily pad made from green paper to stand on. You might wish to make a black fly from construction paper or a glove puppet (see page 7 for directions) and pretend to be the fly buzzing as children act out the rhyme.

Classroom
Additions

Center Ideas

Here are some suggestions of materials that can be placed in the learning centers in addition to your regular materials.

- Housekeeping: lily pad placemats (make like art activity and cover with clear contact paper)
- Circle: balance beam (Pretend to be frogs sitting on a log.)
- Books: books about frogs
- Table Activities: file folder activities listed
- Blocks: lily pads, frog fishing
- Puppets: frog stick puppets
- Science: frog growth chart
- Science Activities

  Set out frog eggs. If possible use a magnifying glass to see them.

Teachers Aids

- File Folder Activities: Choose the skills you wish to emphasize this week. See directions on pages 5 and 6.
- Match The Frog Spots   • Lily Pad Counting
- Match The Frogs

Bulletin Board Ideas:

- Frogs
- Lily Pads   • Water   • Display children's art work.

For Parents

- Check out books about frogs at the library.
- Take your child to a pond to find frog eggs. Notice their development and discuss with your child.
- Go frog hunting.
- Find items that are the color green.
- Provide child with crayons and paper so he/she can draw the development of the eggs through frog stage.

Bibliography

Children's Books

Kalan, Robert. ***Jump Frog Jump.*** Morrow, 1989
Kent, Jack. ***The Caterpillar and the Polliwog.*** Simon & Schuster, 1985
Schneider, Rex. ***The Wide Mouthed Frog.*** Stemmer House, 1980

Records

Hap Palmer. ***Walter the Waltzing Worm.*** Educational Activities, Inc., 1982

Patterns

Patterns

Patterns

Weekly Theme: _Butterflies_   **Week of:** _____

	Monday	Tuesday	Wednesday	Thursday	Friday
Date					
Sharing Time	Finger Play: Fuzzy Caterpillar	Finger Play: Sleepy Caterpillar	Discuss the Color of Butterflies	Poem: Caterpillar	Flannel Activity: Caterpillar
Art	Caterpillar	Cocoons	Butterfly	Finger Paint	Rolly Caterpillar
Story Time	Flannel Story: The Butterfly Tray	Book: _Cathy Caterpillar and Betty Bee_	Book: _From Egg to Butterfly_	Book: _The Caterpillar_	Book: _The Very Hungry Caterpillar_
Circle Time	Activity: Caterpillar Wiggle	Activity: Butterfly Development	Activity: Dance Like a Butterfly	Activity: Butterfly Emerging	Book: _The Butterfly_
Food Experiences	Vegi Caterpillars	Fuzzy Caterpillar	Butterfly Salad	Cocoon Snacks	Buttery Foods
Theme Activities	Book: _Terry and the Caterpillar_	Book: _It's Easy to Have a Caterpillar Visit You_	Book: _Caterpillar and the Polliwog_	Book: _Look. . . A Butterfly_	Butterfly Emerging

Monday

Materials Needed For The Week:

celery, cream cheese, raisins, lettuce, crushed pineapple, cherries, refrigerator biscuits, parsley flakes, "butter" foods, egg cartons, pipe cleaners, scarves, cheese, pimentos, pretzel sticks

Sharing Time: Finger Play

"Fuzzy Caterpillar"

Fuzzy little caterpillar, *(Hold up thumb.)*
Into a corner will creep.
He'll spin himself a blanket, *(Put thumb inside hand.)*
And then go fast asleep.
Fuzzy little caterpillar,
Wakes up by and by.
To find he has wings, *(Put thumbs beside each other and hold fingers outward.)*
And has turned into a
Butterfly! *(Hold hands same as above and move fingers.)*

Discuss what "fuzzy" means. Make a feelie box. See page 7 for directions.

Art: Caterpillar

Use egg cartons. Cut in half lengthwise. Add pipe cleaners for antennae. Add facial features with permanent markers. Let children color or paint the caterpillars.

Story Time: Flannel Story
Patterns are on page 362 and 363.

"The Butterfly Tray" (A Zuni Indian Legend)

Long, long ago there lived in New Mexico a very beautiful Indian girl named Dove Wing. She was the best weaver of the beautiful wicker trays for which the Zuni tribe was famous. Girls from the other nearby cities came to learn the skill of weaving from Dove Wing.

Dove Wing's father was the village rain chief. Each year when the crops needed rain, her father would prepare for the rain ceremony. He would take the specially dyed feathers and lay them on the wicker trays for the ceremony. This ceremony never failed to please the rain god Sayatasha, and the clouds sent the life-giving rainwater.

Monday (cont.)

One year all this changed. The rain didn't come. The ground was cracked and dry. Dust was everywhere. The rain god, Sayatasha, was not pleased with the offering this year. The villagers were alarmed and a special council meeting was called.

It was decided that Dove Wing must weave a special prayer tray with the most beautiful design that she had ever made. The young Indian girl wandered out into the fields searching for a design that would please the rain god. She realized that the future of her whole tribe depended on her.

In the fields she saw the most beautiful butterfly she had ever seen. She tried to catch it but each time she got close, it fluttered just beyond her. Soon, the chase after the beautiful butterfly had taken her far from home to new and strange lands.
She found herself in front of a very beautiful tree. Instead of leaves it had millions of butterflies on its branches.

Dove Wing knew it must be a meeting place of all the butterflies. She walked up to the tree and suddenly was face-to-face with a beautiful girl dressed in the same heavenly blue as the wings of the butterfly.

The Butterfly Girl took Dove Wing into a large, open room where beautiful girls sat weaving beautiful wicker trays with butterfly designs. The girls helped Dove Wing to weave the perfect design for her special tray. When Dove Wing brought the new butterfly tray to her father, he was very pleased. The next day he offered the special tray to Sayatasha. The rain god must have been very pleased, for the rain began to fall steadily and gently. Everyone said it was the best harvest that they could remember.

Circle Time: Caterpillar Wiggle
   Children can wiggle on the carpet like caterpillars.

Food Experiences: Vegi Caterpillars
   Spread cottage or cream cheese on a stick of celery. Add raisins for eyes.

Theme Activities: Book
   Read *Terry and the Caterpillar* by Millicent E. Selsam.

Tuesday

Sharing Time: Finger Play

"Sleepy Caterpillars"

"Let's go to sleep," the caterpillars said, *(Hold up thumb.)*
As they tucked themselves into their beds. *(Put thumb inside hand)*
They will awaken by and by, *(Take thumb out of hand)*
And each one will be a beautiful butterfly. *(Put thumbs together and "flap" hands.)*

Discuss the life cycle of a caterpillar. Explain cocoons.

Art: Cocoons
Let children wrap cotton batting around a craft stick or a small tree branch to simulate a cocoon.

Story Time: Book
Read *Cathy Caterpillar and Betty Bee* by Sally Rippon.

Circle Time: Butterfly Development
Using scarves, children can pretend they are caterpillars turning into a butterfly. Let them start by being rolled up in a ball, with the scarves scrunched into their hands. Slowly, let them unroll themselves to become butterflies and spread their wings.

Food Experiences: Fuzzy Caterpillar
Soften 8 oz. (2.25 g) of cream cheese and 12 oz. (340 g) of shredded American cheese. Mix together. Let each child make five small round balls and roll balls in parsley flakes. Arrange on a lettuce leaf. Add pimento pieces for eyes and nose. Use pretzel stick for antennas.

Theme Activities: Book
Read *It's Easy to Have a Caterpillar Visit You* by Caroline O'Hagen.

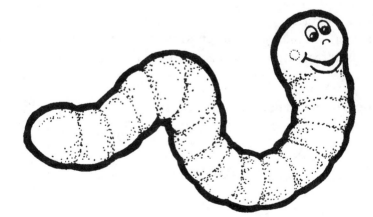

Wednesday

Sharing Time: Colors of Butterflies

Discuss the colors of butterflies. Butterflies can be cut from different colors of felt and put on the flannel board. Let children name the colors.

Art: Butterfly

Using tempera paint, paint the bottom of the children's feet. Have paper nearby and have them put one foot down towards the bottom of the paper. Then put the heel for the other foot down, touching the toe of the other foot. This will become the butterfly body. Then paint children's hands and place one on either side of the body to create the wings. After the paint has dried, decorate the wings by gluing small paper or bits of fabric to it.

Story Time: Book

Read *From Egg to Butterfly* by Marlene Reidel.

Circle Time: Dance Like a Butterfly

Using scarves or streamers, encourage children to dance like a butterfly. Children can hold streamers in their hands or you can attach scarves to their shoulders.

Food Experiences: Butterfly Salad

Place crushed pineapple in the center of a lettuce leaf. Add cherries for decoration to create a butterfly salad.

Theme Activities: Book

Read *The Caterpillar and the Polliwog* by Jack Kent.

Thursday

Sharing Time: Poem

> ***"Caterpillar"*** (Traditional)
> Caterpillar, caterpillar, brown and furry,
> Winter is coming and you'd better hurry.
> Find a leaf under which to creep.
> Spin a cocoon in which to sleep.
> Then when springtime comes one day,
> You'll be a butterfly and fly away!

Art: Fingerpaint
Using fingerpaint (see recipe on page 6), let children create caterpillars and butterflies.

Story Time: Book
Read *The Caterpillar* by Christina Rossetti.

Circle Time: Butterfly Emerging
Use a large cardboard box that has both end flaps. Let children crawl in one end of the box as a caterpillar and then emerge from the opposite end as a butterfly. Have them roll or creep into the box and come out flying. Put some scarves or streamers in the box so they can emerge as butterflies.

Food Experiences: Cocoon Snacks Use refrigerated biscuit dough and put a chunk of cheese into each one before baking. As children bite into them explain what it might be like to be in a cocoon.

Theme Activities: Book
Read *Look...A Butterfly* by David Cutts.

Friday

Sharing Time: Flannel Activity
   Use the poem "Caterpillar" from Thursday as a flannel activity. Use the patterns on page 363.

Art: Roly Caterpillar
   Have children cut out round colored circles to form a caterpillar. Add facial features. Then glue the caterpillar onto white construction paper.

Story Time: Book
   Read *The Very Hungry Caterpillar* by Eric Carle.

Circle Time: Book
   Read *The Butterfly* by Paula Z. Hogan.

Food Experiences: Buttery Foods
   Give children the experience of trying foods with the word butter in them. Some foods to include are peanut butter, apple butter, buttermilk, butter flavored crackers.

Theme Activities: Butterfly Emerging
   Repeat this activity from Circle Time on Thursday. Put streamers or scarves in the box for children to use as they emerge as butterflies.

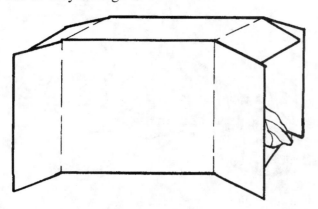

Classroom Additions

Center Ideas

Here are some suggestions of materials that can be placed in the learning centers in addition to your regular materials.

- Housekeeping: pictures of butterflies on the wall
- Circle: an assortment of colored flannel butterflies
- Books: books about butterflies
- Table Activities: file folder activities listed
- Blocks: cardboard box
- Puppets: butterfly puppet, caterpillar puppet
- Science: magnifying glass, pictures of caterpillars, cocoons, butterflies
- Science Activities

    Catch a butterfly in a net. Look very closely but don't touch. Let the butterfly free.

Teachers' Aids

File Folder Activities: Choose the skills you wish to emphasize this week. See directions on pages 5 and 6.

- Caterpillar Color Matching
- Butterfly Wallpaper Matching

Bulletin Board Ideas:

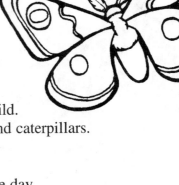

- Caterpillars
- Cocoons
- Butterflies
- Trees

For Parents

- Discuss the development of the butterfly with your child.
- Go to the library and check out books on butterflies and caterpillars.
- Talk about the different colors of butterflies.
- Go on a butterfly hunt with your child.
- Let your child prepare the butterfly salad for lunch one day.
- Dance like a butterfly.

Bibliography

Children's Books

Carle, Eric. *The Very Hungry Caterpillar.* Philomel Books, 1981

Cutts, David. *Look... A Butterfly.* Troll, 1982

Hogan, Paula Z. *The Butterfly.* Raintree, 1979

Kent, Jack. *The Caterpillar and the Polliwog.* Simon & Schuster, 1985

O'Hagan, Caroline, ed. *It's Easy to Have a Caterpillar Visit You.* Lothrop, 1980

Reidel, Marlene. *From Egg to Butterfly.* Carolrhoda Books, 1981

Rippon, Sally. *Cathy Caterpillar and Betty Bee.* Rourke Corporation, 1982

Rossetti, Christina. *The Caterpillar.* Calico Books, 1988

Selsam, Millicent E. *Terry and the Caterpillars.* Harper, 1962

Patterns

Patterns

Weekly Theme: *Mice*   Week of: _____

	Monday	Tuesday	Wednesday	Thursday	Friday
Date					
Sharing Time	Glove Puppet: Five Little Mice	Finger Play: Mousie Brown	Finger Play: Hickory, Dickory, Dock	Finger Play: A Mouse Lived in a Hole	Finger Play: This Little Mouse
Art	Heart Mouse	Mouse Stick Puppet	Paper Plate Clock	Mouse Print	Mouse Puzzle
Story Time	Flannel Story: Mouse and the Thunder	Book: *Whose Mouse Are You?*	Book: *Mouse Tales*	Book: *Anatole*	Book: *The Country Mouse and the City Mouse*
Circle Time	Song: Three Blind Mice	Activity: Farmer in the Dell	Song: Mousercise	Activity: Mouse, May I?	Activity: Find the Cheese
Food Experiences	Green Cheese and Crackers	A Mouse for Lunch	Cheese Popcorn	Mouse In a Hole	Taste Different Cheeses
Theme Activities	Poem: The Little Mouse	Rhyme: Six Little Mice Sat Down to Spin	Book: *The Dragon and the Mouse*	Flannel Activity: Little Mousie	Book: *A Mouse In My House*

Monday

Materials Needed For The Week:

glove for glove puppet, play food (cheese), cream cheese, crackers, green food coloring, spray cheese, pears, raisins, cheese popcorn, bread, cheese slices

Sharing Time: Glove Puppet

Make a glove puppet for "Five Little Mice." See instructions on page 7. Use any of the patterns throughout the mice unit.

"Five Little Mice" (Traditional)

Five little mice came out to play,
Gathering crumbs along the way.
Out came pussycat sleek and fat;
Four little mice go scampering back.

(Continue until no mice are left. This can be done from 10 to 1.)

Art: Heart Mouse

Out of gray construction paper cut a large heart. The pointed part will be the head of the mouse. Draw facial features and add a piece of yam for the tail. Cut out pink ears and glue to the side of the head.

Story Time: Flannel Story

See patterns on page 372.

"Mouse and the Thunder"

Once there was a little mouse who was afraid of thunder. When she saw thick, dark clouds in the sky she would run and hide.

"Thunder! Thunder scares you!" the other mice would cry. They would chase her and cry, "Thunder! Thunder! Run!" And it scared the little mouse so she ran and hid.

One day she went for a walk. She was far, far away. It was hot. "I'm thirsty," said the mouse. "Oh, I want a drink. I am so thirsty!" Just then it began to thunder, but the little mouse was so thirsty that for a moment she didn't hear the thunder. Then a great clap of thunder rolled out of the sky. It scared her and she cried and began to run. Then she saw a frog.

"Thunder!" he said. "I'm glad. Now my pool won't dry up." The frog liked thunder.

Then she saw a duck. "Thunder! Hurrah!" he said. " Mud is nice." The duck liked thunder.

"They are glad it thunders," said the mouse. She thought and thought. "I knowl When it thunders we have rain," she thought. "And rain is good. If it rains, I can have some water. And I'm so thirsty!"

The mouse was right. Soon it rained. She got her drink of water, and thunder didn't scare her after that.

Tuesday

Circle Time: Song

"Three Blind Mice" (Traditional Tune)

Three blind mice,

Three blind mice.

See how they run.

See how they run.

They all ran after the farmer's wife,

She cut off their tails with a carving knife.

Did you ever see such a sight in your life,

As three blind mice.

Food Experiences: Green Cheese and Crackers

Using green food coloring, color cream cheese green and serve with crackers.

Theme Activities: Poem

"The Little Mouse" (Mother Goose)

I have seen you, little mouse,

Running all about the house;

Through the hole your little eye,

In the wainscot peeping sly,

Hoping soon some crumbs to steal,

To make quite a hearty meal.

Look before you venture out,

See if kitty is about.

If she's gone, you'll quickly run,

To the larder for some fun;

Round about the dishes creep,

Taking into each a peep,

To choose the daintiest that's there,

Spoiling things you do not care.

Tuesday (cont.)

Sharing Time: Finger Play

"Mousie Brown" (Old Chinese Rhyme)

Up the candlestick he ran,

Little Mousie Brown,

To go and eat the tallow,

But he couldn't get back down.

He called for his Grandma,

"Grandma, Grandma,"

But his Grandma was in town.

So he doubled up into a ball,

And rolled right down.

Art: Mouse Stick Puppet
Use the pattern on page 372 and cut out a mouse's head. Color and tape on a craft stick.

Story Time: Book
Read *Whose Mouse Are* You? by Robert Kraus.

Circle Time: Activity/Song
Do the "Farmer in the Dell." See Farm week, page 335.

Food Experiences: A Mouse for Lunch
Place a pear half upside down on a small paper plate. Use spray cheese to make a tail. Raisins attached with a dab of the cheese will work for eyes.

Theme Activities: Rhyme

Six Little Mice Sat Down to Spin (Nursery Rhyme)

Six little mice sat down to spin,

Pussy passed by, and she peeped in

"What are you at, my little men?"

"Making coats for gentlemen."

"Shall I come in and bite off your threads?"

"No, no, Miss Pussy, you'll snip off our heads

"Oh, no, I'll not, I'll help you spin."

"That may be so, but you don't come in!"

Wednesday

Sharing Time: Finger Play

"Hickory, Dickory, Dock" (Traditional)

Hickory, Dickory, Dock,

The mouse ran up the clock,

The clock struck one,

The mouse ran down,

Hickory, Dickory, Dock.

Art: Paper Plate Clock
Use a nine inch (23 cm) paper plate. Write clock numbers around the rim. Cut one small hand and one large hand out of tag board. Fasten hands to the center of the plate with a brass paper fastener.

Story Time: Book
Read *Mouse Tales* by Arnold Lobel.

Circle Time: Song
Sing and do "Mousercise" from the record *Mousercise.*

Food Experiences: Cheese Popcorn
Buy and serve already-made cheese popcorn or pop some in the classroom and add grated cheddar cheese or parmesan cheese to it.

Theme Activities: Book
Read *The Dragon and the Mouse* by Timm.

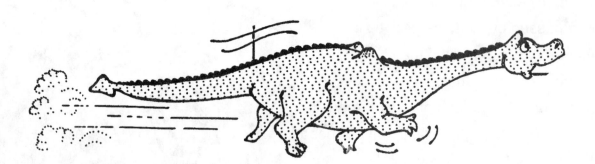

Thursday

Sharing Time: Finger Play

"A Mouse Lived in a Hole"

A mouse lived in a hole, *(make circle of thumb and index finger)*

Lived softly in a little hole. *(put index inger of other hand in hole)*

When all was quiet as can be (sh! sh!) *(put index finger to lips)*

When all was quiet as can be (sh! sh!) *(put index finger of other hand in hole)*

Out popped HE! *(pop finger out of hole)*

Art: Mouse Prints

Have children use their fingerprints to make mouse pictures. Use fingerpaint or tempera paint.

Story Time: Book

Read *Anatole* by Eve Titus.

Circle Time: Mouse, May I?

Play "Mouse, May I?' like "Mother, May I?" Encourage children to take steps such as little mice steps or to run very quickly.

Food Experience: Mouse in a Hole

Let children poke a hole or tear a piece out of a slice of bread as a mouse might. Lay a slice of cheese over the hole and melt it.

Theme Activities: Flannel Activity

Use the patterns on page 374.

"Little Mousie"

See the little mousie

Creeping up the stair,

Looking for a warm nest.

There-Oh! There.

Friday

Sharing Time: Finger Play

"This Little Mouse"
Five little mice on the pantry floor;
This little mouse peeked behind the door;
This little mouse nibbled at some cake;
This little mouse not a sound did make;
This little mouse took a bite of cheese;
This little mouse heard the kitten sneeze.
"Ah-choo!" sneezed the kitten.
And "Squeak!" the mice cried
And they found a hole and ran inside.
(Hold up one finger, then two, etc.)

Art: Mouse Puzzle

Draw a large mouse on tag board or use one of the patterns at the end of the unit. Cut the mouse shape out. Have children color the mouse. Cut the mouse up into several pieces.

Story Time: Book

Read *The Country Mouse and the City Mouse* told by Patricia Scarry.

Circle Time: Find the Cheese

Use the pattern on page 370. Cut out pieces of cheese and hide them around the room. Have children find them.

Food Experiences: Cheese Tasting

Bring in several different types of cheese. Give the children the opportunity to taste them. Take a poll and see which type they like the best.

Theme Activities: Book

Read *A Mouse In My House* by Houston.

Classroom Additions

Center Ideas

Here are some suggestions of materials that can be placed in the learning centers in addition to your regular materials.

- Housekeeping: cheese play food or real containers
- Circle: cheese flannel pieces for counting
- Books: books about mice
- Table Activities Area: file folder activities listed
- Blocks: plastic mice, mouse house (cut hole in a cracker box)
- Puppets: mice stick puppets
- Science: pictures of mice
- Science Activities: Bring in a pet mouse. Let children help take turns caring for it.

Teachers' Aids

File Folder Activities: Choose the skills you wish to emphasize this week. See directions on pages 5 and 6.

- Cheese Matching
- Count The Mice
- Mouse Quilt

Bulletin Board Ideas:
- Mice   • Cheese
- Mouse House

For Parents

- Take your child to the pet store. Look at the mice. Discuss what mice look like.
- Read mice stories to your child.
- Buy your child a stuffed mouse.
- Make available crayons and paper to draw.

Bibliography

Childrens Books

Houston. *A Mouse In My House.* Addison-Wesley, 1972

Kraus, Robert. *Whose Mouse Are You?* Macmillan, 1970

Lobel, Arnold. *Mouse Tales.* Harper, 1978

Scarry, Patricia. (told by), *The Country Mouse and the City Mouse.* Golden Press, 1961

Timm, Stephen. *The Dragon and the Mouse.* Steppingstone Ent., 1981

Titus, Eve. *Anatole.* Bantam Little Rooster Book, 1990

Records

Mousercise. Disneyland/Vista Records.

Patterns

Patterns

Patterns

Weekly Theme: _Families_   Week of: _____

	Monday	Tuesday	Wednesday	Thursday	Friday
Date					
Sharing Time	Poem: Grandma's Spectacles	Finger Play: Baby Grows	Finger Play: Fine Family	Poem: The Family	Poem: I Asked My Mother
Art	Easel Painting	Friendship Chain	Special Bouquet	Family Tree	Family Card
Story Time	Book: *Just Me and My Mom*	Book: *Just Me and My Dad*	Book: *What is a Family?*	Book: *When the Relatives Came*	Book: *When I Was Young in the Mountains*
Circle Time	Flannel Story: The Bundle of Sticks	Song: Friends	Folk Song: Hush Little Baby	Finger Play: Good Little Mother	Song: What a Miracle
Food Experiences	Family Favorites	Gingerbread Family	Family Style	Family Dessert	Take Home a Treat
Theme Activities	Book: *Love You Forever*	Flannel Story: Old Mother Hubbard	Song: The Hugging Song	Book: *Your Family Tree*	Book: *Are You My Mother?*

Materials Needed For The Week:
   tissue paper, pipe cleaners, paper doilies, gingerbread cookies, frosting, vegetables, cupcakes, candy decoration

Sharing Time: Poem
   "Grandma's Spectacles" (Traditional)

   These are grandmother's spectacles, *(Make circles around eyes with fingers.)*
   This is grandmother's hat. *(Use both hands and cup on head.)*
   This is the way she folds her hands, *(Fold hands.)*
   And puts them in her lap. *(Put hands in lap.)*

   Discuss children's family members.

Art: Easel Painting
   Let children create their own picture to take home to their parents.

Story Time: Book
   Read *Just Me and My Mom* by Mercer Mayer.

Circle Time: Flannel Story
   See patterns on page 382.

   "The Bundle Of Sticks" (Aesop)

   A certain father had a family of sons, who were forever quarreling among themselves. No words he could say did the least good, so he tried to think of a way to show them that quarreling would lead them to misfortunes.

   One day when the quarreling had been much more violent than usual and each of the sons was gloomy and cross, he asked one of them to bring him a bundle of sticks. Then handing the bundle to each of his sons in turn, he told them to try to break it. But although each one tried his best, none was able to do so.

   The father then untied the bundle and gave the sticks to his sons to break one by one. This they did very easily.

   "My sons," said the father, "do you not see how certain it is that if you agree with each other and help each other, it will be impossible for your enemies to injure you? But if you are divided among yourselves, you will be weaker than a single stick in that bundle."

Food Experiences: Family Favorites
   Have children share their family's favorite dessert. Then either ask a parent to contribute it to the class or make a version of it on your own.

Theme Activities: Book
   Read *Love You Forever* by Robert Munsch.

Tuesday

Sharing Time: Finger Play

"Baby Grows" (Traditional)

Five little fingers on this hand, *(Hold up five fingers.)*

Five little fingers on that. *(Hold up five fingers on the other hand.)*

A dear little nose, *(Point to nose.)*

A mouth like a rose, *(Point to mouth.)*

Two little cheeks so tiny and fat. *(Point to cheeks.)*

Two eyes and two ears *(Point to eyes and then ears.)*

And ten little toes, *(Point to toes.)*

That is the way the baby grows.

Discuss friends and families.

Art: Friendship Chain
Put children into small groups to work together to make a friendship chain. Have strips of construction paper already cut for children to glue together. They can wear their own chain or exchange with a friend.

Story Time: Book
Read *Just Me and My Dad* by Mercer Mayer.

Circle Time: Song
Sing "Friends" from the record *On the Move With Steve and Greg,*

Food Experiences: Gingerbread Family
Give each child a ready-made gingerbread cookie and frosting. Have them decorate it to look like a member of their family.

Theme Activities: Flannel Story
Do "Mother Hubbard." The poem and patterns are located in Mother Goose week, pages 148 and 151.

Wednesday

Sharing Time: Finger Play

"Fine Family" (Traditional)

Here is the family in my household.
Some are young,
And some are old.
Some are tall,
Some are small.
Some are growing just like me.
Together we all live as a family.

(Hold up one finger for each line, starting with thumb.)
Have children bring family photographs.

Art: A Special Bouquet

Help children make flowers out of tissue paper and attach to pipe cleaners. Tie a few together with ribbon or yarn. Attach a note to their mother or another special person in their life.

Story Time: Book

Read *What is a Family?* by Gretchen Super.

Circle Time: Folk Song

"Hush Little Baby" (*Folk* Song)

Hush little baby, don't say a word.
Papa's gonna buy you a mockingbird.
If that mocking bird won't sing,
Papa's gonna buy you a diamond ring.
If that diamond ring turns brass,
Papa's gonna buy you a looking glass.
If that looking glass gets broke,
Papa's gonna buy you a billy goat.
If that billy goat won't pull,
Papa's gonna buy you a cart and bull.
If that cart and bull turn over,
Papa's gonna buy you a dog named Rover.
If that dog named Rover won't bark.
Papa's gonna buy you a horse and cart.
If that horse and cart fall down,
You'll still be the sweetest little baby in town.

Food Experiences: Family Style

Prepare vegetables in advance. Let children then place them on platters and have everyone participate in serving, eating, and cleaning up "family style."

Theme Activities: Song

Sing "The Hugging Song" from the record ***Kidding Around With Steve & Greg.***

Thursday

Sharing Time: Poem

"The Family"

This is the Daddy who bakes the bread,

This is the Mother who tucks us in bed.

This is the brother who cuddles the doll,

This is the sister who bounces the ball.

This is the baby, the last one of all.

Oh! How we love them all.

Discuss grandparents.

Art: Family Tree

Gather family names of each child back to their grandparents. Let the child draw a tree and you write in the names of the family members.

Story Time: Book

Read *When the Relatives Came* by Cynthia Rylant.

Circle Time: Finger Play

"Good Strong Mother"

Good strong mother, how do you do? (Hold up thumb.)

Dear strong daddy, glad to see you; (Hold up next finger.)

Big, tall brother, pleased to see you are here; (Hold up next finger.)

Kind little sister, you need not fear; (Hold up next finger.)

Glad welcome we'll give you, and baby dear too,

Yes, baby dear, how do you do? (Hold up last finger.)

Food Experiences: Family Dessert

Get a parent or grandparent to come in and help prepare a favorite dessert for the children.

Theme Activities: Book

Read *Your Family Tree* by Jean Komaiko.

Friday

Sharing Time: Poem

"I Asked My Mother" (Anonymous)

I asked my mother for fifty cents,

To see the elephant jump the fence.

He jumped so high that he touched the sky,

And he never came back till the Fourth of July.

Art: Family Cards

Fold construction paper and use paper doilies to let each child make a card for his or her family. Encourage children to draw pictures of their family's favorite activity. Write any special notes that they want to send.

Story Time: Book

Read *When I Was Young in the Mountains* by Cynthia Rylant.

Circle Time: Song

Sing "What A Miracle" from the record *Walter the Waltzing Worm*.

Food Experiences: Take Home a Treat

Provide cupcakes or cookies for decorating. Give children frosting and some kind of candy decoration. Let each child decorate enough to take home one for each member of his or her family.

Theme Activities: Book

Read *Are You My Mother?* by P.E. Eastman.

Classroom Additions

Center Ideas

Here are some suggestions of materials that can be placed in the learning centers in addition to your regular materials.

- Housekeeping: pot of flowers for the table, family pictures hung on walls
- Circle: flannel family figures
- Books: photo album with children's pictures, pictures of different types of families, photographs of children's grandparents
- Table Activities: file folder activities listed
- Blocks: plastic family figures
- Puppets: family puppets (can be purchased at local school supply store)

Teachers' Aids

File Folder Activities: Choose the skills you wish to emphasize this week. See directions on pages 5-6.

- Glasses Matching
- Houses

Bulletin Board Ideas:

- Display photos of children
- Display children's baby pictures
- Display family trees
- Display pictures of families of different cultures

For Parents

- Discuss family trees with children.
- Visit grandparents and listen to stories of the past.
- Visit the library.
- Look at old family photographs with your child. Tell him or her who is each family member.

Bibliography

Childrens Books

Berenstain, Stan and Jan. *Papa's Pizza.* Random House, 1978

Eastman, P.D. *Are You My Mother?* Random House, 1960

Komaiko, Jean, & Kate Rosenthal. *Your Family Tree.* Parents' Magazine Press, 1963

Mayer, Mercer. *Just Me and My Dad.* Western, 1977

Mayer, Mercer. *Just Me and My Mom.* Western, 1990

Munsch, Robert. *Love You Forever.* Firefly Books Ltd., 1986

Rylant, Cynthia. *When the Relatives Came.* Bradbury, 1984

Rylant, Cynthia. *When I Was Young in the Mountains.* E.P. Dutton, 1985

Super, Gretchen. *What is a Family?* Troll, 1991

Records

Steve Millang and Greg Scelsa. *On the Move With Steve and Greg.* Youngheart Records, 1983

Steve Millang and Greg Scelsa. *Kidding Around With Steve And Greg.* Youngheart Records, 1985

Hap Palmer. *Walter the Waltzing Worm.* Educational Activities, Inc., 1982

Patterns

Weekly Theme: _Circus_   Week of: _____

	Monday	Tuesday	Wednesday	Thursday	Friday
Date					
Sharing Time	Finger Play: The Animal Fair	Let's Act: Tiger Walk	Let's Act: Five Big Elephants	Rhyme: Simple Simon	Finger Play: Balloons
Art	Ringmaster Hat	Clown Hats	Elephant Ears	Lion Masks	Paint Clown Faces
Story Time	Book: *Bearymore*	Book: *At the Circus*	Book: *Bear Circus*	Book: *Bozo the Clown the Beast With the Least*	Book: *Dumbo the Flying Elephant*
Circle Time	Book: *Circus*	Book: *Morris and Boris Go to the Circus*	Book: *Small Clown*	Book: *The Teddy-Bear Circus*	Book: *Morris and Boris at the Circus*
Food Experiences	Clown Salad	Clown Hats	Peanuts	Snow Cones	Popcorn in Bags
Theme Activities	Activity: Clown Act	Activity: Tight Rope Walk	Activity: Act Like an Elephant	Activity: Roar Like a Lion	Activity: Peanut Toss

Monday

Materials Needed For The Week:

pineapple slices, raisins, cherries, carrots, peanuts, popcorn, ice cream or frozen yogurt, frosting, small candies, paper plates, ice cream scoop, styrofoam packing peanuts, balloons, corn starch, cold cream, food coloring cotton swabs, crushed ice, fruit flavored syrup or juice, small paper cups, straws, yarn or ribbon, sugar ice cream cones, small paper sacks, brown spray paint

Sharing Time: Finger Play

"The Animal Fair" (Traditional)

I went to the animal fair.

The birds and the beasts were there.

The old baboon by the light of the moon

Was combing his auburn hair. *(Comb hair.)*

The monkey sure was spunk.

He climbed up the elephant's trunk. *(Walk first 2 fingers upward.)*

The elephant sneezed and fell to his knees, *(Achoooooo!)*

And that was the end of the monk, monk, monk, monk!

Discuss who has been to the circus before. Talk about what they saw.

Art: Ring Master Hat

Use black construction paper and cut out a top hat. Cut a rectangle for the front and a band to fit around the child's head.

Story Time: Book

Read *Bearymore* by Don Freeman.

Circle Time: Book

Read *Circus* by Lois Ehlert.

Food Experiences: Clown Salad

Put a pineapple slice on plate for a face, put two raisins for eyes, a cherry for the nose, and shredded carrots for hair.

Theme Activities: Clown Act

Children can pretend they are clowns. They can dance, sing, and act silly.

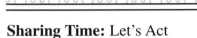

Tuesday

Sharing Time: Let's Act

   "Tiger Walk" (Traditional)

   Walk, walk, softly-slow- *(Children walk around the room.)*

   This is the way the tigers go. *(Children continue walking.)*

   Walk, walk, get out of the way, *(Children walk fast and hide.)*

   Tigers are coming to school today! *(Teacher can call them back when all is safe.)*

Art: Clown Hats

   Take a paper plate, cut a slit to the center, form into a cone, and staple together. Glue on any type of scrap tissue paper, cloth, or ribbon. Punch holes in each side and add yarn or ribbon. Tie under children's chins.

Story Time: Book

   Read *At the Circus* by Eugene Booth.

Circle Time: Book

   Read *Morris and Boris Go to the Circus* by Bernard Wiseman.

Food Experiences: Clown Hats

   Give each child a scoop of ice cream or frozen yogurt on a plate. Let children place a sugar ice cream cone on the top. Let them use frosting and small candies to decorate it and make a clown.

Theme Activities: Tight Rope Walk

   Use a balance beam or masking tape on the floor. Children can pretend to be walking on a tight rope high up in the air.

Wednesday

Sharing Time: Let's Act

"Five Big Elephants" (Traditional)

Five big elephants, oh, what a sight! *(Five children stand.)*
Swinging their trunks from left to right. *(With hands together, in front of them, swing arms gently.)*
Four are followers, and one is king. *(Children stand behind each other.)*
They all walk around in the circus ring! *(The other children sit in a circle with the five children-elephants in the center.)*
Continue until every one has been an elephant.

Discuss how large elephants can grow. Find a rope that long and show it to the children.

Art: Elephant Ears
Use the elephant ear pattern on page 390. The pattern given is for the left ear. To make the right ear, simply flip the pattern over. Then cut out the ears from gray construction paper and attach to a band to fit around a child's head.

Story Time: Book
Read *Bear Circus* by William Pene du Bois.

Circle Time: Book
Read *Small Clown* by Nancy Faulkner.

Food Experiences: Peanuts
Let each child decorate a small paper sack. Fill the sacks with peanuts in the shell. Serve the peanuts for a snack.

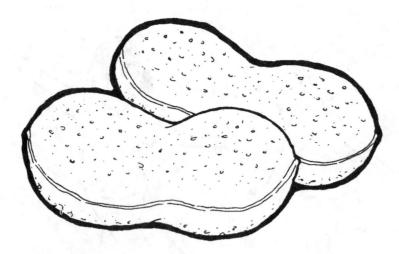

Theme Activities: Act Like an Elephant
Have children pretend they are elephants walking around the ring at the circus. Let them put their arms in front of them, with their hands joined to act as a trunk. Have them parade around the room.

Thursday

Sharing Time: Rhyme

> *"Simple Simon"* Simple Simon met a pieman
>
> Going to the fair;
>
> Says Simple Simon to the pieman,
>
> "Let me taste your ware."
>
> Says the pieman to Simple Simon,
>
> "Show me first your penny."
>
> Says Simple Simon to the pieman,
>
> "Indeed, I have not any."

Substitute the word "circus" for the word "fair." Or talk about the difference between a fair and a circus. Ask children who has been to a fair and how it differed from the circus.

Art: Lion Masks
Use paper plates. Draw lion faces on them. Glue on yarn for the mane.

Story Time: Book
Read *Bozo the Clown the Beast With the Least* by Carl Buettner.

Circle Time: Book
Read *The Teddy-Bear Circus* by Eleanor Conrad.

Food Experiences: Snow Cones
Bring in crushed ice and a fruit flavored syrup. Place a scoop of ice in a paper cup, then pour a little syrup over it. Give children straws to drink it with.

Theme Activities: Roar Like a Lion
Have children roar like a lion. One child can be the lion tamer and the other children can be the lions. Let the children form a circle around the lion tamer. The children can do what the lion tamer says.

Friday

Sharing Time: Finger Play

"Balloons"

This is the way we make a balloon, so, so, so. *(Cup hands in a circle.)*
This is the way we blow our balloon, blow, blow, blow. *(Pretend to blow up a balloon.)*
This is the way we break our balloon, oh, oh, oh. *(With hands cupped, squeeze hands inward until balloon pops.)*

Art: Paint Clown Faces

Use the recipe below to make clown face paint. Let the children use it to paint clown faces on each other. Cotton swabs work well for painting. (Children should wear aprons or smock to protect their clothing.)

Clown Face Paint

- 1 teaspoon (5 mL) cornstarch

- ½ teaspoon (2 mL) water

- ½ teaspoon (2mL) cold cream

- few drops of food coloring

   Mix cornstarch and water until smooth, stir in cold cream. Add food coloring. Make a batch of paint for each color.

Story Time: Book

Read *Dumbo the Flying Elephant* by Disney.

Circle Time: Book

Read *Morris and Boris at the Circus* by Bernard Wiseman.

Food Experience: Popcorn in Bags

Give each child a small paper bag to decorate. Pop popcorn and serve it in bags that the children have decorated.

Theme Activities: Peanut Toss

Use peanuts in a shell and let children try to toss them into a bucket. Styrofoam peanut packing can be used; spray lightly with brown spray paint.

Classroom Additions

Center Ideas

Here are some materials that can be placed in the learning centers in addition to your regular materials.

- Housekeeping: circus costumes
- Circle: flannel circus animals
- Books: books about the circus
- Table Activities: file folder activities listed
- Blocks: plastic circus animals
- Puppets: clown paper plate puppet
- Science: peanut plant
- Science Activities: Try a few of the following activities. Let each child blow up a balloon. Compare types of peanuts. Use shelled peanuts with and without red skins, and dry roasted peanuts.

Teachers' Aids

File Folder Activities: Choose the skills you wish to emphasize this week. See directions on pages 5 and 6.

- Clown Face - Making Different Facial Features
- Clowns and Balloons Color Matching
- Peanut Matching

Bulletin Board Ideas:

- Circus Tent   • Peanuts   • Clowns   • Balloons

For Parents

- Take your child to a circus if possible.
- Take your child to the library to check out books about the circus.
- With your child discuss circus animals and how they are treated.
- Buy some peanuts in the shell for snacks.
- Hang all of your child's art work up at home and discuss it.

Bibliography

Children's Books

Booth, Eugene. *At the Circus.* Raintree, 1985

Buettner, Carl. *Bozo the Clown the Beast With the Least.* Western Publishing, 1971

Conrad, Eleanor. *The Teddy-Bear Circus.* T.S. Denison, 1969

Disney. *Dumbo the Flying Elephant.* Random House, 1978

Ehlert, Lois. *Circus.* Harper Collins, 1992

Faulkner, Nancy. *Small Clown.* Doubleday, 1960

Freeman, Don. *Bearymore.* Viking, 1976

Pene du Bois, William. *Bear Circus for our Friends the Kangaroos.* Puffin, 1987

Wiseman, Bernard. *Morris and Boris Go to the Circus.* Harper and Row, 1988

Wiseman, Bernard. *Morris and Boris at the Circus.* Harper and Row, 1988

Patterns

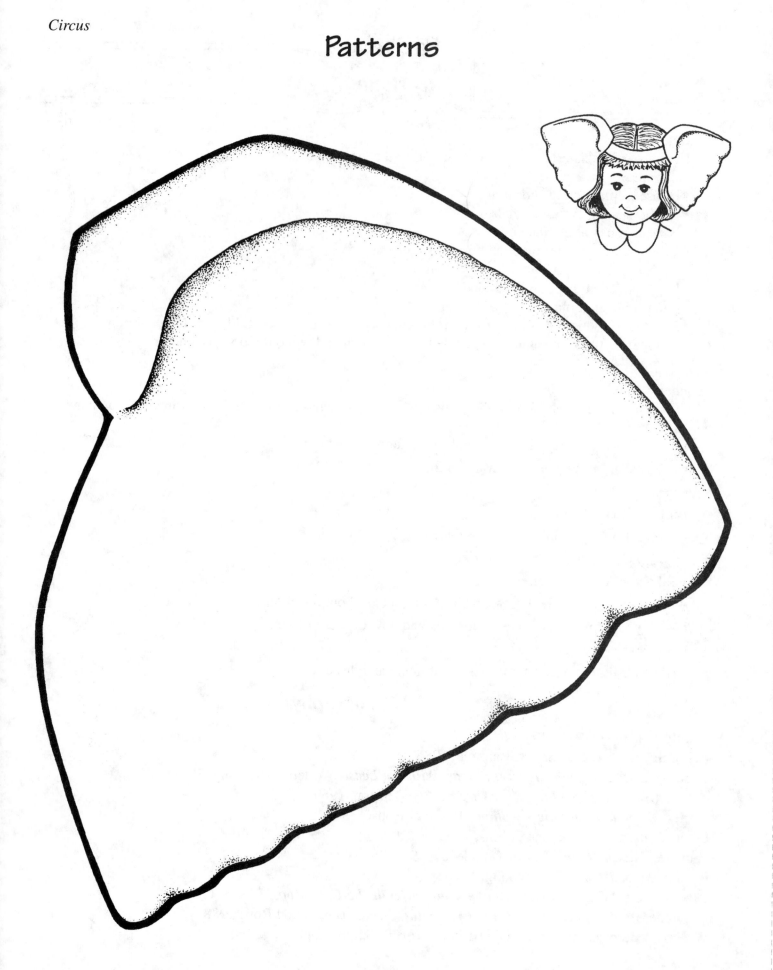

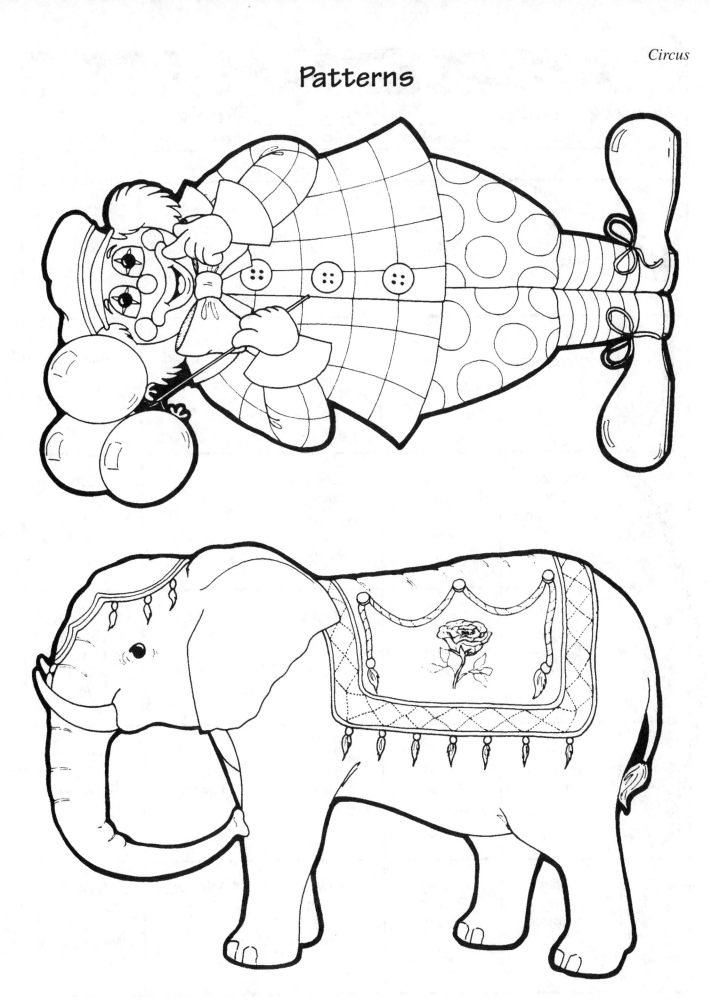

Weekly Theme: *Summertime*   Week of:

	Monday	Tuesday	Wednesday	Thursday	Friday
Date					
Sharing Time	Poem: Little Drops of Water	Poem: August Heat	Poem: A Kite	Finger Play: Baby Bumblebee	Let's Pretend: I Love to Row
Art	Fingerpainting	Starfish	Beach Scene	Sandpaper Seahorse	Sailboats
Story Time	Flannel Story: The Dog and the Bumblebee	Book: *At the Beach*	Book: *Teeny Witch Goes on Vacation*	Book: *Under the Sea*	Book: *Mr. Bear's Boat*
Circle Time	Song/Activity: Down in the Sea	Song: The Magic Coin	Flannel Story: The Ants and the Grasshopper	Activity: Play in a Wading Pool	Flannel Story: The Boy and the Worm
Food Experiences	Slush Drinks	Sand Dollar Cookies	Fruit Salad	Ice Cream	Fish Crackers
Theme Activities	Activity: Flying Streamers	Activity: Bubble Blowing	Activity: Let's Go Fishing	Activity: Kite Flying	Activity: Sailboats in a Wading Pool

Monday

Materials Needed For The Week:

sand, sandpaper, fresh fruit, fish crackers, ice cream, plastic shovels and buckets, beach balls and towels, large umbrella, juice, ice cube trays, crepe paper streamers, refrigerator or cookie dough, bubble liquid, wading pool, kites, styrofoam meat trays, clay, toothpicks

Sharing Time: Poem
"Little Drops of Water" (Traditional)

Little drops of water,

Little grains of sand

Make the mighty ocean

And the pleasant land.

Discuss going to the beach. Ask how the sand feels on bare feet.

Art: Fingerpaint with Sand
Add sand to fingerpaint. Use recipe on page 6, or buy fingerpaint from the store.

Story Time: Flannel Story
Do "The Dog and the Bumblebee." See story and patterns on page 22, Pet week.

Circle Time: Song/Activity
Sing "Down in the Sea" from record *Monsters and Monstrous Things.*

Food Experiences: Slush Drinks
Let children freeze juice in ice trays. Don't let them freeze totally. Drink for a summertime afternoon treat.

Theme Activities: Flying Streamers
Enjoy being outside. Use crepe paper streamers and have children take them outside to fly.

Tuesday

Sharing Time: Poem

"August Heat" (Traditional)

In August, when the days are hot,

I like to find a shady spot,

And hardly move a single bit—

And sit—and sit—and sit—and sit!

Art: Starfish

Give children a piece of construction paper and some sand. Have them put some glue on the paper and sprinkle sand over it and then let it dry. Have the children cut a starfish from tag board. You will need to enlarge the picture. Glue onto the sand and let dry.

Story Time: Book

Read *At the Beach* by Eugene Booth.

Circle Time: Song

Listen to "The Magic Coin" from the record *Quiet Moments With Steve and Greg.*

Food Experiences: Sand Dollar Cookies

Use a basic cookie dough recipe or refrigerated dough. Give each child some cookie dough and have them shape their own cookie in the shape of a sand dollar before baking.

Theme Activities: Bubble Blowing

Purchase some bottles of bubbles. Use the plastic rings from six packs of pop. Cut them in individual sections. Pour bubbles in a shallow pan. Children can put rings in bubble mixture and blow.

Wednesday

Sharing Time: Poem

"A Kite"

I often sit and wish that I,
Could be a kite up in the sky,
And ride upon the breeze and go
Whichever way I chanced to blow.

Art: Beach Scene

Have children draw beach scenes. Sprinkle sand on glue for the sandy beach. Blue tissue paper can be glued on for the water.

Story Time: Book

Read *Teeny Witch Goes on Vacation* by Liz Matthews.

Circle Time: Flannel Story

Use the patterns on page 399 to tell this Aesop's fable.

"The Ants and the Grasshopper"

Once a family of ants lived on a hillside. They were very busy ants. They took good care of the baby ants, and they stored up food for the winter.

In a field nearby lived a grasshopper. He did not work. All day long he danced and sang. When he saw the ants hard at work, he said, "Why do you work so hard?"

"We must work," said the ants. "We must get ready for winter. We cannot find food then."

"I have never been hungry yet," said the grasshopper.

"You will be hungry when winter comes," said the ants.

"Winter is a long way off," said the grasshopper. Then he danced away.

"That grasshopper will be sorry when it is too late," said the ants.

By and by winter came. How cold the mornings were! The long grass was stiff with frost. The birds had gone away to their winter homes. The ants ran into their house and shut the door. It was warm in their house.

But where was the grasshopper? He had no home, and he could find nothing to eat. The ground was covered with snow. His legs were stiff with cold. He could not dance anymore, and he did not feel like singing. He went to the ants' house.

"Please give me some food, dear ants," he said. "I am very hungry."

"But we have only enough food for ourselves," said the ants.

"While we were working and gathering food, you were dancing and singing. Now see if your dancing and singing will get you through the winter."

And the grasshopper was turned away. The ants never saw him again.

Food Experiences: Fruit Salad

Use various types of fresh fruit. Cut into chunks. Stir in a large bowl. Chill and have for a snack or with lunch.

Theme Activities: Let's Go Fishing.

See fishing pole instructions on page 7. Cut out the different shapes throughout the book. See patterns on page 30. Put a numeral on one side and the same number of dots on the other side.

Thursday

Sharing Time: Finger Play
   "Baby Bumblebee" (Traditional)

   I'm bringing home a baby bumblebee. *(Cup one hand over the palm of other hand.)*

   Won't my mommy be so proud of me? *(Move hands up and down, hold hands as above.)*

   I'm bring home a baby bumblebee. *(Continue the same.)*

   OUCH! He BIT me! *(Open up hands.)*

Art: Sandpaper Seahorse
   Have children cut a seahorse from various textures of sandpaper. Have them feel the texture.

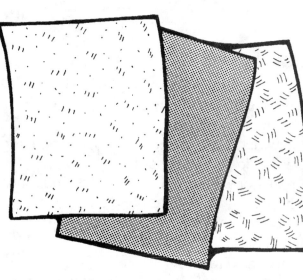

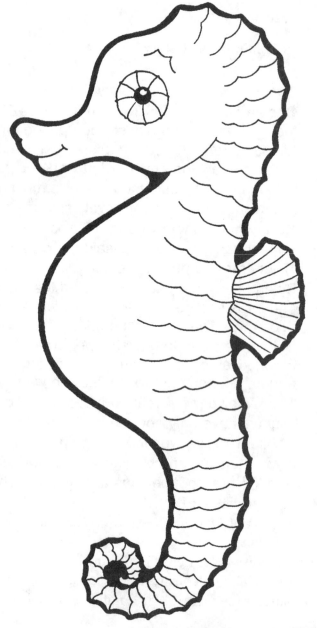

Story Time: Book
   Read *Under the Sea* by Eugene Booth.

Circle Time: Wading Pool Fun
   Let children play in a wading pool. Note: Careful supervision is essential for all to have a good time.

Food Experiences: Ice Cream
   Have a few different flavors of ice cream on hand. Let children choose their own and tell why they chose that particular flavor.

Theme Activities: Kite Flying
   Purchase a kite or several kites. Let children take turns flying them. See how high they can fly.

Friday

Sharing Time: Let's Pretend

Play let's pretend. Children can pretend they are rowing in a boat out on the sea as they say poem below.

"I Love To Row"

I love to row in my big blue boat,

My big blue boat, my big blue boat;

I love to row in my big blue boat

Out on the deep blue sea.

My big blue boat has two red sails,

Two red sails, two red sails;

Out on the deep blue sea.

So come for a row in my big blue boat;

My big blue boat, my big blue boat;

Come for a row in my big blue boat,

Out on the deep blue sea.

Art: Sailboats

Cut sailboats from styrofoam meat trays. Put a small lump of clay on the bottom of the tray. Cut a small square sail from paper and attach it to the top of a toothpick. Poke the bottom of the toothpick into the clay.

Story Time: Book

Read *Mr. Bear's Boat* by Thomas Graham.

Circle Time: Flannel Story

Do "The Boy and the Worm." The story and patterns are located on pages 37 and 42 in Apples and Worms week.

Food Experiences: Fish Crackers

Serve fish crackers on a napkin for a snack.

Theme Activities: Sailboats In Wading Pool

Give children the chance to float their sailboats they made during Art in the wading pool.

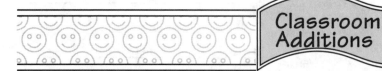

Classroom
Additions

Center Ideas

Here are some suggestions of materials that can be placed in the learning centers in addition to your regular materials.

- Housekeeping: beach towels, hats, empty suntan oil containers, sunglasses, beach bags
- Books: books about beaches and summer activities; a large umbrella, beach towels can also be used for children to lay on while looking at a book
- Table Activities: file folder activities listed
- Blocks: shovels, sand pails, plastic wading pool with sand
- Art: sand mixed in paint, construction paper, paint brushes, (Coarse sand paper cut in 1"/ 2.54 cm. strips can be dipped in paint and used as a paint brush.)
- Science: real shells, or plastic shells, different textures of sandpaper, sand
- Science Activities: Let children try some of the following: bubble blowers and bubble mixture, food coloring and bowls for mixing colors, prism for making rainbows on walls

Teachers' Aids

File Folder Activities: Choose the skills you wish to emphasize this week. See directions on pages 5 and 6.

- Matching Sand Buckets With Shovels (colors, numbers, shapes)
- Beach Hats - numbers
- Sunglasses
- Matching Beach Towels

Bulletin Board Ideas:
- Sand Scene • Water • Sand • Buckets
- Beach Umbrellas • Fish • Sea Shells

For Parents

- With your child pretend you're at the beach.
- Purchase a shallow wading pool for outside play.
- Have a picnic or go fishing
- Play outside games with your child.
- During the summer take your child to the library weekly; join the summer reading program.

Bibliography

Childrens Books

Booth, Eugene. *At the Beach.* Raintree, 1985

Booth, Eugene. *Under the Ocean.* Raintree, 1977

Graham, Thomas. *Mr. Bear's Boat.* Dutton, 1988

Matthews, Liz. *Teeny Witch Goes On Vacation.* Troll, 1991

Records

Steve Millang and Greg Scelsa. *Quiet Moments With Steve and Greg.* Youngheart Records, 1983

Kathleen Patrick, *Camille Core Gift,* Libby Core Bearden. *Monsters and Monstrous Things.* Kimbo Education, 1986

Patterns

Teacher Planned Themes

The months of June, July, and August are often seen as a transition to a more relaxed learning program. This is an excellent time to renew skills acquired throughout the year. Since the weather is often mild, take advantage of being outside with the children. Allow them opportunities to play games, run, jump, use riding toys, wading pools or sprinklers, and paint with water. Move your story time outside under a large shady tree, with the children sitting on a blanket. Give them experiences with food associated with summer. Barbecue hot dogs, have slices of watermelon, serve corn on the cob, and make popsicles from juice.

If you wish to continue to structure your lessons in the pattern set forth in this book, there are many themes that are appropriate for the early childhood classroom. These include:

fairy tales	nursery rhymes
big and little	colors
flowers	water
Father's Day	airplanes
insects	Fourth of July
machines	books
food	puppets

Use the blank calendar on page 8 to plan appropriate activities for Sharing Time, Art, Story Time, Circle Time, Food Experiences, and Theme Activities.

Some ideas for each category follow.

Sharing: books, songs, people with experience in the theme area, rhymes, finger plays, children's toys and games

Art: finger paints, collages, easel painting, bag puppets, clay, play dough, crayons

Story Time: books on the subject (from the local library), books that parents send or children may have, outings to story time at the library or a children's book store, parents coming in to share stories

Circle Time: books, songs and records, fingerplays, games

Food Experiences: summer foods such as fresh fruits and vegetables, foods to create projects, simple no-bake recipes

Theme Activities: field trips, poems, finger plays, group projects, speakers, movies or videos about the subject, stories, book

Use the various file folder games you have created during the year, let children play with glove puppets, and with fishing games you have made.

Give children a fun learning experience, as they get through the warmer days of summer, using the time to energize for the fall.